The Clergyman and the Phychiatrist— When to Refer

The Clergyman and the Psychiatrist— When to Refer

Robert L. Mason, Jr.
Carol B. Currier
John R. Curtis

Nelson-Hall, Chicago

Library of Congress Cataloging in Publication Data

Mason, Robert Lee.
    The clergyman and the psychiatrist—when to refer.

    Includes index.
        1.   Pastoral psychology.   2.   Pastoral counseling.
3.   Mental illness.   I.   Currier, Carol B., joint author.
II.   Curtis, John Russell, 1934–   joint author.
III.   Title.
BV4012.M35   253.5   77–22597
ISBN 0–88229–260–9

Contents

Foreword

This book should fill a great need for those members of the clergy who are seeking to be of maximum use to their parishioners (or to troubled people everywhere). Obviously meeting spiritual needs is a first priority for all clergymen but when psychological distress becomes overwhelming any person who experiences it becomes limited in his capacity for achievement or enjoyment. Consulting a psychiatrist is still a difficult problem for most people, whether because of internal or external considerations.

Clergymen, as well as psychiatrists and psychologists, have complex problems of identity. The unlimited fields in which they operate are noted for their variety, rapid change, and multiple methods of approach. All must often make decisions on the basis of constantly changing and insufficient facts. In addition they must often deal with problems of their parishioners or patients for which the causes are obscure and acceptable solutions are not apparent. This book beautifully organizes a vast range of human problems that inevitably impair, in varying degrees, both spiritual and mental health.

Although all periods of history have varying degrees of suffering and disillusionment, the present age seems to have more than any previous one, possibly because an in-

creasing number of people have become aware of how emotional conflict can affect personal health, both mental and
physical. While this has been going on, from Phillipe Pinel
to Dorothea Dix to Clifford Beers, both progress in treatment and attacks on those who attempt to furnish it occur
in irregular spurts. The present series of controversies regarding psychiatry largely consist of attacks on the "medical model" as applied to emotional and mental disorders, together with heated assertions that there is no such thing as
mental illness, and that emotional conflicts are a result of
society's shortcomings rather than anything within the individual. It seemingly never occurs to some of the more ve-
hement critics that treating the suffering individual along
the lines of the medical model and at the same time working
toward the removal of inequities in our social system are
not only compatible but highly desirable.

The fact that psychiatric disorders have many sources
has been ignored by those who would decry the medical profession's attempts to treat individuals. All persons of good
will can be of help in relieving the sufferings of the mentally ill, but special knowledge of the factors behind their
illnesses is essential in planning treatment. In this area the
collaboration of psychologists, family physicians, psychiatrists, clergymen, and representatives of government can
be productive as they share their special spheres of knowledge and responsibility.

All persons have emotional problems, but most of them
are able to surmount them, especially when their relations
with their relatives, friends, and associates are warm and
rewarding. Efforts to correct the highly undesirable practice of sending patients to hospitals where the facilities for
caring for them, let alone treating them, are grossly inadequate, have resulted in many thousands of patients in many
states being discharged to their communities where the neglect is of a different kind, often tinged with exploitation
and tragedy.

Coincident with these developments, new and far more

effective drugs have been isolated or synthesized which aid emotionally disturbed persons in dealing with their symptoms. These have been helpful, though at times they may be overused or misused.

This bare outline of problems facing psychiatry emphasizes the need for all persons of goodwill to unite in their efforts to try to remove or improve any conditions which impair human welfare or dignity. Herein lies great opportunities for collaboration between psychiatrists and many other disciplines.

The authors' warning that clergymen should not become so preoccupied with the emotional problems of their parishioners that they subtly or overtly display lack of interest in their spiritual welfare is a sound one. Spiritual growth and psychological maturity can and should be furthered by their proponents with mutual cooperation and respect, since both are necessary for maximum personal development.

This book is valuable reading not only for clergymen but for psychiatrists and other mental health workers as well, demonstrating as it does the various ways in which they can all be helpful to one another. Even for those who have been working in this field for many years, the book offers a much needed review with many new ideas being advanced. In a time when psychological misery and confusion are so pervasive in our society it is a welcome aid in their resolution.

Dana L. Farnsworth, M.D.
Henry K. Oliver Professor of Hygiene Emeritus
Harvard University
Cambridge, Massachusetts

Preface

Chaplain Lee, as portrayed in the pages of this book, is not intended to represent any particular religious faith or church denomination. We have deliberately refrained from referring to race, color, and creed throughout the entire book for the problems presented in this book are not peculiar to any particular race or faith. To be human is to have problems. The problems dealt with in this book are indeed the problems of mankind. Though some people may be more susceptible than others, no human being is totally immune to the disruptions and ravages of mental illness.

Chaplain Lee was created for the role of pastoral counselor, and as such, he represents the multitude of sensitive and intelligent men and women who are engaged in a ministry without boundaries, who have expressed interest in the psychological and physical, as well as the spiritual well-being of those with whom they labor. Religious work, as a profession, has its share of quacks, charlatans, and misfits as does medicine, psychology, law, teaching, and sundry other professional groups. Though not always recognized and appreciated for such, the majority of those engaged in the performance of religious duties are dedicated and sincere in their efforts to build and promote a better life for the many who look to them for guidance. We hope that

Chaplain Lee will serve as the embodiment of the principles adhered to by these men and women who have answered the call to serve their fellowman in this fashion, for it is to these individuals that this book is dedicated.

We would like to express our gratitude to our colleagues and fellow workers, who have chosen to work in the field of mental health, for their encouragement and suggestions regarding this manuscript. We are also indebted to Michelle LaMort for her typing and to Babs Austell, without whose help this book would still be unfinished.

Prologue

At 4:30 A.M. the phone began to ring in Lee Richards's bedroom. Though he had grown accustomed to the ringing at all hours and its impact on his life during his sixteen years as minister to various congregations, he still answered the phone at such a late hour with a sense of foreboding. On the other side of town, Lynn Wildman, sobbing softly, listened on the extension as her husband, Frank, a prominent attorney, informed Chaplain Lee, as he was affectionately called, that Marsha, their nineteen-year-old daughter, had killed herself in her room at the nearby university.

Stunned by the news, but ever mindful of the needs of those who turned to him in time of tragedy, Chaplain Lee promised to drive over immediately. Aware that Marsha's death would rate no more than one short paragraph on the back page of the city newspaper, he knew that he was about to share an experience of such personal and tragic proportions that the lives of Lynn and Frank Wildman and their four remaining children would never again be the same.

Hanging up the receiver, Chaplain Lee dressed hurriedly in the early morning chill. Anticipating the snow and the predicted drop in temperature, he reached for his topcoat and overshoes left the previous night in the passageway between the kitchen and the garage. Backing from his garage he noticed that the snow had been falling for some time, with several inches already visible in the early morning darkness. Still struggling with the impact of the message he had just received, he steered his battered, but dependable, seven-year-old sedan slowly and cautiously through the city streets, now silent and deserted. For the moment, oblivious to the postcardlike stillness and beauty of the night, Chaplain Lee thought of Marsha, the young dark-haired girl, who had visited his office for the first time only a few short weeks before seeking some measure of relief from the problems that she had finally found too burdensome to bear. Taking little solace from the fact that his untiring labors in his own church, as well as in various local schools, hospitals, prisons, and homes, had earned him the respect of the community, he was reminded of the never-ending stream of human problems brought before him and of the inevitable feelings of frustration and inadequacy resulting when tragedy or failure occurred despite his efforts to help. As in the past, he was consumed with the questions, "Could the tragedy have been prevented?" or "Did I do the right thing?"

Painfully conscious of the loneliness and the awesome sense of responsibility known only to those forced to be so many things to so many people, the burst of lights from the Wildman's home, on an otherwise darkened avenue, forced a return of his thoughts to the present and to the bereaved family awaiting his arrival with pain and bewilderment far greater than his own.

Chapter 1
Introduction

This book is addressed to those clergymen who have expressed a desire to know more about mental illness. More specifically, this book will attempt to alert clergymen to possible nervous and emotional disorders in their parishioners. While most books of this sort are directed to mental health professionals, we have chosen clergymen as our audience since it is to this professional group that most people with emotional problems first turn for help before seeking the services of a psychiatrist. Cloistered in their paneled offices, protected by appointment books, zealous secretaries, and the omnipresent mystique surrounding their field, psychologists and psychiatrists are often perceived as inaccessible.

Clergymen, dealing with personal tragedy, death, bereavement, and myriad other emotional crises, are both literally and figuratively entrenched in the front lines, "on call" twenty-four hours each day, wherever and whenever the cry for human assistance is heard.

In response to this plea for help, many clergymen have in recent years become increasingly sensitive to the emotional and physical needs of those individuals in their care and have gone to great lengths to prepare themselves to better serve their constituents in these areas as well as in spir-

1

itual areas. Since we are fully aware that many clergymen are already well trained in pastoral counseling and in the treatment of mental illness, this book is primarily directed to those clergymen who have not had the opportunity to prepare themselves for work with the emotionally disturbed.

Rather than a collection of theories on the origins of mental illness or a discussion of the many ways of treating the mentally ill, this is a book of case studies in which we attempt to demonstrate the wide spectrum of mental illness and its many manifestations. Though the cases range from the mildly disturbed to the more seriously ill, the emphasis is primarily on the more severely disturbed individual, since it is with this group that clergymen have expressed the greatest need for guidelines in the recognition of psychopathology.

As we have in recent years become more aware of the magnitude of mental illness in this country, the role of the clergyman has become of major significance. It is estimated that over 20 million Americans, or as Nina Ridenour says, one out of every ten Americans, will spend some part of his life in a mental hospital.[1] At least one-half of all our hospital beds are occupied by patients with emotional problems! Though of lesser concern than the pain and suffering engendered by emotional problems, the economic factors cannot be totally ignored. Ridenour says that some states spend more than one-third of their total state budget in the care of the mentally ill.[2] In addition, the enormous economic losses suffered annually in this country due to the loss of energy and skills from those forced from their jobs for emotional reasons is without measure.

When one considers the shortage of professionally trained mental health workers, along with the prohibitive costs of psychiatric care for many individuals in our society, the number of individuals who turn to clergymen for assistance with their emotional problems becomes a matter of major importance. Again and again in professional meetings and seminars, as well as in less formal encounters, ministers have demonstrated an awareness of what is expected of them in regard to the emotional well-being and mental health of those who look to them for guidance and assistance. As a result of this awareness and of the acceptance of this role, clergymen of all faiths are increasingly turning to psychiatrists and other mental health professionals for assistance, frequently raising questions about the recognition, treatment, and referral of emotionally disturbed individuals.

In a recent meeting with clergymen, one minister mirrored the anxiety, apparently shared by a large number of his fellow clergymen when a member of his church had threatened suicide. Faced with a problem requiring immediate attention, those present seemed confused and uncertain as they wrestled with the question, "What would I do in a similar crisis?" One question seemed to be of paramount concern: "Was the crisis of such magnitude or was the behavior being exhibited symptomatic of an emotional problem severe enough to warrant referral to a psychiatrist or mental health agency?"

Similar questions have been raised by campus ministers as well as military and hospital chaplains who have allotted considerable time in their schedules for the counseling of individuals experiencing personal problems. Though they perceive themselves as quite competent in many areas of pastoral counseling, many have expressed a distinct need for guidelines to distinguish between those individuals who need psychiatric referral and those who might better profit from the skills and services of pastoral counselors.

Any psychologist or psychiatrist, working in a mental health clinic to which referrals are made from physicians, teachers, school counselors, or clergymen, is well aware of the incertitude and vagueness characterizing many referrals and of the loss of time for all involved as a consequence. Of even greater concern, however, are those referrals which are never made, or those which are made at such a late date that they often result in an intensification of the problem, prolonged treatment for the patient, or even death. Serving as a consultant in a relatively isolated and rural community, a visiting psychiatrist recently spoke with dismay of his therapeutic encounters with three individuals who had been involved in counseling sessions with an older minister in the community. Though aware that the individuals had problems before they visited the minister, the psychiatrist was convinced that the near psychotic state they were in had been helped along by the counseling sessions with the minister despite his good intentions.

Clergymen, as well as other professional persons, often feel the need to consult with some mental health specialist concerning the problems they encounter working with people experiencing emotional stress and confusion. Has there ever lived a person in any helping profession, no matter how competent or experienced, who has not known the loneliness and burden of responsibility involved when the emotional or physical well-being of another human hinges on his decisions and recommendations? Rare indeed is the person who would not welcome at these times the opportunity for discussion and consultation with another qualified and concerned professional. Even rarer is the person, working to help other human beings, who has not at some time felt the need to share personal feelings of inadequacy and guilt when things go wrong.

To whom does the clergyman turn for assistance when confronted by a parishioner with emotional problems which he finds perplexing or which he considers to fall outside the realm of his professional training and responsibility? Often the only professional person in smaller communities with any training in psychological counseling, the clergyman is frequently viewed as the mental health expert in residence. Though they may do so with some misgivings, clergymen are frequently compelled to evaluate individuals with emotional problems and to make decisions and render opinions with far reaching consequences.

Hopefully we can provide some assistance in the recognition of signs or symptoms which might give some clues as to the severity of the emotional problems to those clergymen who have had relatively little training in the recognition of psychopathology, but who must make decisions about the mental health of their parishioners. Despite their lack of training in this field, clergymen, as a group, are more apt to possess both the potential and the inclination to recognize emotional problems and to have an awareness of the available resources necessary for appropriate referral and treatment than are peers, parents, and relatives.

Where questions of referral or psychiatric treatment are concerned, we believe that case studies, gleaned from years of clinical experience in hospitals, counseling centers, schools, and mental health clinics, are the most meaningful and direct way of communicating ideas and recommendations to clergymen.

We are in no way suggesting that clergymen become highly proficient in the practice of attaching diagnostic labels to individuals who seek their help in times of emotional stress. In the discussion of cases, psychiatric jargon is kept to a minimum. We present in nonmedical language the sorts of problems which may be brought each day before clergymen, physicians, teachers, counselors, nurses, and social workers in the performance of their professional duties.

The cases were chosen because they represent the types of emotional problems most often seen in the offices of clergymen, physicians, social workers, teachers, and school counselors and because they are also indicative of the magnitude and scope of emotional illness and the many ways in which these problems become manifest. Through our presentation and discussion, we hope the reader will become familiar with some of the various and subtle ways in which emotional problems manifest themselves, and as a result, become more proficient in the recognition and handling of them. If such is accomplished, those clergymen who have more than a passing interest in the emotional well-being of the people with whom they work will help to relieve the critical shortage of individuals trained in the field of mental health.

Chapter 2
Going Crazy

Going crazy! Nuts! Flipping out! Cracking up! Weird! Freaked out! Lest we be accused of trying to be flippant or speaking disparingly of those suffering from mental illness let us hasten to explain that it is not at all uncommon for those experiencing emotional problems to express the fear that something is wrong through the choice of such words and phrases as those above. Perhaps they are attempting to inject a bit of lightheartedness into an otherwise frightening and anxiety-provoking awareness that all is not well. Or it may be seen, for those relatively unsophisticated about mental illness, as the most accurate way to communicate those things which they are feeling and experiencing. Whatever the cause, many individuals in the initial stages of counseling openly and bluntly inform the counselor of their fear of going crazy.

While perhaps not as widespread, more sophisticated labels are used by others in their attempts to acquaint the counselor with their problems. Such psychiatric terms as "paranoid" and "schizophrenic" are being increasingly used by the man in the street, either in jest or in earnest, even when he is uncertain as to their meaning. Nor is uncertainty always restricted to those untrained in the ways of diagnosing mental illness. There are times when even those highly

7

educated and skilled in the diagnosis of psychopathology are hard pressed to define or distinguish between emotional illness and behavior which may be distracting and discomforting, but still a part of the more normal pattern involved in living in a highly technical and competitive society which tends to breed distrust and suspicion.

To varying degrees all human beings, adults as well as children, live a Walter Mitty type of existence. All fantasize and daydream. All do irrational things and have irrational thoughts. All experience doubts and fears and feelings of inadequacy. All experience feelings of distrust and suspicion —sometimes with good reason, at other times without any basis. Most people have at one time or another walked into a room or approached a crowd to have the conversation stop as they near. Rare is the individual under these circumstances who has not wondered if people were talking about him. One has only to travel a short distance on one of our modern freeways before he begins to suspect that the famed six cylinder revolver of the Old West has been replaced by the eight cylinder automobile from the Midwest as man's chief means of expressing aggression and hostility. After a series of near misses by automobiles hurtling by at record breaking speeds, even the best adjusted individual may begin to be suspicious that people are out to "get him."

Though such feelings are shared by all human beings it is important to distinguish between the individual who is suspicious to the point that he exercises reasonable caution, and the person who is actively paranoid to the extent that he refuses to drive a car for fear that someone is out to kill him. It is important to distinguish between the person who occasionally has irrational thoughts or fantasies and the individual approaching a state in which he is no longer able to function in the day-to-day world.

Recognizing that the line between normal and abnormal behavior is a fine one indeed, we offer the following cases to assist those clergymen called on to make such distinctions and decisions.

David

Remaining late in his office to put the final touches on his sermon for the following Sunday morning, Chaplain Lee was surprised to hear a knock at his door. No appointments had been scheduled as he seldom remained this late at night at the church. Greeting Chaplain Lee with a lifeless handshake, David seemed unaware that his visit at this hour of the night might be considered anything out of the ordinary. He said that he had seen the lights on in Chaplain Lee's study and stopped by. He had been walking due to his highly agitated state of mind and his inability to concentrate on his studies. His major concern at the moment was the fear that he was falling apart and might have to leave school.

In the following hour, Chaplain Lee learned that David, twenty-eight years old and a junior at the university, had been in and out of several colleges due to academic difficulties. Although he stated that he had an I.Q. of 135 and had been on the dean's list on several occasions, he would at other times become unable to study or concentrate on his studies and consequently find himself on academic probation. Viewing himself in negative terms, he indicated that he had had only two or three dates in his entire life. For the most part he attributed his poor relationship with girls to his physical appearance which in his opinion had suffered irreparable damage as the result of obesity in childhood. Though now a lean and physically well-developed male, he had been overweight to the point that his peers had referred to him as "fatty" in school. Fifteen years later he still saw himself as fat, believing that no girl could possibly be interested in him as a date.

In the initial meeting with Chaplain Lee, David appeared to be somewhat removed from the matters he discussed. He sat quietly, smoked a great deal, and wore a fixed, but distant, expression on his face. He talked at some length in an unexpressive fashion of being depressed and indicated that he felt so bad at times that he got down on his knees and asked God to take him out of his troubles.

In a later session Chaplain Lee was able to learn that David's mother and father had divorced two years earlier with David feeling that he really had no one to turn to with his problems. Though viewing himself as a near genius, David indicated that he had been seen as a stupid child not only by his parents, but by his teachers and peers as well. This, along with his perception of himself as marred physically for life, had caused him to withdraw more and more from social situations to the point that he now had little contact with anyone, either male or female. Careerwise he had considered a number of vocations including physician, lawyer, and mathematician. More recently he described events in which God had appeared to him in a dramatic fashion which he interpreted as a sign that he should be a minister. On other occasions he felt that he had been appointed by God to write great novels and compared himself to Tolstoy, often bringing samples of stories he had written to Chaplain Lee. On still another occasion he felt inspired to write poetry, and in one of the sessions he presented Chaplain Lee with a copy of his poem which he equated in greatness with the works of the Biblical writers. Though his compositions were for the most part unintelligible, David would visit teachers and professors in the area begging them to read and use his stories and poetry in their classes. When refused he viewed the rejection as a testing of his faith and the result of the spiritual blindness of his critics. He compared his lack of acceptance to that of Christ during his earthly ministry. Dissatisfied with his lack of acceptance in these areas, he turned to mathematics, comparing himself to Einstein and other great mathematicians, though he was at the same time finding it difficult to complete his classroom assignments in these areas.

In subsequent sessions David appeared depressed and weary, or panicky and highly agitated. Though often referring to his relationship with God he would in the same session resort to the use of profanity. He also referred on several occasions to his use of alcohol. Feeling guilty about such behavior which he viewed as un-Christian he would then apologize to Chaplain Lee. Repeating that he felt that he was falling apart, he complained of losing control of his emotions. Though he often talked of his need to improve his relationships with girls and to find himself a wife, David volunteered the information in the fourth session with Chaplain Lee that he had decided to give up girls for life. This decision had been reached after he had concluded that girls were a millstone around his neck and a hindrance in reaching his goal of writing great novels. Pointing to his stomach he then proceeded to describe the desire to have an operation which would remove all the bad feelings he had inside. Once this thing inside him was cut out, he believed that things would improve for him.

Frightened by his confusion and feeling that things were slipping away, David indicated that he had attempted to contain his fears through organization. As a result he placed all his change in one pocket, his paper money, keys, etc. in another pocket, and rearranged his room in a certain fashion with particular articles placed so that he could locate them by categories. He had nightmares when sleeping and fantasies when awake in which fighting and violence were being experienced by those around him. Though still denying any intention of suicide or harm to others he described several episodes with brothers, roommates, and other relatives in which he struck out in anger, either physically or verbally.

Believing God called individuals to serve him in various ways, Chaplain Lee, with some hesitation in the earlier sessions, had begun to suspect that David's behavior and revelations from God were indicative of severe psychological disturbances. No longer able to ignore his suspicions, Chaplain Lee arranged, with David's consent, an appointment with a psychiatrist. When David failed to respond favorably to the medication and sessions with the psychiatrist, he agreed against his family's wishes to enter the hospital for psychiatric care. After his release from the hospital two months later, he resumed his visits with Chaplain Lee on an irregular basis. Continuing to have both good and bad quarters in school, he was later admitted to the hospital again for psychiatric reasons. Returning to school for the second time, he continued to see Chaplain Lee occasionally while under the care of a psychiatrist until he graduated from the university.

Discussion

Beginning with the initial session with Chaplain Lee, David displayed symptoms of severe emotional disturbance to the degree that immediate psychiatric referral should have been made. The need for hospitalization and medication was probably indicated. His late night appearance without an appointment in Chaplain Lee's office and his fear of falling apart hint that all is not well. Even more suggestive of psychological trauma: his preoccupation with his earlier obesity as a reason for not dating; his grandiose thinking in which he compares himself to Christ, Tolstoy, and Einstein while finding himself unable to complete his math assignments or to write stories which are even readable; his almost total lack of socialization though he desired human contacts in a desperate fashion; his vacillation between doing what God wanted and behavior which he saw as being inappropriate and inconsistent with his belief that he had been visited and appointed by God to be a minister; and his feeling that an operation would cure him.

While not necessarily symptomatic of severe emotional disturbance when coupled with the other evidence, David's low self-esteem, his depression and anxiety, his nightmares, indecision as to a college major at age twenty-eight, his fighting with peers and relatives add up to a rather dismal picture of a person experiencing major disruption and emotional upheaval in his life. Of major significance is his attempt, described in the last session, to save himself from his chaotic thought processes through organization and structure. Such thinking and behavior are frequently seen in the borderline person who, realizing that he is losing his grasp on reality, reaches out in desperation to cling to anything which will provide the stability and assurance that he is still in control of his life.

In his attempts to allow David freedom and responsibility for himself Chaplain Lee encouraged and permitted a wide range of strange and unrealistic behavior. Chaplain Lee's acceptance of such could well be interpreted by David as support or reinforcement of the unrealistic view he had of himself and the world. Often aware that some of their thinking is unreal, the confused person will reach out asking for realism and structure for his crumbling world. It appears that David did so initially by seeking Chaplain Lee out for help. However, not until the latter sessions did Chaplain Lee begin to respond in a fashion so as to provide the help David asked for. With clients such as David, the counselor must often assume some responsibility for the patient when he is obviously unable to do so himself and render the structure which he needs.

After David's hospitalization, Chaplain Lee was of considerable assistance to him in regard to the transition and adjustment which all mental patients must make upon release from a mental hospital. Apparently David will need ongoing help for a long time of the sort which might be best achieved through the cooperative efforts of clergymen and psychiatrists.

Miles

Miles, a twenty-three-year-old disc jockey, opened the conversation by saying that his fear of being poisoned had become so intense that he had begun to alienate himself from his friends and, to a lesser degree, his co-workers. Usually extroverted and involved in numerous activities, he did not appear to be depressed nor did he give the impression that he would have any difficulty in relating well to people. However, he used the word "paranoid" on several occasions during the first session to describe himself and expressed the fear that he was about to crack up. In recent weeks his obsession with "being paranoid" had worried him to the point that he was afraid to use salt from a shaker in a cafeteria for fear that it might have poison in it. In the weeks that followed, his fears expanded to include soft drinks, ice machines, food served in restaurants and at parties. In his third week he informed Chaplain Lee that he had eaten lunch in a local restaurant the day before. Leaving his glass of tea on the table, he went to the restroom. When he returned he suspected that his tea had been poisoned. Though he found it difficult to do, he told himself that such thinking was irrational and drank the tea. On another occasion he had spilled some lighter fluid on his hands at work. Forgetting to wash his hands before lunch, he completed his meal before he remembered the incident. He spent the next twenty-four hours concerned that he would suffer effects from the lighter fluid. In each case a similar pattern seemed to emerge. His fear of being poisoned would occur. He would usually convince himself, however, that such thinking was absurd and go ahead with his food or drink, followed by a period of anticipated disaster. The fear had become so great that he had cut down on his meals with a loss of weight resulting. Talking the matter over with his father usually helped to reassure him that he would be all right. He denied any fears in other areas of his life.

Though Miles talked primarily about his fear of being poisoned, Chaplain Lee was able to learn that Miles had hoped to become station manager in the near future. Though he wanted the job, his young age and lack of experience had led him to have doubts as to whether he could handle the work or not. In addition, two older employees thought that they should be promoted first and had begun to give Miles a hard time when it was rumored that he was about to be promoted. As a result of the friction and anxiety, his work had begun to suffer. Though he insisted that he had an excellent relationship with his parents, he made several comments which would lead one to suspect that problems did exist with his father who entertained high hopes for his son. Miles showed no inclination, however, to pursue any discussion along these lines. He continued to insist that his father was a perfect parent. Several weeks later when one of the other employees was promoted to station manager with Miles becoming assistant manager much of the friction disappeared. No longer feeling that he had to compete, he changed his attitudes and behavior around the station. While still present his fear of being poisoned decreased. After several more visits, he terminated the sessions.

Discussion

Although Miles had developed some exaggerated responses to anxiety and pressures in life, he obviously had a number of strengths. He was apparently well socialized and expressed concern about the growing distance he felt from friends and co-workers. He also recognized his behavior as being irrational and referred to himself as being paranoid. This ability to distinguish between the real and imaginary is usually lacking in the true paranoid. Despite his suspicions that his drink had been poisoned, he went ahead and drank it anyway. In Miles's situation the target of his immediate fears is clear: his anticipated promotion and his concerns that he might not be able to handle the job or live up to the expectations of others, including his father.

Because Miles does have a tendency to react in such an exaggerated fashion to stressful situations, he could probably profit from psychiatric assistance. He apparently needs help in separating himself from his family as he does appear to be emotionally over-dependent on them, particularly his father. The most positive indicator in Miles is his ability to modify his behavior with minimal assistance from Chaplain Lee when he did not receive the promotion he had anticipated. This flexibility and realistic adaptation to a disappointing and frustrating situation seems to indicate that Miles is not yet locked into a rigid style of responding to stress. He is a good candidate for psychotherapy.

Warren

Warren, a forty-one-year-old foreman in a large manufacturing plant, gave as his reason for coming to see Chaplain Lee his growing fear and distrust of people in social situations. As a result he indicated that he was spending more and more time alone. Married for the first time at age thirty-eight, he had lived with his wife for less than six months. More recently his distrust of people had led to difficulties in his work. He had begun to suspect that workers in his charge were deliberately slowing down production in an attempt to get him fired. Beginning to distrust those in similar positions of leadership in the plant, he complained to Chaplain Lee that they were always insinuating negative things about him. When pressed to elaborate, he had difficulty in remembering any specific events to substantiate his beliefs. He had noticed that conversation came to a halt when he entered the foremen's locker room, leading him to conclude that he had been the topic of conversation. As a result he had begun to turn down all invitations to participate in activities with his colleagues and usually ate alone. On the way over to see Chaplain Lee, though denying delusions or hallucinations, he had fallen in, unable to pass, behind a large slow moving truck. As his irritation increased, he became certain that the driver was deliberately trying to provoke him. When he eventually reached an open stretch of the highway, he refused to pass for fear that the truck would deliberately run him off the road. On another occasion, just before his appointment with Chaplain Lee, he had stopped in a barber shop for a haircut. Displeased with the results, he complained to Chaplain Lee that the barber had on purpose cut his hair in such a fashion as to make him look ridiculous. On still another occasion he appeared in a highly agitated state with the accusation that his noonday meal in the plant cafeteria had been tampered with, perhaps poisoned. So firmly convinced was he that he left his tray of food untouched. A bonus at Christmas time from his employers for a job well done and a Christmas present which those under his supervision had chipped in to buy were ignored by Warren as were other compliments or positive comments.

Chaplain Lee's attempts to persuade Warren that such was proof that his suspicions were unfounded were either ignored or met with an argument. Seeking relief from headaches and depression which had plagued him recently, Warren had seen a physician several days before seeing Chaplain Lee. In response to Warren's queries about the medicine prescribed, the doctor had gone to some length to discuss the medicine, dosage, and anticipated effects. Despite his efforts, however, Warren again complained to Chaplain Lee that the dosage was much higher than the doctor had led him to believe. Consequently he stopped the medicine the second week after complaining of numerous side effects.

In the fourth session Chaplain Lee, thinking he had made some progress in establishing Warren's trust in him, began to probe and interpret more than he had in previous sessions. As a result, Warren confessed for the first time that he had been approached by a homosexual male recently. Though he had refused to become involved in a sexual relationship with him, Warren related that he had since found himself thinking of his desire to do so. In his mind, to think about such was as bad as if he had submitted. Attempting to convince Warren that he still cared for him as a person and that such thoughts were engaged in by many men, Chaplain Lee was surprised when Warren failed to keep his next appointment and was not heard from again.

Discussion

While similarities in the behavior and feelings expressed by Warren and Miles exist, there are significant indicators that Warren is much more disturbed than is Miles at the moment. Though Miles spoke freely of being paranoid, while Warren never mentions the word, it is significant that Miles recognized the irrationality of his fears and proceeded to drink and eat his food in spite of his fears. Warren never relented in his belief that people were out to harm him or admitted to the irrationality of his fears even when confronted with evidence that he was misinterpreting events. Clinging tenaciously to his suspicions, he withdrew more and more from contact with people and his environment. Already in serious trouble emotionally, Warren encountered the homosexual, which apparently aroused some latent fears of homosexuality in him and pushed him over the edge into a more open state of psychosis.

Failing to recognize the amount of distrust and distortion of reality, Chaplain Lee attempted to get closer to Warren and to show him that he cared. In doing so, he ignored Warren's history and need for distance in interpersonal relationships. The constant vigilance and the extreme degree of suspicion which could not be lessened through reason and explanations—both signs of severe emotional problems— were apparently not viewed as that significant by Chaplain Lee. With Warren's distrust and suspicion rampant, Chaplain Lee's attempts to be a friend in need only served to drive Warren further away. While an honest approach is most helpful in working with this type of person, a cautious approach with minimal interpretation is best. Frequently weeks, even months, of building trust are required before attempts to interpret or present solutions are acceptable to such individuals.

Obviously Warren does need psychiatric help. Such extreme reactions as evidenced by Warren are usually not modifiable by counseling or supportive therapy alone. Cooperation between Chaplain Lee and Warren's physician could be helpful in getting Warren to seek the psychiatric care he needs. Unfortunately, individuals like Warren are often too distrustful to get help until they are forced to do so by family or by circumstances out of control.

While most mental patients are not a threat to others, the potential to harm others does exist with individuals like Warren because of their anger and suspicion that others are out to get them. When they become convinced that they have been pushed into a corner with their life or well-being at stake, they may lash out to protect themselves from the perceived threat or danger. Since there is usually some element of truth or basis for distrust on the part of the patient, the therapist is often hard pressed to distinguish between truth and fantasy. Unless care is exercised, the therapist can be led into helping, even supporting, the distrust and suspicion revealed by the patient.

Tony

Tony appeared in Chaplain Lee's office without an appointment, indicating that he had not slept in three nights and convinced that he was losing control of his emotions with confinement to a mental institution on the horizon. After some effort to maintain his composure, Tony informed Chaplain Lee that he was a twenty-eight-year-old junior executive for a large department store. Though he believed himself to be in the right career field, he indicated that he had been under great pressure recently and did not like his boss. After dating for two years, he had married and his first child was expected in the near future. As the session progressed, Tony referred on numerous occasions to the many weird thoughts and feelings he experienced. He was especially anxious in new situations and at times felt disoriented and quite depressed. He discussed concerns he had experienced as a child about death which had prompted his mother to caution him against such thinking with the admonishment that only crazy people thought about such things and if he persisted in such thinking he would also go crazy. Indicating that thoughts of death were not the only ones frowned on in his house, Tony then proceeded to discuss in some detail how anger, sadness, and other emotions were also discouraged. He concluded with the statement that no one became angry or raised his voice in his parents' household.

More recently, Tony's thoughts had turned to doing harm to himself or others. He cited specific examples of thoughts of killing his wife which aroused his anxiety to the point that he was afraid to take his wife fishing for fear that he might lose control of himself and push her out of the boat. In his work, he often became anxious over thoughts of wanting to strike out physically in his anger at his boss and co-workers. In church, he had on occasion wondered what it would be like to shatter the silence with an obscenity. At times such as these he would grip his seat with all his might lest such a thought became reality. His wife's efforts to convince him that all people had similar thoughts and feelings at times failed to change Tony's opinion that he was about to crack up.

In an attempt to explain the necessity to rid himself of such thoughts, Tony indicated that if he could not control his thoughts then someday he would be unable to control his behavior. As a result, he had resolved never to let himself become angry, and, if angry, he forced himself to keep his emotions under tight control with no venting of feelings permitted.

His fear that he might lose control and eventually follow through with some of his "insane" thoughts had reached a peak several days prior to his visit to see Chaplain Lee. At this time he had panicked when he found himself without any apparent reason, crying, cursing, and saying things to his wife which he found altogether unacceptable and contrary to the way he had been raised.

Though Tony remained quite lucid and rational during the session, his behavior, in Chaplain Lee's opinion, indicated psychiatric referral. Two weeks later Tony returned with his wife after two visits to a psychiatrist stating that psychiatric evaluation had turned up no evidence that he was approaching a nervous breakdown. The psychiatrist had recommended that Tony and his wife seek counseling together with Chaplain Lee. Tony, obviously relieved to hear that he was not crazy and that all people did indeed experience similar thoughts, appeared for the sessions with enthusiasm and interest in working on problems in the relationship with his wife.

Discussion

Tony's major problem seems to be one of impulse control which he felt necessary to maintain the approval of others. The need for such rigid control, learned from his mother in his earlier years, existed to the point that even the thought of expressing any negative feelings caused him to panic. While his wife is correct in saying that all people have similar thoughts and feelings at times, Tony's unrealistic ways of dealing with his anger and fears seem to be so deeply ingrained that he will probably need psychiatric help in dealing with this problem. While psychiatric consultation in the case seemed to reassure both Tony and Chaplain Lee that his problem was not a serious one, there seems to be some reason to suggest that further consultation be considered. In regard to the matter of killing his wife, it would be most important to explore further Tony's feelings about his marriage.

While psychiatric consultation can be of valuable assistance, clergymen should be encouraged not to ignore their own feelings or opinions when they differ from that of the psychiatrist being consulted.

Whenever any mental status examination is conducted in a brief period of time, as was Tony's, there is always the possibility that the examiner can miss or overlook important clues due to his own limitations or those imposed by time. It is also possible in a series of brief interviews for the patient to successfully minimize or cover up his problem. With clergymen who have known the patient for longer periods of time, it may be more difficult to mask or conceal significant behavior or attitudes. If such is the case and the clergyman remains concerned about the diagnosis and treatment received by the psychiatrist, he should not hesitate to ask for further consultation or referral to still another psychiatrist.

Barry

Barry, a seventeen-year-old high school senior, came to Chaplain Lee complaining that his preoccupation with death and fear of dying had become so intensified in recent weeks that he found himself unable to concentrate on anything else. When seen by Chaplain Lee he was in a state of near panic—nervous and anxious, and unable to eat or sleep well. He would often experience difficulty in breathing and was convinced that he was dying. Things had become so bad and his fears increased to the point that he feared he was going to lose his mind. The fact that his father was an alcoholic and his mother a highly nervous person only served to reinforce his feeling that he had inherited an unsound mind also. Inquiries from Chaplain Lee revealed that Barry's father had walked out of the house one morning, leaving a note that he would return shortly. Barry, five years of age at the time, recalled the event with considerable feeling. He had not seen his father since.

Due to his father's absence and his mother's emotional problems, Barry had assumed much of the responsibility for the care of his younger brother and sister. His mother, apparently willing to let him assume responsibility, leaned heavily on her son for support, financially and otherwise, and frequently shared with him her emotional problems and feelings.

In attempting to understand Barry's preoccupation with death, Chaplain Lee was able to learn that in addition to the disappearance of his father, several other males, including his uncle and grandfather, who had in part assumed the role of father substitute, had died before Barry was age ten. His other grandfather, now seriously ill, was expected to die soon.

In later discussions, Barry described the home environment as depressing, indicating that financial hardships forced his family to live in a small house trailer with little privacy possible. His mother, still bitter over the desertion of her husband and plagued with financial and emotional worries, tended to infect those around her with a pervasive spirit of gloom and hopelessness. To make matters worse she had begun drinking heavily in recent months, relinquishing even more of the responsibility of rearing a family to her son. In addition to his work at school and at home, Barry had a paper route in the morning and worked evenings at a drive-in restaurant.

In subsequent sessions Barry indicated that he was sleeping more but attributed it to medication prescribed by his family physician. His fear of dying remained strong, and on two occasions he described events which reaffirmed his opinion that he was losing his grip on reality. In each of these episodes, though brief in duration, Barry described the feeling of not being himself, crying hysterically and saying things, according to his friend, which he could not recall saying later. Preceding each episode, he felt closed in and panicky with the desperate need to escape.

A handsome and intelligent young man, Barry had no difficulty in establishing relationships with others of either sex. However in recent months he had limited his dating to one girl with whom he was discussing marriage. Due to Barry's heavy work load and financial condition, most of their time together was spent in Barry's home watching TV. Also a senior in the same school, Barry described his girl friend as possessive and moody, quite satisfied to sit at home with limited social or recreational activities outside the house.

In later weeks with Chaplain Lee's assistance, Barry was slowly able to become more assertive with both his girl friend and mother. Although he strongly resented having to assume the responsibility placed on him, he had for the most part previously suffered in silence. In his work in a local drive-in restaurant, he often felt that he was manipulated into doing the work of others. Here again, though resenting it, he usually concealed his anger and found himself complying with requests from his fellow employees and manager that he do work which he felt to be more than his share.

By this time, convinced that Barry's mother should be involved in the sessions, Chaplain Lee suggested that he encourage her to attend the next session. Though somewhat apprehensive, Barry's mother agreed to come. Already alarmed over Barry's withdrawal and moodiness in recent weeks, his mother began to respond by assuming some of the responsibilities she had earlier delegated. Deciding to go into business for herself she opened a small catering service which soon prospered beyond her expectations. Drinking less, she became more aware of conditions in the home and encouraged Barry to spend more time in pursuits enjoyed by young people his age.

As the sessions continued, Barry was able to discuss with Chaplain Lee his desire to go to college and enjoy life more. In a later session, after much discussion and with the promise of financial assistance from a local bank, a plan was devised whereby Barry could attend college the next year. He also gave up the paper route and his grades improved rapidly.

With this turn of events, Barry began to see Chaplain Lee less frequently. His last week before leaving for school, he dropped by in good spirits to inform Chaplain Lee that things were going well. Rather than suffering in silence, he was now able to be open in the expression of his feelings, both positive and negative. No longer satisfied to sit around the house and watch TV, he had begun to date other girls with interests more in keeping with his own. Intrigued with the idea of college and escaping the morbid environment of his home, he was for the first time in many months enjoying life and looking to the future with some enthusiasm. Though still concerned with thoughts of death at times, he was no longer obsessed with such, apparently seeing it in a somewhat different perspective.

Discussion

Though Barry expressed genuine concern about his emotional stability, he was still able to continue his routine, functioning quite adequately in two jobs as well as in school.

He was also alert to some of the factors and causes involved in his difficulties and expressed an awareness of being closed in with a need to escape and become more independent. This awareness and the desire to establish his own identity, along with his continued success in carrying on the responsibilities of work and school, are positive indications often lacking in the person losing contact with reality. The chaotic family structure, the loss of his father and other significant males, the disturbed mother, too much responsibility for a young boy his age, the depressed girl friend, and financial problems are all major reasons for concern, often contributing to emotional problems in young people. However, the fact that Barry was able to persevere and to endure such hardships and make it as far as he had without major upheaval is also reason for optimism. This, along with his ability to respond favorably to counseling after only a few sessions, becoming more assertive with his mother and girl friend, gives some indication that the basic character and skills needed to improve his situation were already existent.

Chaplain Lee's efforts to get the mother involved are to be commended as she was a prominent figure in the relationship. Her willingness and ability to modify her own pattern to a more constructive one was extremely helpful in bringing about a change in Barry and the happy ending in this situation. She was able to permit her son to separate despite her previous high level of dependence on him. Through Chaplain Lee's efforts she was enabled to discover a greater sense of purpose which motivated her to return to the main stream of activity, so necessary, if she is to maintain a meaningful existence.

Nancy

Nancy, a twenty-one-year-old college student, first appeared in Chaplain Lee's study early one evening accompanied by her roommate who felt that Nancy was too upset to drive a car. Requesting that her roommate wait outside, Nancy began to discuss with Chaplain Lee in a rather agitated fashion her fear of going crazy. Working part time in a department store to help with school expenses, she indicated that she had been unable for the past two days to concentrate on her work and had been making numerous mistakes in writing up sales and operating the cash register. She also found it impossible to concentrate in classes. Although a good student, she had flunked two tests in the past week. She described feelings of confusion and disorientation, having to stop and remind herself on several occasions where she was. In talking with associates, she appeared to be in a fog and had to ask them to repeat themselves two or three times before she was able to comprehend.

In replying to Chaplain Lee's questions as to whether she had experienced similar episodes before, Nancy volunteered the information that as a freshman she smoked marijuana on several occasions and experienced similar feelings for several days afterwards. However, she denied the use of any drugs in several months.

Though Nancy appeared much calmer as the hour passed, she continued to discuss her fear that she was on the verge of a nervous breakdown. Despite her concern that she was losing her mind, Nancy appeared to Chaplain Lee to be well oriented with no evidence of confusion or bizarre thinking. Though crying briefly at the beginning of the session and indicating that she was unhappy with herself, she denied any thoughts of suicide. Before the session was over, Chaplain Lee was able to learn that Nancy was the only child of exceedingly demanding parents who had given her little opportunity to make any of her own decisions. In addition to being a full-time student, Nancy was also involved in numerous activities in her sorority which she served as president. She also maintained a busy schedule in other extracurricular activities, serving as an officer in several clubs and groups on campus. Her rigorous schedule left her with little time for rest, sleep, or food. Though a senior, she was also undecided as to what she would do after graduating and indicated that her uncertainty was a constant source of anxiety to her as well as to her mother.

By the end of the hour, Chaplain Lee was convinced that Nancy had calmed down enough that he need not be concerned for her immediate safety. However, he did insist that she come in again the next evening and discuss her situation with him further. Since she had appeared to be so upset and concerned in the initial meeting, Chaplain Lee was surprised to hear from his secretary the next afternoon that Nancy had called and rescheduled her appointment for a week later.

Beginning her next session with Chaplain Lee with an apology for not keeping her appointment, Nancy indicated that she had cancelled due to a conflict with her work schedule. Other meetings during the week prevented her from coming in earlier. She appeared to be much calmer and stated that things were back to normal with no recurrence of the confusion and panic which she had experienced earlier. In the next two sessions, she focused primarily on her relationship with her boyfriend and parents. She described her father, who had died when she was fourteen, as a quiet and easy going person with whom she had little communication. Her mother, now a successful real estate agent, was portrayed as domineering and demanding, both with her daughter and husband. Her mother, always on the alert for good marriage prospects for Nancy, had put her stamp of approval on Russell, a young lawyer with whom Nancy had been going for two years. Convinced by her mother and boyfriend that he could provide the security she yearned for, Nancy was for the first time beginning to raise questions about her feelings for Russell and the impending marriage, now only three months away. When she had attempted to discuss her doubts with her mother, however, she found herself labeled immature and selfish for considering her own feelings in the matter. The wedding announcements and invitations already out, her mother appeared to be more concerned with what others would think if the wedding was called off than with her daughter's welfare.

Chaplain Lee's attempts to convince Nancy that it was her life and that she should make a decision regarding marriage to Russell based on her feelings rather than as a result of pressure from Russell or her mother met with little success. Her response to such was that children who love their parents want to make them happy. Though obvious to Nancy that her mother's wishes and expectations were in conflict with her own, Nancy continued to insist that she had no right to hurt her mother or her fiancé, concluding that her mother would be unable to hold her head up in the community if the wedding was cancelled.

Not only did her mother exert pressure on Nancy in regard to marriage, she also refused to consider Nancy's interest in attending a school of fashion design in New York City after graduation. She insisted instead that Nancy marry with the understanding that she would perhaps one day teach after her own children were in school. Nancy's desire to pursue any career other than marriage she found unthinkable. In regard to school work, Nancy was constantly being admonished to perform at a level better than other children and relatives and when she failed to do so her mother would make it a point to embarrass her in front of relatives.

In spite of her mother's insistence that she marry Russell, Nancy became involved with a young man on the faculty. Though not anticipating marriage, she found him more attractive and adventuresome than her fiancé and had decided that the experience had whetted her appetite for a lifestyle more in keeping with his.

Though Nancy found it impossible to confront her boyfriend or mother with her desire to stop the wedding, she did agree to ask her boyfriend to attend a session with Chaplain Lee. Much to her surprise, her fiancé agreed to a postponement of the wedding until Nancy could resolve some of the conflict regarding her marriage to him. They did agree to continue seeing one another. Quite upset when she heard the news, Nancy's mother insisted on seeing Chaplain Lee also. In the course of the hour she was quite critical, not only of her daughter, but of Chaplain Lee and the role he had played in the decision to postpone the wedding. She left demanding that Nancy see her own pastor who had known her all her life. Nancy agreed to do so but returned the following week to inform Chaplain Lee that she had refused to change her mind. She indicated that she would rather die than go through with the marriage.

Nancy continued to see Chaplain Lee for several months on a weekly basis until she graduated. Russell, anxious for marriage, had by this time stopped dating her and had become engaged to someone else. After considerable anguish and several setbacks, Nancy gradually began to assume more responsibility for herself. Though sometimes depressed and plagued with feelings of guilt when opposed by her mother regarding some decision, she suffered no further attacks similar to the one which brought her in to see Chaplain Lee.

Discussion

Nancy's situation is in some ways similar to Barry's as both were reacting to perceived pressures from others to do things they were not able to do or interested in doing. Both experienced periods of disassociation, during which they did not seem to be themselves, were in a "fog," couldn't comprehend, and were not aware of their surroundings. Happily, for both, this confusion led to their getting help in time to deal more directly with the pressures they were experiencing.

Nancy did have a more extensive set of needs, since she had not developed the degree of maturity expected for her age. Her needs to develop a pattern of making decisions and setting goals for herself, and the need to separate herself from her mother who seemed to overwhelm her, will take a long time. It was fortunate that Nancy could respond to the situation by dealing with Russell and agreeing to a meeting with Chaplain Lee. The support she received from Chaplain Lee was apparently the impetus needed for her to assume more responsibility.

Nancy responded well and positively to the help offered. She is a good counseling candidate and has some solidly established characteristics for continued personal growth. There might be some difficult times for her because of the delay in the developmental process, but she is moving well in her progressive expansion of skills and coping attitudes. Chaplain Lee's efforts seemed to be effective with no indications that she needs to be referred to a psychiatrist. Clergymen can often help in dealing with the guilt aroused in a child as a result of negative feelings toward parents. Though such negative feelings are inevitable in the struggle to establish one's identity and individuality, they are often viewed by the child as unacceptable and by the parent as proof that they have failed as a parent. Chaplain Lee was able to help Nancy see that she could disagree with her mother and still be a good person, thus pushing her gently to complete the developmental tasks of adolescence.

Jeff

Jeff, a twenty-six-year-old member of Chaplain Lee's church, appeared for his first visit in a nervous and agitated state. He indicated that he had the feeling that something terrible was about to happen to him. He had been throwing up for several days, unable to sleep, and had lost several pounds in the last three days. Further discussion revealed that he had entertained similar fears since he was ten years of age. However, in recent weeks they had become so great that he felt he would lose his mind if something were not done to provide relief. During the night he woke up with feelings so strong that he could not go back to sleep. Though he perceived the cause to be emotional, he described great physical discomfort in his throat and chest areas. He frequently experienced difficulty in breathing and suffered from dry throat and mouth to the point that he could hardly swallow. He indicated that the feelings could usually be arrested or temporarily alleviated by placing his hand on his chest while lying on his left side. The feelings of discomfort, which seemed to appear when he was alone or with others, had increased to the point that he now found them intolerable.

During the session Chaplain Lee learned that Jeff had been accepted in law school for the coming year after long months of doubt as to whether he could make it or not. Though he expressed pleasure in getting in, he showed no real enthusiasm in being accepted, indicating that he did not deserve to get in and that he had expected rejection as a form of punishment which he had brought upon himself. Again he stated that he had a tendency to look on the dark side of life and always expected things to turn out bad. However, any attempts to get him to discuss reasons for his guilt were useless. Denying any pressure from his parents to go to law school, he expressed the opinion that his father, who had high hopes for his son, would have been disappointed had he been turned down. In all areas mentioned Jeff insisted that he felt adequate and competent with the exception of his physical appearance. Of slight build, he expressed a desire to be more muscular.

In the following sessions, Jeff continued to insist that he was not really concerned with anything other than the discomfort in his throat and chest. Attempts by Chaplain Lee to get him to talk about his childhood or parents resulted in the answer that his Mom or Dad were ideal parents and his childhood a good one. He answered any question with as few words as possible and openly displayed his hostility and resistance whenever Chaplain Lee attempted to discuss his earlier years. Any probing into other facets of his life he perceived as being totally unrelated to his problem and a complete waste of time.

On several occasions he brought up the matter of hypnosis and desensitization as a possible cure for his problem. He indicated that he had done considerable reading in this area in regard to his own discomfort and that a friend had seen a psychologist for desensitization purposes with good results. However, when he had approached the psychologist he had been told that such treatment was not appropriate in his case. When Chaplain Lee continued to insist that he was not trained to work in these areas, Jeff decided not to return for further sessions.

Discussion

The chronicity of symptoms seen in Jeff's life, going back to age ten, gives us some clue as to the depth of Jeff's disturbance. Jeff clearly signals he does not want to deal in any depth with any psychological problems he might have. The physical symptoms seem to be his way of saying that he needs an excuse for any failure or difficulty he might have. He will not disappoint others if a physical problem prevents his completing a task, since he (as most people do) views illness as something beyond his control. He is apparently seeking someone to take responsibility for him, to perform some magical cure.

Unfortunately, until Jeff overcomes his disinclination to consider what he is doing and to deal with his problem more in depth, the symptoms will probably continue in stressful situations. His lack of motivation to change gives us strong reason to suspect that any sort of intervention will meet with resistance and defeat. Suffering from doubts and low self-esteem, he nonetheless appears to be demanding of himself and has chosen a career requiring considerable ability and dedication.

As absurd as his ritualistic behavior may appear to some, it is Jeff's way of escaping from or reducing by magic means, tensions or anxiety which he finds intolerable. Though he insisted that he be desensitized in order to rid himself of his disturbing behavior, caution should be exercised in recommending such a procedure. Attempts to alleviate symptoms through desensitization or other methods without dealing with the underlying causes of the problem could destroy the defenses which Jeff has unconsciously erected to protect himself from certain anxiety-arousing situations or events. Removal of the defenses or pressure to deal with his problem before he is prepared to do so could possibly evoke primitive or undesirable responses on the part of Jeff. In situations such as Jeff's, psychiatric referral should be encouraged with more intensive and long-term therapy usually indicated.

Summary

How does one recognize or identify the individual who is about to "crack up" or have a "nervous breakdown"? What signs or symptoms should one look for which might indicate the presence of mental illness and the need for psychiatric help?

Admittedly the task of identifying the emotionally disturbed individual is by no means an easy one. However, the questions raised above by clergymen and others in the helping professions are legitimate inquiries and warrant some answers. The following, while not exhaustive by any means, summarizes in readable form and language, some of the symptoms most frequently manifested in the more severe forms of mental illness. Such a list can guide clergymen in the recognition of emotional illness, although it should be emphasized that all human beings at some time or other display some, or all, of the symptoms listed below. For this reason, caution is urged in the labeling of anyone as emotionally disturbed on the basis of any one, or several, of the following symptoms without a more comprehensive personal history. On the other hand, the presence of any one, or combination, of the symptoms listed below should alert clergymen to the possibility that the individual may be emotionally disturbed and in need of psychiatric help. Further evaluation is encouraged if the individual:

- clings to irrational beliefs rigidly despite substantial evidence that he is wrong.
- sees, hears, feels, smells, or tastes things that are not present.
- feels that he is unable to control his thoughts or behavior, or feels that he is being told what to do or compelled to act by some unseen force.
- shows evidence of excessive lying, stealing, cheating, or engages in other unlawful or immoral acts with or without any sense of remorse or conscience.
- suddenly or dramatically changes his behavior or lifestyle for no apparent reason.
- distorts reality with bizarre thoughts or irrational behavior displayed.
- withdraws from social contacts.
- is hypersensitive or unduly irritable, distrustful, or hostile without cause.
- experiences excessive or irrational fears, panic, terrors, tensions, or anxiety.
- is suspicious beyond reason, making wild accusations, or feels persecuted beyond reason.
- shows evidence of grandiose thinking, exaggerates his own importance, takes on Godlike qualities, seeing self as center of attention.
- fantasizes excessively, unable to distinguish between fact and fantasy.
- shows evidence of overwhelming depression, extreme moodiness, stupor.
- shows neglect of children, home, or personal appearance, particularly if previously conscientious and neat.
- is unable to feel or express emotions, appears lifeless, apathetic, aloof.
- experiences rapid or variable swings in moods, from elation to sadness, etc.
- shows undue elation or sadness.
- responds to given circumstances in inappropriate fashion, laughing when crying seems called for, etc.

- displays excessive guilt, low self-esteem, and feelings of worthlessness.
- gives evidence of acts or thoughts of violence involving harm to self or others.
- displays excessive or abnormal physical concerns or seriously distorts body image.
- exaggerates or overresponds to situations.
- loses sense of identity, fears loss of grip on reality, falling apart, going crazy.
- appears disorganized or confused, uncertain as to the time, place, or events.
- shows poor judgment, inability to make decisions.
- has difficulty in communicating, jumps from one topic to another, goes off in many different directions at one time, is incoherent, shows evidence of disconnected thoughts.
- shows feelings of hopelessness, helplessness, and worthlessness.
- has robotlike body posture, in a stupor, dresses inappropriately, stares at floor, covers face with hair, etc.
- is preoccupied with ritualistic behavior.
- is hyperactive, highly agitated, restless, fidgety.
- is disorientated, has blackouts, loss of consciousness, loss of memory, convulsions, etc.
- is overly concerned with mystical or metaphysical matters, witchcraft, reincarnation, etc.

In any diagnosis of mental illness, appropriateness is the key word. Whenever a person responds to a familiar situation or event in a manner far out of proportion to what is usually acceptable or expected, there is some reason to suspect that all is not well. If further investigation proves this to be true then psychiatric referral should be made.

Chapter 3
Grief and Depression

No human being, whether living in a penthouse or a hovel, is immune to grief and depression. All humans at one time or another experience the loss of a loved one through death or separation. Depression, ranging from a light case of the blues to chronic or psychotic states, has been referred to as the most common ailment of our age. Of the many complaints heard by clergymen, mental health workers, and others in the helping professions, no other is so frequently voiced as that of depression. It may be cited as the major reason the individual came for counseling or as only one of many symptoms listed as prompting him to seek help. But more often than not depression is present in some form or other whenever emotional problems are discussed. Though common, it should never be ignored or go untreated for any length of time. At best it is a miserable feeling, often crippling and disabling. At its worst it may result in suicide. If there is a positive side to depression, victims can be assured that depressed individuals usually respond to treatment and eventually recover, though some do so much more slowly than others.

Though the ultimate goal in treating the depressed person is to restore him to a normal and productive way of life, the major goal in the initial stages may be to protect him from his suicidal impulses or thoughts. In order to accomplish these goals, one must recognize the illness and begin treatment as soon as possible. The cases presented in this chapter hopefully will enable the counseling clergymen to recognize some of the more common symptoms displayed by the person suffering from depression.

Hilary

Hilary, an eighteen-year-old college freshman, complained of depression, going crazy, thoughts of suicide, inability to concentrate on her studies, crying a lot, and missing class. She stated that she had already made an attempt at suicide in the eleventh grade but had been discovered by her mother in time to be rushed to the hospital. The attempt had been preceded by an argument with her parents who had refused to let her date a young man of whom they disapproved. On other occasions in high school she had run away from school when things went wrong at home or in school, only to return a short time later in response to her parents' frantic pleas.

She attributed her most recent state of depression to difficulties in a math course which she was failing and to troubles with her boyfriend who was threatening to break off their relationship. She had scheduled an appointment with Chaplain Lee due to her fears that she might attempt suicide again if things continued as they were. She confided in Chaplain Lee that if she could get out from some of the pressures she was then under that things would improve. She then concluded the session by requesting that a letter be written to her math professor expressing the opinion that her mental condition might be improved if she were permitted to withdraw from the course. Unaccustomed to such requests, Chaplain Lee consented to write her professor after Hilary disclosed that she had been turned down by the University Counseling Center when she had made a similar request.

Permitted to drop the course Hilary, one week later, was led into Chaplain Lee's office by his secretary in a distraught condition, crying and screaming that she was afraid that she was about to have a nervous breakdown. After some moments of loud crying and violent sobs in which she appeared dazed and confused, answering Chaplain Lee's questions in a vague manner, Hilary calmed down enough to relate the events of the day which had precipitated her current state. Earlier in the day at her boyfriend's apartment he had told her they were not going steady anymore and that he was going to date another girl that night. Jumping into her car Hilary sped away and for the next forty-five minutes drove through the streets unaware of what she was doing or where she was going. In relating the events to Chaplain Lee, she stated that she felt the urge to drive her car into a tree. Sometime later she returned to her boyfriend's apartment complex, where in a highly agitated and dramatic fashion, she prevailed on one of his neighbors to drive her to see Chaplain Lee. While driving around alone, as well as later in Chaplain Lee's office, she described voices and sounds inside her head speaking in unintelligible terms. Viewing this as proof that she was at the breaking point and fearful that she might make another suicide attempt she cried and pleaded with Chaplain Lee to help her. Apparently relieved at such a suggestion she accepted Chaplain Lee's invitation to visit the emergency room at the city hospital where she was admitted overnight.

Once admitted, Hilary changed her behavior rather drastically. No longer crying she became rather coy and "girlish" in her attitude toward Chaplain Lee and one of the hospital doctors. She discussed rationally her off and on again relationship with her boyfriend. In previous episodes when he had left, she had managed to get him back by threatening suicide or displaying symptoms of crazy behavior which she had convinced him resulted from his indifference to her and attention to other females.

As Chaplain Lee left her room for the evening, Hilary supplied him with her boyfriend's phone number requesting that he call and let her boyfriend know that she had been hospitalized. Agreeing to do so, Chaplain Lee was surprised when Hilary scheduled another appointment but cancelled it a week later informing him that she and her boyfriend were back together and that she was no longer in need of counseling.

Discussion

Any therapeutic efforts on the part of either Chaplain Lee or a psychiatrist will probably result in considerable frustration as Hilary will be a difficult person with whom to work. She is unwilling to deal with things beyond a superficial level. She is not apt to change since she has experienced much success in manipulating people. Exceedingly immature, self-centered, and manipulative, she has developed a way of shifting responsibility for herself to others. Despite her theatrical behavior and claims that she wants help, there is little evidence of any sincere desire to change. Refusing to deal with her real feelings, she chooses to relate to the world in a distorted fashion. It is interesting, however, that despite the distortion and claims of falling apart, she appears able to pull herself together with fairly little difficulty after things have gone her way. Once in the hospital, for example, and her boyfriend contacted, there is no further reference to suicide, depression, hearing voices, or going crazy.

Failing to confront her immediately with her manipulation when asked to write an excuse, Chaplain Lee continued to let himself be trapped into relating to Hilary as had others in the past. Attempting to use therapy for wrong and shallow purposes, Hilary was able to maneuver Chaplain Lee into being a pawn in her continued efforts to control. Writing letters to professors is not an effective and appropriate way to resolve difficulties any more than is the threat of suicide in squabbles with boyfriend and parents.

Though such goals will be difficult to achieve, it would be a major therapeutic achievement if Hilary could be helped to meet such crises in interpersonal relationships in a more realistic manner and learn to accept responsibility for herself. As theatrical and superficial as they may be, however, her threats and need for help should not be dismissed lightly. Her high degree of distortion along with the dramatic and unnatural lengths to which she goes to meet her needs and call attention to her problems indicate that she does need help. Psychiatric referral may be made at some future date when she appears more ready to work on her problems. However, there is strong reason to suspect that without motivation stronger than is reflected here, Hilary would not accept such a suggestion at this point in her life or remain in therapy for any length of time even if she did.

Robbie

Robbie, a twenty-six-year-old female secretary, opened her session with Chaplain Lee complaining of depression and inability to stop crying. Obviously sad and unhappy, she was of the opinion that these feelings had been precipitated by an encounter group she had attended led by a young man the week before in her home town. A first year graduate student in psychology, he had become involved with group therapy as a result of his own participation in a group several weeks before. Lacking any formal training, he had asked for and accepted all volunteers with no attempt to screen out those who might not be ready for such an experience. During the session, she had been confronted by the group concerning her feelings toward her father. Unable to deal with the many hostile and negative feelings toward her parents, she had returned to her job the following day anxious and confused. The next night her father called her accusing her of ignoring him and no longer loving him.

During the sessions, Chaplain Lee learned that Robbie's father, a prominent lawyer, had been divorced by his wife when Robbie was three years of age. Her father, hurt and bitter, had never ceased to let Robbie know that he had been treated unjustly. Her mother later remarried and maintained minimal contact with her daughter over the years. In recent months, however, she had made an effort to re-establish the relationship with her daughter, asking Robbie to come and live with her. Convinced that she had been deserted and unloved for years, Robbie was confused by her mother's belated attempts to salvage the relationship. When unsuccessful in her attempts to arrange a visit from Robbie to her home, she also accused Robbie of not loving her.

Feeling that she had been rejected by her mother, Robbie was of the opinion that no one could be trusted. As a consequence, she had few dates and felt inept in all social situations. Though an attractive girl she saw herself as unattractive. Obviously intelligent, an honor graduate from college and successful in her work, she still viewed herself a failure. In general, her concept of herself was low, reinforced by her parents, who either ignored her or showered her with advice, making all her decisions. A shy, withdrawn person, who seldom ventilated her feelings, she found herself unable to express the resentment and anger she experienced toward her parents. Though twenty-six-years-of-age, she referred frequently to her disappointment that she had not had a normal family life and even now spoke as if she still expected such to materialize if all the fragments of her family could be brought together again.

Obviously depressed, Robbie denied that she would make any attempt at suicide. During the two sessions with Chaplain Lee, she sat still, speaking in a low voice, crying softly most of the time. She continued to downgrade herself both physically and socially. Her few friendships were with girls and existed due to the initiative of the other girls. With boys she felt even more incompatible than with girls. A beautiful girl, she attracted numerous males. However, after the first date they seldom called again which only seemed to reinforce Robbie's negative image of herself. Though hostile and resentful toward her father, she remained silent, continuing to allow him to manipulate and control her life. If she failed to satisfy his demands, she was made to feel guilty of deserting him as had her mother. Her greatest fear was that she was coming unglued and falling apart. Confused, she appeared to be unable to concentrate or think clearly. She denied hallucinations or delusions but expressed concern over the nightmares she had experienced with increasing frequency in recent weeks. She had difficulty going to sleep as a result of the anticipated dreams and often woke up during the night unable to go back to sleep. Frequent headaches, loss of energy, and little desire to study prevailed with the result that she anticipated poor grades for the first time in her life.

Still confused and depressed Robbie scheduled a third appointment with Chaplain Lee. However, she cancelled, indicating that she had quit her job and planned to return home to live with her father, giving as her reasons her father's loneliness and her uncertainty regarding the future. Several months later Chaplain Lee received a letter from Robbie written from a hospital where she had gone for treatment after a suicide attempt.

Discussion

As compared to Hilary, Robbie represents a deep and genuine depression. She feels worthless, rejected, and unloved, and she is confused. Her reported feelings of helplessness, hopelessness, and distrust seem sincere and pervasive. The unhappy relationship and experiences with her parents appear to have been generalized to all people with little evidence that she feels that she can trust anyone or that things will ever improve. She appears sad, as did Hilary, but in a quieter and much more profound way. While both distort reality, Hilary appears able to pull things together when necessary and to reach out to others when in need, though she does so in unhealthy ways. Robbie does not appear to have the capacity to do even this much because of her lack of trust and feeling that all is hopeless anyway. Though Robbie never complained of hearing voices or reported any history of suicide attempts (behavior usually associated with the more severely ill), she seems to be much more disturbed and more apt to kill herself or need hospitalization than Hilary. Immediate psychiatric referral in cases such as Robbie's should be encouraged with long-term therapy probably indicated.

Returning home was in itself probably a serious mistake due to Robbie's unhealthy relationship with her father and her unresolved feelings. Her situation is made even more precarious by her willingness to participate in groups of the sort described above. While groups can be beneficial as instruments for growth and therapy, they can be extremely harmful to some individuals and particularly in borderline cases such as Robbie. Under the control of an inexperienced leader who made no attempts to screen the applicants, the group confronted Robbie with things which she was unprepared to face. As she was stripped of her defenses, the group confrontation, followed by her father's accusations, pushed Robbie to the brink of an emotional breakdown.

It should be stressed that any clergyman in the position to refer individuals for group participation should first know something of the qualifications of the group leader as well as goals and purposes of the group.

Connie

Connie, a twenty-eight-year-old director of religious education in a nearby church, had been in and out of therapy, both individual and group, for several years. She complained of frequent depression and stated that she had made two attempts at suicide as an undergraduate. She came to see Chaplain Lee due to a recurrence of suicidal thoughts and increasing depression after a period of two years in which she described herself as relatively free of such feelings. She attributed her recent feelings to the fact that her application to become a foreign missionary had been turned down by her denomination. In addition, her parents were considering divorce. Further discussion revealed that they had been threatening divorce as long as Connie could remember. Connie also described herself as lonely, having moved to the community only three months before. Though not dating regularly, several weeks earlier she had become involved sexually with a man for the first time in her life. He had found her depression and attitudes toward life in general intolerable, however, and had broken off the relationship. Already experiencing feelings of guilt about her sexual involvement, she felt even more unworthy when he left her after she had given herself to him sexually.

Since Connie had looked with great favor on her previous group experience, she requested that Chaplain Lee refer her to a group which met weekly in the city. Responding to her request, Chaplain Lee was informed several weeks later by the group leader that he had asked Connie not to attend the group meetings any more due to the turmoil which she created. When in the group, she manipulated members with her threats of suicide to the point that little else was being dealt with in the sessions. Between group meetings, she would call the leader or individual group members on the phone for hours, crying, and threatening to kill herself. As a result, after several weeks, the group members were responding negatively, offering little in the way of support to Connie. At this point, the leader referred her back to Chaplain Lee.

Calling Chaplain Lee late one evening the following week, Connie expressed the fear that she was about to kill herself. Accepting Chaplain Lee's invitation to come to his office, she appeared in a distraught and hysterical fashion, spending the hour attempting to convince Chaplain Lee how desperate she was. Though she cried a lot, she appeared to be intact and later relaxed during the session.

In the following weeks, Connie continued to see Chaplain Lee, entering his office, dropping in a chair in a relaxed fashion followed by the comment, "What now?" Any suggestions made, however, she turned aside with arguments, appearing quite content to come forever on a weekly basis with things remaining as they were. Whenever Chaplain Lee referred to Connie's lack of progress or to termination of the sessions, she would then become more dramatic and expressive with her tears, accusing Chaplain Lee of destroying her and tearing down the progress she had made through his indifference and lack of concern for her. Through such maneuvers, she managed to manipulate Chaplain Lee into continuing the sessions, adopting the role of a rather passive and helpless person who saw the counseling sessions as an end in themselves rather than as a means to an end.

The sessions continued for two more months with little change evident until her church asked her to resign due to her inability to relate to young people with whom she worked. Taking a job as a school teacher in another state, she made no further contacts with Chaplain Lee.

Discussion

Connie will in all probability be difficult to work with as she also shifts responsibility for herself to others. Having successfully developed a pattern in which she arouses guilt in others when they cannot respond in ways which are helpful to her, she is not likely to let go easily her sick dependency on other people. An angry, infantile, and narcissistic person, it is interesting that she has chosen a profession which requires a giving of herself to others. As with Hilary, emphasis on her unrealistic demands on other people and her interpersonal interactions in the here and now should be stressed with the hope that she will learn to assume more responsibility for herself and develop better ways of relating to others. For the most part, however, motivation for change seems to be lacking. Any counselor working with Connie will, as did Chaplain Lee, probably be confronted sooner or later with her lack of motivation to change. Rather than a means to an end, Connie in both group and individual sessions with Chaplain Lee, seemed to use therapy as an end in itself, content to remain in counseling forever.

With individuals like Connie, Chaplain Lee should maintain realistic therapeutic goals, realizing that counselors cannot be expected to meet all the sick needs of emotionally disturbed individuals no matter how much they threaten, plead, or demand. Connie's demands upon the world are such that psychiatric referral is indicated and treatment should be encouraged. While her threats of suicide should not be ignored, permanent damage or death is more apt to occur through an accident or miscalculation on her part in one of her suicide gestures rather than through any deliberate intent to kill herself.

Nita

Nita, a thirty-three-year-old secretary, scheduled an appointment with Chaplain Lee following complaints from her boss regarding her work. Though she had worked for nine years as his secretary and had acquired the reputation of a highly efficient employee, she had recently begun to make numerous typographical errors and often found herself unable to add correctly a simple column of figures. In addition, she had difficulty remembering names or events, something she had always prided herself on doing. As a result of her boss's criticism and her recent unexplainable behavior, she had become depressed and thought that she was losing her mind. She frequently found herself going to sleep at her desk during the day and on several occasions had been unable to stay awake in church or at the movies.

Though appearing quite normal during the initial visit, Nita complained, in addition to depression, of extreme nervousness and anxiety with crying spells over which she had little control. Usually a pleasant person, she had recently lost her temper with co-workers and had become sarcastic and biting in her comments at home as well as in the office. A good mother, she had become short tempered with her children and husband. Her sexual interest had declined to the point that sexual intercourse with her husband was a rare event. Concerned with her weight and dieting for several months, Nita ventured the opinion that some of her difficulties might be attributed to a lack of wholesome food.

Reassured by Chaplain Lee that she did not appear to be crazy, Nita returned for several sessions in which she discussed her relationships at the office and with her husband. Three weeks later, however, she reappeared without an appointment in a state of panic indicating that she felt as if she were turning into stone with no feelings toward anything or anyone. Again depressed, with little energy, she related that she found it almost impossible to get out of bed in the morning.

On several occasions, she had done so quite late and had reported to work tardy. Even this, however, failed to alleviate her ever increasing feelings of fatigue and apathy. She had again experienced temporary losses of memory and periods of confusion in which she found it near impossible to concentrate or work.

Concerned about the physical aspects of her case, Chaplain Lee encouraged Nita to see a physician. Hospitalized for tests, Nita was discovered to be suffering from hypoglycemia, a condition in which periods of low blood sugar occur related to dietary intake. Once proper treatment was begun, many of her symptoms disappeared. Continuing to see Chaplain Lee for several sessions, she struggled with the fact that she must live with the disorder. Successful in doing so, her problems at home and in the office gradually subsided.

Discussion

While it has been estimated that more than half of the patients seen by physicians are suffering from psychosomatic illnesses, counselors should not ignore the physical aspects of emotional problems. Though counseling is often used as an adjunct in the medical care of patients suffering from such disorders, it would be unfortunate indeed if, for example, counseling was the sole treatment in the case of sexual impotence in a male later found to be suffering from diabetes or cancer of the prostate gland. Much to their sorrow, some people can attest that both physical and emotional complaints were ignored or treated solely as emotional problems when in fact they were dying from some physical disorder. While these cases may be exceptions rather than the rule, one should never assume that "one's problems are all in the mind." The adage "when in doubt, refer" seems appropriate for the nonmedical person involved in counseling whenever he is confronted with cases in which there is some reason to suggest that the emotional problem has a physical base or when the symptoms displayed may call for medical treatment. Such was the case with Nita, and Chaplain Lee is to be commended for his alertness in recognizing the possibility of physical causes underlying her depression and his referral for appropriate medical treatment.

His help enabled Nita to make a good adjustment to a situation which will involve some change in lifestyle for her in the years ahead.

Ken

Ken, a sixteen-year-old high school student, was brought by his stepmother to Chaplain Lee's office in a state of depression. After his mother left Ken sat quietly, avoiding any sort of eye contact with Chaplain Lee. When he did speak, he spoke in an almost inaudible tone with each word seemingly a great effort. He indicated that he was depressed so much of the time that he was surprised when he was not. He attempted to cope with his depression by writing poetry, painting, and, on occasion, taking drugs. With intense feelings of inadequacy, he reacted negatively to any form of criticism. Most of Chaplain Lee's questions were usually answered, after a long pause, with "I don't know." He admitted that he had no desire to do anything. He did not want to go to school nor did he wish to withdraw and stay home. He indicated that he was so tense that he had difficulty in going to sleep. If he did, he usually woke up during the night or early morning and could not go back to sleep. He ate a lot because it was something to do rather than because he was hungry.

When Chaplain Lee attempted to question him as to the possible causes of his depression, he became outwardly irritated at this misdirected intrusion, as he perceived it, into his life. In a loud voice he informed Chaplain Lee that his depression did not have a cause and that he did not understand him. He immediately apologized and lapsed again into silence answering any questions begrudgingly.

Attempts by his peers to involve Ken in their activities usually resulted in a similar response. Indicating that he was usually tired, he left school each day and retired alone to his room to rest. The previous day he had exploded when an acquaintance had dropped in. Admitting that he had no reason to do so, Ken had resented his presence and angrily demanded that he shut up and leave. Ken later confessed that he was never permitted to be depressed at home lest his stepmother scream at him that he was behaving in a disgusting fashion and ungrateful for the good home she had provided for him. Though usually depressed, he felt compelled to feign happiness and enthusiasm.

However, the strain of being nice to people and keeping

up a good appearance had become near intolerable for Ken in recent weeks. When questioned about suicide, Ken responded that it didn't matter whether he lived or not and that no one would care. He just wanted to be out of it all.

After considerable effort, Chaplain Lee was able to learn that Ken's parents had divorced when he was five following his mother's nervous breakdown. His father had remarried twice. In between marriages Ken had lived in foster homes but had moved in again with his father and stepmother six months earlier. Indicating that he was never given a room or bed of his own for the six months, but forced to sleep on a pull-out sofa in the living room, which he interpreted as proof that his stay was only a temporary one, Ken bitterly informed Chaplain Lee that such had not contributed to feelings of security or trust in others. At this point in the session, Ken indicated that he was not getting any help from the session and wanted to leave. Expressing the opinion that he had probably come in the first place with unrealistic expectations in regard to relief from his depression, he left the room despite Chaplain Lee's plea that he remain. He was still crying and apparently quite angry.

Discussion

With his unstable background, Ken is understandably having difficulty in establishing any sense of trust or personal identity. He had apparently expended a great deal of energy trying to buy security by pleasing other people rather than developing adequate ways to express anger and frustration or to define his internally selected goals. These negative feelings seemed to be bottled up until an explosive reaction overwhelmed him.

Much work is needed with Ken. He shows a lack of trust as he has experienced little security with many rejections, both real and imaginary, as he was shifted from home to home. He needs a stable and steady person who can serve as a role model as well as a counselor. Chaplain Lee, if given the chance, could possibly fill this requirement. Along with working on more adequate ways to meet his needs for love and security, Ken must also find ways to express his angry feelings more appropriately. Modification of environmental and family expectations on his part will probably be necessary also.

A high level of family involvement in the counseling process is called for as Ken is still a minor. If the family refuses to be seen as a unit, either referral to a group with a male and female co-therapist serving as parental figures and group members as siblings might be of assistance to Ken in reliving and working through some of the chaotic family experiences he has endured.

Because of his age, Ken has problems which fit into a developmental pattern. If he were older, his chaotic behavior would be viewed as even more serious. If some vigorous attempts at intervention are not undertaken soon then permanent and even more crippling results are highly probable.

Lydia

Lydia, the thirty-eight-year-old mother of two teenage daughters, came to see Chaplain Lee after being told by a neurologist that Tracy, her fifteen-year-old daughter, had an inoperable brain tumor and could not expect to live more than one year at the most. Although Lydia had received the news three weeks before her visit to Chaplain Lee, she confessed to him that she still could not believe that her daughter was going to die. Refusing to accept the doctor's opinion, she had arranged to have her daughter admitted to a well-known clinic for further tests. When the previous diagnosis was confirmed, she arranged to see Chaplain Lee still unable to believe that this was happening to her. In the first two sessions, she continued to raise the question as to what she had done to bring about such a tragedy in her daughter's life and even went far back into her past seeking an answer. A religious person, she had become concerned at one point that she was being punished for an affair which she had engaged in briefly when she was in college.

By this time, beginning to suffer from severe headaches and spells of dizziness, Tracy, a sensitive and intelligent young girl, was certain that something was seriously wrong. In spite of her daughter's suspicions that she was gravely ill, Lydia and her husband had decided not to share with Tracy the nature of her illness. Too alert to ignore the deterioration of her condition however, Tracy soon came to the conclusion on her own that she would not get well. Despite this awareness on Tracy's part, Lydia continued to tell her daughter that she was mistaken and that she would get well.

After two months in which Lydia saw Chaplain Lee on a weekly basis, Tracy's condition continued to worsen even more rapidly than had been expected. No longer able to ignore Tracy's accusations that something was being kept from her, Lydia informed her daughter that she had a brain tumor and that her doctors were concerned about her recovery. Aware that her daughter had suspected for several weeks that she was seriously ill, Lydia was unprepared for Tracy's reaction. On hearing her suspicions confirmed, Tracy cried hysterically, insisting that she had been in perfect health only a few short months ago and could not possibly be about to die. In the days immediately following her mother's announcement, Tracy alternated between periods of crying and long intervals of quiet and depression, refusing to see her friends and classmates who dropped by to visit. At other times she too would raise the question, "Why did it have to happen to me?" At times, seeming to resent her younger sister's good health, she would lash out at her in anger. On still other occasions, she angrily dismissed her religious beliefs insisting that no God of love and kindness would ever permit such suffering to endure. At other times she would pray in earnest for long periods of time, promising God that if he would let her get well that she would dedicate her life to his service as a medical missionary.

As the weeks progressed, Chaplain Lee, who had continued to see Lydia, also came to see Tracy in her home where she was now confined largely to her bed. Though with obvious pain and reluctance, Tracy began to discuss with Chaplain Lee her impending death, her desire to live, her belief in God and immortality. Slowly but gradually, Tracy and her family, with Chaplain Lee's assistance began to accept the truth that Tracy would soon die. As a result, they became more open in their discussion of death with the topic no longer hushed up in Tracy's presence. Within the limits set by her doctor, Tracy began to read and study again with visits from her friends resumed. With Lydia, in the initial stages of counseling, her guilt and acceptance of the inevitable had taken precedence. In later weeks, emphasis was placed more and more on the future with Lydia's responsibility to herself and other family members being considered.

Returning to the hospital several weeks later, Tracy died in her sleep during the night. Several days before she lapsed

into unconsciousness and aware that the end was near, she had
for the last time talked with her family in a serene manner of
her acceptance of death and her hopes for the future. Lydia,
who continued to see Chaplain Lee after her daughter's death,
was gradually able to resume the role of wife and mother to
her family.

Discussion

The matter of death raises many questions not easily
resolved and involves philosophical and religious, as well as
physical and psychological, issues. Faith in God, life after
death, sin, guilt, forgiveness, meaning and purpose of one's
existence, once discussed only as interesting topics of conversation, become matters of utmost personal importance
when one is confronted with the lonely and inescapable process of dying. At such times when one's faith and philosophy of life receive their severest test, clergymen are in
many cases in a better position to provide comfort and assistance than are psychiatrists.

Regardless of the time or the way in which such news
is communicated, an awareness of one's own impending
death or the death of a loved one is usually met with shock
and numbness. Such is nature's tranquilizer, a way of pro-
tecting human beings from pain and trauma, either physical
or psychological, which they find intolerable. During this
period the person experiencing grief may appear confused,
refusing to believe or denying that which has happened.
Life may seem unreal with the person incapable of responding rationally to even the smallest details of living. This
may be followed by a period in which any one or a combination of the following may occur: guilt, resentment, anger,
depression, crying, anxiety, withdrawal, thoughts of suicide, doubt, and confusion. Whenever possible, the individual should be encouraged to ventilate his grief and to discuss his feelings rather than coaxed to "bear up," or "be
strong and don't cry." This is often followed by a period
of bargaining in which the individual may, as did Tracy,
promise God something if He would only restore health.

When such does not work, a gradual acceptance of the situation usually follows.

While there is by no means any consensus of opinion as to whether a person afflicted with a terminal illness should be told of his condition or not, and if so, when, there are several general suggestions which can be made. First, it is our opinion that the patient should be permitted to set his own pace in the matter of facing up to the reality that he is about to die. This may be achieved through cooperation from family members, clergymen, and physicians as they create an environment in which the patient is permitted to learn as much about his condition as he desires. If there is deliberate avoidance of the facts on the part of the patient or some other clear cut indication that he is not ready to deal with his condition, in most cases he should not be confronted with the truth. On the other hand, if he demands to know the details of his condition, honesty is the best policy.

The second suggestion offered concerns hope. Even when the patient demands that he not be spared any of the details, honesty tempered with hope, whenever possible, is the most appropriate course to pursue. Patients suffering from diseases believed to be incurable have been known to recover much to everyone's surprise and for reasons which doctors have been unable to explain. Also, there is always the chance that science may achieve some breakthrough resulting in a long sought for cure in diseases which result in death for thousands each year like Tracy. On the other hand, while hope should not be destroyed, it is just as cruel, no matter how unintentional it may be, to build up false hopes or to deceive the person suffering from a terminal illness through a denial of his real condition or with the promise of a cure when none seems near.

Once death has occurred, family members should be encouraged, and helped if necessary, to work through the stages of grief involved in the loss of a loved one. Grieving is a painful process and human beings will often go to great lengths to avoid the ordeal and the agony involved. A num-

ber of excellent books can offer assistance to clergymen who
feel the need for such. If, after several weeks, Lydia had remained withdrawn, moody, and unaccepting of her daughter's death or if she had displayed other signs of prolonged
depression, psychiatric referral would have been important.

Sandy

Sandy, a twenty-six-year-old female, came to see Chaplain
Lee nine months after the death of her brother in Viet Nam.
Her chief complaint centered on her depression and hopelessness. She described these feelings as having existed for many
years to the point that she was convinced there was no place
in the world in which she could fit and be reasonably happy.
Now a graduate student in nursing, she was managing to keep
her head above water but doing so with considerable difficulty.
At other times she described her feelings as that of having
her head beneath water and unable to come up. She had considered dropping out of school but had no idea as to what she
would do if she did. Her previous work experience as a public
health nurse had left her frustrated and depressed. She experienced great difficulty in getting up in the morning and
going to class after spending a large portion of her nights
worrying rather than sleeping. When she did try to study, she
had difficulty concentrating on her studies.

Under the care of a neurologist since age five for epilepsy,
she felt that life had played a cruel joke on her from which
she would never recover. In addition, her mother was an alcoholic and her father a man who had spent much of his life
on the road as a salesman. Describing herself as a religious
person at one time, she had lost her faith in God after the
death of her brother. Though still attending church and hold-
ing rigidly to her earlier moral values, she appeared to achieve
little success from such. Obviously experiencing a great deal
of resentment toward God, her church, and her parents, she
struggled to contain her anger and seldom permitted herself
to ventilate any of the feelings which dominated her life.
Even in the sessions with Chaplain Lee, it took considerable
time to cover simple events with Sandy concerned that every
sentence be grammatically correct or else repeated. Apologizing for every mistake no matter how minute, she returned
again and again to the same theme, refusing to look at alternatives or new approaches to her situation.

As the sessions continued it was apparent that Sandy had
not accepted the loss of her brother nine months after his

death, nor had she learned to live with the fact that her mother was an alcoholic. Now living alone in an apartment, Sandy had moved from one place and roommate to another, always finding something unacceptable about each situation. Having dated little in the past, she now refused to date at all or to become involved with either males or females beyond a superficial relationship. She refused to attend any social functions, indicating that her interests and values were not shared by her peers in a secular world she viewed as moving in the direction of moral decay. On the other hand, she also refused to become involved in church groups with people her age, rushing to leave the church after the service was over each Sunday.

In the following weeks, her situation seemed to deteriorate even more with her self-esteem such that she referred with increasing frequency to her hopeless and meaningless sort of existence and lack of purpose in living. Chaplain Lee's attempts to lead her in the discussion of more positive things in her life and involvement with other young people in the church met with debate, something Sandy seemed facile in doing.

Frustrated in his every attempt to deal with Sandy's anxiety and depression, Chaplain Lee suggested that she see her family physician for medication for her depression. Though she agreed, even with medication prescribed, Sandy complained that she could not take it because of the many side effects which she experienced. After several weeks Sandy discontinued her sessions with Chaplain Lee indicating that she did not feel them to be of benefit in the relief of her depression and loneliness.

Discussion

Without psychiatric intervention, Sandy will probably continue to be chronically depressed, becoming even more angry and dissatisfied with life. Since such rigid, compulsive, and perfectionistic people also possess the potential for more serious emotional problems, psychiatric referral with more intensive exploration and treatment should be encouraged. Though she does not appear to be in danger of commiting suicide at the moment, it would be wise to explore this more explicitly with her.

In general, Sandy seems to have established a rigid pattern of bitterness, suffering, and pessimism, with strong feelings of not being appreciated. While most people are willing to try something new when they are painfully unhappy, Sandy was unwilling or unable to do so. This type of person is usually resistant toward therapy and is difficult to work with despite his unhappiness. The family background of an alcoholic mother and traveling father often contributes to a closer than average sibling relationship as more needs must be met within the brother-sister relationship. With the death of her brother, such was no longer possible, decreasing even further Sandy's already limited opportunities for meaningful relationships and communication. The death of her brother is an area which needs more work as it appears that the working through of grief remains incomplete in Sandy's case. Chaplain Lee's "happy talk" was perhaps too leading and gave Sandy no real opportunity to work out some of these feelings or to make a choice.

Another problem area obviously in need of additional work is that of Sandy's epilepsy. Many people with chronic disorders, such as epilepsy, diabetes, hypoglycemia, and arthritis, need help in working through their feelings and learning to live with diseases for which there is no known cure. For example, many epileptic patients are often self-pitying and angry with feelings such as Sandy's that life has dealt them a cruel blow. Diabetics may respond to their illness with self-abuse or in lack of care for themselves. Whatever the cause, Sandy is apparently receiving some sort of gain from her suffering and as a result displaying considerable resistance toward efforts on the part of Chaplain Lee to alleviate her pain. Though it is important to deal with the death of her brother and her attitudes toward her epilepsy, if Sandy is to achieve any lasting rewards from therapy, changes in more basic personality structure will probably have to be considered. For this reason psychiatric referral is recommended in cases similar to Sandy's, with long-term psychotherapy probably involved.

Joyce

Joyce, a twenty-eight-year-old divorcee, complained of depression, loneliness, and lack of purpose or goals in her life. Married for four years, she had been divorced for seven months. With no children from the marriage, she lived alone in a swinging apartment complex. Though opposed to divorce, she had quietly succumbed to her husband's demands and the divorce was completed as quickly as possible; open conflict was kept to a minimum. Thinking it best, Joyce followed advice given by well-intentioned friends and plunged immediately into a round of parties and sexual activities in an effort to prove she was still attractive and could hold her own as a woman. A typical evening might find her attending several parties, often ending up in bed with some male she had met for the first time earlier in the evening. Attempting to deny her loss and hurt over the breakup of her marriage, she refused to think about it through involvement.

Apparently successful in hiding her grief, she was unable to account for the periods of depression which she had begun to suffer in recent weeks. Puzzled and unhappy, she called Chaplain Lee. In the initial sessions, she discussed her relationships with several males. Though insisting she had a satisfying relationship with her current boyfriend, she expressed feelings of being empty inside. Whenever any reference was made to her ex-husband, her eyes would fill with tears and she had difficulty in speaking. As the sessions continued and with Chaplain Lee's encouragement, she began to talk more openly about her marriage. Though admitting that she had no right to be concerned, she displayed considerable interest in her husband's activities and the woman he was now dating. She insisted that they would never get together again and that a marriage between them could never work; however, she tended to focus on the good times they had together. In the following sessions, she was eventually able to discuss in depth and with great feeling her intense sense of loss, as well as feelings of inadequacy and failure as a result of her unsuccessful marriage. In the next few weeks, her social activities were curtailed drastically though she did continue to see her boyfriend occasionally. Aided by his patience and the sessions with Chaplain Lee, she gradually began to feel less depressed.

Discussion

Avoiding pain is not an appropriate or adequate means of dealing with the loss of a significant person in an individual's life, as well demonstrated by Joyce. No matter how bad the marriage, divorce almost inevitably results in feelings of failure and loss, accompanied by a major sense of upheaval. Even when seen as the only answer, divorce represents a major change in lifestyle with some doubts of one's masculinity or femininity often present. Ideally, the ground-work for dealing with these and similar feelings and reper-cussions should be begun when divorce first becomes a strong alternative. Plunging into a divorce without some prepara-tion for the trauma involved is a serious error. When such does occur, it is not uncommon to experience a delayed grief reaction and depression as did Joyce.

While not in total agreement, many authorities believe that depression may be classified as either situational or re-active as opposed to endogenous or chemical. With Joyce, it seems fairly obvious that her depression is a delayed reac-tion to a grief provoking situation, the loss of her husband. Attempting to deny the loss through a merry-go-round of sex, parties, and involvement in numerous activities, Joyce failed to complete the task of grieving.

Chaplain Lee's efforts in working with Joyce were ap-propriate and successful as he encouraged and permitted her to acknowledge her loss and subsequently to begin the other tasks involved in a successful coping with her grief. Once feelings of pain, anger, and frustration were dealt with the slow, but necessary, process of regaining confi-dence and a sense of adequacy and effectiveness as a woman could begin.

Situations similar to Joyce's in which there is a reality base to one's depression are treatable by clergymen. Since moral issues are usually involved in divorce in our society, clergymen can be especially helpful to divorced persons as well as to those contemplating divorce.

Summary

When should clergymen refer depressed individuals to a psychiatrist? In any discussion of depression one comes across such words as reactive, endogenous, exogenous, neu-rotic, psychotic, chronic, and acute. For our purposes how-ever, it seems more appropriate to place depression on a con-tinuum ranging from transient and mild cases of the blues to severe and incapacitating feelings of hopelessness and helplessness. Referral to a psychiatrist is recommended if the depressed person:

- continues to be depressed or grieves beyond a reasonable length of time.
- fails to respond to counseling by the clergymen.
- is believed to be suicidal.
- shows evidence of confusion, undue suspicion, withdrawal, bizarre or irrational thoughts or behavior, losing touch with reality.
- expresses an overwhelming sense of hopelessness and helplessness.
- has attempted suicide before.
- drinks a lot or uses drugs.
- suddenly appears to be no longer depressed or seems calm and accepting of his situation.

The real danger is that depression, whatever the cause, may go undetected due to the individual's conscious or unconscious efforts to mask it beneath a smiling face, complaints of anxiety, tension, or a host of physical complaints, such as backaches, stomach problems, headaches, or chest pains. For this reason, clergymen should familiarize themselves with the nonverbal, as well as the verbal ways, in which depression may be communicated. Major warning signs include loss of weight and appetite, sleep disturbance, decreased sex drive, facial expressions, body posture, lassitude, and decrease or slowing down of motor and intellectual functioning.

Whether mild or severe, depression should never be ignored or go untreated for any length of time. When properly treated, depressed patients recover at a rate higher than that of persons with any other emotional problem or illness. Treatment may involve the use of antidepressant medication or hospitalization and shock therapy in the more severe cases when other treatment fails. In either event, counseling should be a part of the total therapy program, and clergymen may well be an important member of the treatment team.

Chapter 4
Suicide

The decision to kill one's self is not usually made suddenly. Instead, it is the result of a gradual process in which the individual has, in his thinking, exhausted all other means of coping with a life which he is no longer able to tolerate. Most individuals who think or talk of suicide never follow through to kill themselves or even make an attempt to do so. While this may be true, it is a serious mistake to assume, as many do, that individuals who talk about suicide will never kill themselves. If the experts on suicide are correct, then relatively few individuals who commit suicide fail to talk about it to someone or to communicate in some way their intentions of doing so.

If one accepts these facts, then the need to distinguish between "talker" and "doer" becomes a matter of paramount importance to those who must make such an assessment and, of even greater importance to the individual contemplating suicide. For this reason, this chapter is directed toward the recognition of clues regarding the potential for suicide rather than to any discussion of theories or causes.

In the following cases, suicide was introduced, with one exception, in the initial stages of counseling with Chaplain Lee by the counselee. Though the matter of suicide was injected by the counselees, each is different, as will be demonstrated. Hopefully the situations selected for presentation and discussion will provide clergymen with at least some of the basic information necessary to distinguish between suicidal ideation as a passing occurrence and suicidal thoughts portending more serious and destructive behavior or emotional disruption in which psychiatric referral would be indicated.

Of the many histories readily available, those chosen are representative of the types of problems involving suicide or threats of suicide which pastoral counselors might expect to encounter.

Marsha

Marsha had been attending services at Chaplain Lee's church since his arrival eight years ago. Though involved in a number of church groups and activities for young people, Chaplain Lee was aware that he did not really know this quiet, introverted, nineteen-year-old girl of pleasing personality with whom he shared a rather vague relationship. He was therefore somewhat surprised when she called for an appointment while home for the Christmas holidays from the nearby university which she attended as a sophomore.

In the initial session with Chaplain Lee, Marsha not only complained of being depressed but also looked depressed and displayed little interest in anything. Any attempt at movement or conversation seemed to require great effort. For extended periods of time, she would sit looking at the floor in silence, occasionally sighing or moving her hands or feet. Not speaking directly of suicide, she exuded sadness and made several references to her lack of desire to go on living. She complained of difficulty sleeping and a loss of energy although she had recently begun eating at all hours of the day and night. Previously an immaculate person where her physical appearance was concerned, she admitted that she was no longer concerned about how she looked.

Though apparent to Chaplain Lee that Marsha was experiencing considerable difficulty in communicating her feelings and her concerns, he was eventually able to learn from her that she was especially worried about her grades, which would soon be given out for the semester at the university. She anticipated failing at least one subject. In spite of her fears, she had found herself unable to concentrate on her studies even when she tried. Becoming increasingly frustrated in her efforts to study, she had begun to take long walks alone in the evening, often returning late at night, displaying little concern for her safety. Her roommate and dorm counselor, concerned over her emotional state, convinced her to see a university psychiatrist. Marsha reluctantly scheduled an appointment which she failed to keep.

After considerable effort, Chaplain Lee discovered that Marsha had had bouts of depression since early in junior high school. As a ninth grader, she had taken ten aspirins during one of these episodes, which she viewed as being caused by her parents' demands. At age seventeen she had taken a combination of drugs in an attempt to kill herself. However, she only succeeded in becoming so sick that she threw up, much to the disgust of her parents who failed to take her attempt seriously. Chaplain Lee was also able to learn that much of Marsha's concern about grades was related to the anticipated disappointment and anger of her father. At this point in the session, Marsha covered her face and began to sob softly. Speaking with considerable feeling and emotion, for the first time she began to discuss her feelings of being rejected by her father, who was portrayed as a demanding individual toward her entire family. She described her mother as a rather docile and passive woman, who catered to the every whim of her husband. One of her brothers and mother had been seen by a psychiatrist for depression for a brief period of time.

Marsha's father, now enjoying a large and lucrative law practice, viewed himself as a person who had overcome many obstacles to reach his present affluent position. Disappointed that neither of his two sons had chosen law as a career, he had turned his attention to Marsha, seeking in her the fulfillment of his dream that his children would follow in his footsteps.

By the time Marsha saw Chaplain Lee, she had been convinced for some years that her father had been disappointed that his youngest child had been born a girl rather than the son who would later achieve fame as a great athlete, scholar, and lawyer. Carried by her father on numerous hunting and fishing expeditions, as well as to various sporting events, Marsha was permitted little time or opportunity to develop adequate views of herself as a female. Consequently, she had come to perceive of herself as being unattractive and lacking in the feminine traits which she so admired in other girls her age.

Unable to satisfy her father's demands in the masculine world in which he lived, Marsha subsequently turned to academics in an attempt to make herself more acceptable to her father. Though achieving some success in this area, graduating with a B average from high school, she never felt her performance good enough to please her father. If she made one of the top grades in the class, he would demand that she shoot for the top on the next test. If she brought home an A, he would ask why she did not make an A+. As a freshman in college she had managed a low B average with nothing lower than a C. However, at the time she visited Chaplain Lee, she anticipated an F on her report card for the first time in her life. The fact that over 60 percent of the class had D's or F's did nothing to alter Marsha's perceptions of her father's reaction when he received her grades. Feeling that she had now finally and completely let her father down and anticipating her rejection and shame in the community, Marsha had in desperation turned to Chaplain Lee.

By now, alarmed and thoroughly convinced that Marsha needed treatment which he could not provide, Chaplain Lee tried to persuade her, as had school officials, to see a psychiatrist. Her only concession was that she would discuss it with her father. Not satisfied with this decision, Chaplain Lee requested that he be permitted to share his concern for her well-being with her father. Marsha agreed, only to withdraw her permission as she rose to leave the office by asking Chaplain Lee to delay contacting her father for one week. Concerned about her safety, Chaplain Lee tried to reach some agreement with Marsha that she would not harm herself. Marsha initially refused to enter such an agreement, indicating that she could make no promises or predict how she might feel or behave in the future. Again, her only concession was that she would promise not to harm herself before her next appointment with Chaplain Lee, scheduled for the next day.

In the next session, Marsha appeared to be in somewhat better spirits, though still depressed. She had approached her father about her grades, attempting to discuss her feelings and concerns. After verbal assurance that he would continue to love her no matter what her grades were, he had launched into his usual pep talk in which he attempted to convince Marsha that she could make acceptable grades if she would quit feeling sorry for herself and buckle down to her studies. Though he had in the past occasionally attempted to persuade Marsha that his love for her would endure no matter how she turned out, Marsha remained unconvinced, feeling instead that her father's acceptance of her was in every way conditional, depending primarily on whether or not she lived up to his expectations and demands.

In the second session, Marsha also began to discuss her relationship with Tom, her only boyfriend, whom she had been dating for the last six months. Prior to her freshman year at the university, she had never had a boyfriend and had dated infrequently. Though she stated that she did not really care that much for Tom, she saw the relationship as better than nothing. In recent weeks, however, Tom had insisted that their physical relationship go beyond the occasional kiss which Marsha permitted. Marsha discussed the physical aspects of their relationship in such grave terms and with such guilt that Chaplain Lee began to suspect that Marsha might be pregnant. He was surprised to learn that the sexual involvement had progressed no further than a hasty fondling of Marsha's breasts. Nonetheless, her guilt was of such a magnitude that she was torn between the fear of continuing in such an immoral fashion and the fear of being alone without a boyfriend should she insist that he "behave himself." Viewing herself as physically and socially unattractive, she could not envision a relationship with any other male. Her low self-esteem and negative views of herself physically had not been helped by the fact that she had gained fifteen pounds over the last three months and now saw herself as grossly overweight and repulsive.

Marsha's father, having met Tom on one of his brief visits to the university, had heartily disapproved of the relationship and questioned Marsha at some length about her relationship and sexual involvement. Convinced that the relationship was interfering with her studies, he had extracted from Marsha a promise that she would terminate the relationship—a promise Marsha failed to keep. Marsha continued to see Tom in secret even when her father threatened to cut off her money supply. In regard to Chaplain Lee's suggestion that Marsha see a psychiatrist, her father denied her permission to do so, citing his disbelief in the use of drugs and his general lack of faith in psychiatry as reasons. He also reminded Marsha that psychiatric intervention had been of little, if any, benefit to either her brother or her mother.

During the third session, Marsha agreed to let Chaplain Lee contact her father concerning his impressions of the turmoil now existing in his daughter's life. Unwilling to take time from his busy schedule to talk in person with Chaplain Lee, Marsha's father in a telephone conversation with Chaplain Lee refused to consider the seriousness of Marsha's mental condition. He insisted that she was just feeling sorry for herself and that her depressed state was no more than that which all normal young people pass through at some point. He also informed Chaplain Lee that in an attempt to shock Marsha out of her depressed state he had suggested that she either go ahead and kill herself or quit talking about it so much.

In the fourth session, Marsha appeared to be somewhat less depressed and calmly expressed her intention of terminating the sessions. At this point, she refused to discuss her feelings or to reach any agreement in regard to her future behavior. Annoyed at Chaplain Lee's persistence that she promise not to harm herself and to contact him if she felt so inclined, Marsha again insisted that she could not predict what she might do when in such a depressed state as experienced earlier, and consequently promises made would be of little worth. Still calm and appearing to be more accepting of the situation than in earlier sessions, Marsha left Chaplain Lee's office.

Though acquaintances and dormitory officials had continued to exert some effort to see that Marsha received psychiatric help, even talking with her father in person when he drove her back to the university after the holidays, Marsha had made no further contacts in this direction. Two weeks after returning to the university, she killed herself with her father's pistol which she had smuggled from his safe while at home.

Discussion

There are some serious issues, philosophical and legal as well as physical and psychological, involved in Marsha's case which render it a somewhat unique situation regarding certain principles usually considered sacred in the counselor-counselee relationship. Not the least of these is the matter of intervention as opposed in this case to that of confidentiality. Of equal importance is the philosophical issue regarding the freedom to make one's own decisions even when the therapist is convinced that such will be detrimental to the patient. There are those who believe that each individual should be permitted the freedom to make his own decisions without interference from the counselor even when harm to self or to others is involved, insisting that the person has the right to commit suicide if he so chooses. As a result, minimal effort is exerted where intervention is concerned. Though some will not agree, it is our opinion that maximum effort should be exerted to prevent suicide for the simple reason that most individuals who express suicidal thoughts eventually recover and live productive and meaningful lives. While confidentiality is of the utmost value in any counseling relationship, we believe that it should rank somewhere below that of life and death whenever a serious threat of suicide or homicide exists in the opinion of the counselor.

As with the Monday morning quarterback, hindsight provides certain clues not always so obvious to the person on the firing line faced with a dilemma requiring an immediate decision. However, counselors who fail to utilize hindsight arising from the failure and tragedy involved in cases such as Marsha's, might be considered derelict in the acceptance of their responsibilities for it is from our failures, as well as our successes, that psychology in general and counseling in particular have been able to record the progress made in recent years. Therefore it is with hope that similar tragedies can be prevented, rather than with any condemnation of Chaplain Lee, that Marsha's case is discussed.

To begin with, it should be noted that Marsha had a long history of depression going back at least to the ninth grade. She had also made two previous suicidal attempts as a teenager. In any counseling situation, considerable attention should be paid to the way in which stressful situations have been handled by the client in the past for the reason that past performance is a good indicator of the way an individual will react in the here and now. Although people can, and do, learn newer and better ways of coping with stress, it is important to remember that at least twice Marsha had considered suicide as a potential means of escape from distressing situations. Though they were abortive attempts, such gestures should not be dismissed as insignificant. At best, any suicide attempt represents a cry for help. Even when the intent to kill oneself is missing, any suicidal gesture should be viewed as serious if for no other reason than that the person has become so desperate and so void of ways to cope with his problems that he feels he must go to such lengths to call attention to, or cope with, his situation.

Another significant clue is that of Marsha's low self-esteem and negative self-concept. Everyone at times suffers from a lack of self-confidence or from feelings of inadequacy and insecurity. Despite these feelings, most people believe that things will eventually get better. In Marsha's case, however, feelings of worthlessness and inadequacy seemed pervasive and overwhelming with no indication that she expected things to improve. Having seen herself a failure as a daughter for many years, she had more recently come to see herself a failure as a student and as a woman, physically unattractive and unable to hold a man without engaging in behavior which she saw as sinful and immoral. Guilt, stemming from her sexual involvement with Tom, had begun to erode even her image of herself as a good and moral person, something she had always taken pride in being.

Still another important clue in Marsha's life is her contrived and never-ending efforts to win approval from a father who continued to reject her no matter what she did. The fact that neither her mother nor her brother had been able to satisfy her father or modify his attitudes was ignored by Marsha, who continued without success even to the final week of her life to struggle for his approval. Such a struggle to achieve goals set for her by her father, which were for the most part unrealistic as well as unattractive to Marsha, represents a serious distortion of perspective and reality by both Marsha and her father. The fact that her mother and her brother were seen by a psychiatrist suggests that the entire family structure was perhaps unstable. Little in the way of help and resources was available to Marsha as she struggled to cope with her problems.

On the physical level, Marsha's long walks alone at night with total disregard for her personal safety is significant. Her rapid gain of weight, along with her difficulty in sleeping, overeating, and neglect of appearance in the latter weeks are also reasons for concern. During the sessions with Chaplain Lee, her lack of animation and stuporlike qualities, a drastic departure from her usual demeanor, are symptomatic of a seriously depressed person.

Of all the clues available to Chaplain Lee in his assessment of Marsha's potential for suicide perhaps none was so ominous as her unwillingness to enter into a "no suicide contract." This procedure, which involves the patient in a contract whereby he agrees not to attempt to kill himself for a given period of time, is an important tool in working with the suicidal person. A group from California recently reported on a study in which thirty-one therapists used the "no suicide contract" while working with 266 patients considered seriously suicidal. Results indicated that only three died or made a serious attempt within the time limit, and only one patient killed himself outside the time period.[1]

Marsha's initial unwillingness to enter into such an agreement was apparent since she either refused to do so or qualified her statement to the point that it had little meaning in terms of intent or prevention.

As for suggestions in regard to treatment in Marsha's situation, the reader is reminded that depression is potentially a serious illness and should never be permitted to continue without appropriate treatment. One of the major difficulties in counseling a severely depressed person is that unlike those of most people, the feelings of the depressed person do not return to a more balanced perspective but tend to get worse if untreated. Though obviously uncomfortable and disturbed about Marsha's suicidal ideation, Chaplain Lee continued to allow her to express self-depreciation, self-pity, and hopelessness in regard to change. Furthermore, though he reacted strongly to her references to suicide, there is no evidence that he explored in depth

Marsha's depression or her plans for suicide. Apparently feeling that he had to honor Marsha's request for confidentiality and to permit her the freedom to deal with her problems in her way, Chaplain Lee failed to realize that Marsha was too upset to function adequately and that she needed protection in a more direct way. While the nondirective approach can be an effective tool in counseling, there are situations in which the individual is too upset or too disturbed to make decisions or behave rationally. In circumstances such as these, the counselor must intervene and assume certain responsibilities for the care of the disturbed person. Marsha seemed to have fallen into this category. While many crises involving depression can be handled by clergymen effectively, once it is established that the individual is as severely depressed as was Marsha, immediate psychiatric referral with possible hospitalization and medication is strongly recommended. Had Chaplain Lee been firmer with Marsha about his concerns for her safety and his own limitations in treating her, and had he insisted that her father become more involved and accept more responsibility for the care of his daughter, the results might have been more favorable.

It is also highly significant that Marsha appeared to be less depressed and calmer in her last session with Chaplain Lee. Special attention should be given to a person once a severe depression begins to lift, for it is at this time that the individual may attempt to kill himself. The severely depressed person is often unable to organize his thoughts or to mobilize the energy necessary to carry out the act of suicide. Once the depression begins to lift, however, and he arises from the stuporlike state in which he has been, the potential to kill himself increases. It is also significant that Marsha appeared calmer and more accepting of her situation during the final session. After making the decision to kill one's self, a person struggling with thoughts of suicide will often display qualities of calmness, acceptance, or resignation. This state of mind must not be misinterpreted to mean that the individual has his depression licked and is out of danger.

Finally, Marsha's choice of her father's pistol as a death weapon is also highly significant. Women usually do not use guns to commit suicide, showing instead a preference for drugs or some other means not so violent or so likely to disfigure. The use of a gun might, therefore, be viewed as further evidence that Marsha suffered not only from depression but from other serious emotional problems as well. Even more noteworthy is the fact that the gun belonged to her father. There is some reason to suspect that Marsha's suicide, as is often the situation, was a deliberate and angry type of retaliation directed at her father, reflecting the build up of years of resentment, hostility, and frustration on her part. His attempt to call her bluff about suicide was apparently the last straw.

John

John, a twenty-seven-year-old shy, sensitive, withdrawn male came to see Chaplain Lee after experiencing the fear that the wind was about to blow him off an overhead bridge which he had to walk across each day on his route as a mail carrier. This fear had become so strong that he went several blocks out of his way in order to avoid the situation. Though he indicated that nothing of the sort had occurred recently, he stated that earlier he had heard voices in the midst of heavy traffic as he waited at downtown intersections to cross the street. In some form or other the message usually transmitted was that he was no good and that the world would be better off without him. At night after going to bed he felt that the designs on his bedroom walls were changing, sometimes into such grotesque patterns that he now slept with the light on. On other occasions he reported that he could hear the wall breathing. He complained of insomnia and nightmares, and he appeared physically and emotionally fatigued. His movements and speech were laborious and slow.

Though John had felt a need to seek help for some time, he had found it impossible to ask for help. His shyness and feelings of unworthiness as a person convinced him that no one could be interested in his problems. John was married when he was twenty-two, and his wife deserted him, taking their one-year-old son after only eighteen months of marriage. In the first session he talked of suicide as well as his fear that he might harm others, particularly his mother and young son. For reasons which he could not explain he had uncontrollable outbursts of temper usually directed at his child. The mere presence of his son in the room would sometimes send John into a rage. On several occasions his wife had intervened when John was screaming at his son for no apparent reason. At other times he admitted that he entertained thoughts of killing his son.

In later sessions John continued to describe himself as always having been a lonely person. His father had deserted his family when John was seven years of age and had not been heard from in years. John stated that he had only one friend of any consequence. Even here it appeared that his friend had homosexual intentions and was deterred only by John's inability to relate sexually to anyone, male or female, in any satisfactory manner.

John indicated that he smoked pot several times weekly and had on several occasions used mescaline and LSD often in combination with other drugs or alcohol. Only under the influence of drugs did he feel the capacity to communicate in a meaningful fashion with others. He also saw in drugs a means of escaping from the unpleasant existence he lived but more importantly felt that they might provide him with the insight necessary to understand himself better. Though he insisted that drugs had been of value to him in this respect, apparently they were adding to his confusion and fears.

Though he saw Chaplain Lee for several sessions, he found it difficult to relate to him. With increasing feelings of alienation and desperation, he withdraw even further from other people, maintaining minimal contact with his fellow employees at the post office. His rounds completed, he returned to his apartment where he spent the night smoking pot, contemplating his situation. When he read he usually turned to mystical or metaphysical matters. His work also began to suffer with his superiors calling him on the carpet after a number of people on his route complained of mail being delivered to the wrong address.

In the fourth week of counseling, he indicated that he had met a young woman at a small pot party with whom he could communicate for the first time in his life. Somewhat elated he expressed the opinion that he no longer needed to talk to

Chaplain Lee. At Chaplain Lee's insistence, he agreed to return one more time to let him know how things were going.
However, he failed to keep the appointment.

Six weeks after the missed session, Chaplain Lee was
notified by hospital officials that John had been seen in the
emergency room the previous evening for an overdose of drugs
with his life hanging in the balance for most of the night. At
the request of hospital physicians, John was visited by Chaplain Lee the following evening in his hospital room. At this
time, John informed Chaplain Lee that his only regret was
that he was still alive, indicating that he was not even successful in killing himself. He stated that he would do a better job
next time.

As he talked, it became apparent that John had been contemplating suicide for several weeks and had gone to great
lengths to obtain and save up the medications he thought
necessary to do the job. He revealed his reasons for doing so
as the breakup of the relationship with the girl who had
found someone else. This he saw as the final proof that he
was totally inadequate and unacceptable in his relationships
with other human beings.

His mother, with whom he had almost no communication,
refused to accept her son's attempt to kill himself seriously,
insisting instead that John had made the mistake of mixing
drugs and alcohol with almost fatal results, but had no intention of killing himself. All of Chaplain Lee's attempts to convince her that her son had made a serious attempt to take his
life and that he was alive only because he had miscalculated
the dosage necessary to kill, were unsuccessful.

Discussion

Early in the first session, John paints a picture of himself as a person desperately in need of psychiatric care. His
needs are for a much more intensive and extensive program
of therapy than Chaplain Lee will be able to provide as evidenced by his irrational beliefs and fears, his seriously depressed state, his thoughts of harm to himself and others,
and his history of poor socialization. His destructive behavior is pervasive, ranging from drugs to unrealistic expectations of other people. His misinterpretations of everyday
sounds as voices telling him that he is worthless and his

fear that he is about to be blown away, an unlikely event, are signs of severe mental disturbance. Hospitalization is likely needed in John's case with appropriate medication and treatment in a nonthreatening environment in which he can be given firm directiveness in regard to interpretations of events.

As disturbing as the idea of suicide may be, John's uncontrollable desire to harm his son is even greater cause for concern. In a society in which suicide is socially unacceptable, killing one's child is far more unacceptable, and serious thoughts of committing such an act is a symptom of grave emotional problems.

As for John's attempts to kill himself, though he had not informed Chaplain Lee that he had been saving up the pills necessary to carry out his plans, he later confessed that he had been saving up for months for this purpose. In working with individuals suspected to be entertaining thoughts of suicide, one must explore the extent of planning which they might have done. The individual who has purchased a gun or pills, made plans to drive his car off a bridge, or written letters putting his affairs in order is generally considered much more apt to kill himself than is the person who has only vague thoughts of killing himself with no real effort or planning evident.

Additional clues that John is a high suicide risk are: his use of drugs and alcohol (a potentially lethal combination), feelings of unworthiness, loneliness, lack of friends, divorce, recent breakup with girl friend, obsession with metaphysical literature, poor work performance, his appearance, insomnia, and nightmares. While none of the above are in themselves necessarily indicators of emotional illness, combined with the earlier symptoms discussed they do contribute to the total picture of a person with serious problems.

In general, whenever a person reports events, concerns, and fears so "far out" that the counselor is unable to identify with or comprehend that which is being related, referral for psychiatric evaluation may be appropriate. This seems to have been the situation with John.

Finally, his regret over being unsuccessful in his attempt to kill himself, along with his stated intentions of doing a better job next time, leave little room for optimism. The situation becomes even more dangerous due to his mother's inability or unwillingness to grasp the seriousness of her son's problem. Even with hospitalization where he can be protected and treatment begun, the prognosis for John is dismal.

Janice

Janice, a twenty-two-year-old file clerk, first came to see Chaplain Lee the morning after she had been released from a local hospital where she had gone after swallowing a bottle of sleeping pills. She complained of despondency over the recent breakup of her relationship with her boyfriend. Though she was extremely attractive physically—a former cheerleader and beauty contestant—she also indicated it was depressing to be growing so ugly and fat that people no longer paid her the attention she had become accustomed to.

Not a member of Chaplain Lee's church, Janice had been referred by her roommate with whom she had shared an apartment for the last three months. Fed up with Janice's outbursts of temper, alternating with periods of moodiness and depression, accompanied with threats of suicide, she had delivered the ultimatum of "get help or get out." Fearful of having to leave the person she depended on most, Janice had reluctantly scheduled an appointment with Chaplain Lee.

Out of school temporarily, Janice had been on and off probation in several colleges. She complained of being inferior to others intellectually and socially and experienced considerable difficulty in relating to other people. She also found it difficult to make decisions, particularly in regard to a college major and career. In an attempt to compensate for her perceived inferiority, Janice dressed in an elaborate and expensive fashion, spending money considerably beyond her means. However, she became convinced that no man would remain with her any length of time after being involved in a number of whirlwind romances in the past three years. In the last year alone, she had had relationships with eight different males.

In discussing the breakup the previous night of the most recent of these relationships, Janice indicated that she had no insight as to the cause of the breakup, insisting that she thought things had been going along well. Further discussion revealed, however, that things had not been going well at all for some time. A member of one of the better sororities in one of the colleges attended earlier, Janice was of the opinion that her status in the community could stand improving. Subsequently she convinced her boyfriend, who was a young but successful businessman, to join one of the more prestigious social clubs in the area. She had also attempted to convince him that he should only associate with people who had acquired a certain standing in the community socially and economically. Such behavior had prompted her boyfriend to label her a snob and social climber. He also became infuriated at Janice's flirtations and seductive behavior with other males. Initially taken in by such behavior himself, as well as finding Janice attractive physically, he had come to learn that for Janice sex was not the enjoyable and delightful experience he had been led to believe. To his great disappointment, instead, she found it distasteful. She engaged in sexual activities only when he threatened to leave and find someone else. His disillusionment in this area along with her constant demands for attention had prompted him several weeks earlier to declare his intentions of terminating the relationship. So informed, Janice returned to her apartment and took fifteen aspirin tablets—after which she immediately called her boyfriend to inform him of her action. In near panic, he responded by rushing her to the hospital where after a brief period of observation she was released. Feeling responsible for her deed, he agreed to a reconciliation with things going along pretty well for a period of weeks. Soon disillusioned again with her inability to relate in a mature and sincere fashion, he once again walked out of the apartment one night, indicating that he would not return. Later the same evening, after several phone calls interspersed with threats of killing herself, to which her boyfriend failed to respond, Janice shut herself in her bathroom. Startled by the sound of broken glass, her roommate rushed to the bathroom to find Janice sitting on the floor, a number of pills in her hand. Janice indicated that she had already taken half the bottle.

Once again Janice was rushed to the hospital where after considerable fanfare she admitted that she had swallowed only five of the pills. In the ensuing turmoil, however, Janice had persuaded her roommate to call her boyfriend and inform him of the most recent attempt to kill herself. When he failed to respond as she had hoped, she arranged the appointment with Chaplain Lee.

In subsequent sessions, Janice behaved in much the same fashion with Chaplain Lee as she had previously with her boyfriend and roommate. Her attendance at the sessions was sporadic. Her conversation was sprinkled with threats of suicide. At times, free with her compliments toward Chaplain Lee, frequently dressed in revealing dresses or the bearer of gifts, she would infer that he was the only one really interested in, and capable of, helping her. On other occasions, appearing to be in a depressed mood, she would accuse him of not caring for her and again resort to threats of suicide or not coming back for further appointments. If neither of these approaches seemed to work, she was apt to leave unexpectedly only to return and repeat the process week after week.

In spite of Chaplain Lee's attempts to convince Janice that her immature, self-dramatizing, and manipulative ways of relating to people were unnecessary to gain the attention she so desperately craved, he was for the most part unsuccessful. Neither her behavior nor attitudes were altered to any significant degree.

After several canceled appointments and one in which she neither called nor showed up, she made one final appearance. At this time, she thanked Chaplain Lee for his time and for being such a nice person, but concluded by saying that she did not find the sessions helpful and would not return for further appointments. Feeling rather frustrated and confused by Janice's behavior (since she had been so complimentary to him in the past), Chaplain Lee attempted to schedule another appointment still convinced that he could help Janice. Appearing to accept the invitation for another session. Janice scheduled another appointment. One week later she called to cancel the appointment and was not seen again by Chaplain Lee. He did hear from her roommate that she continued behaving in much the same fashion with the same predictable results.

Discussion

Janice presents a pattern of behavior which is extremely difficult for friends and helpers. She uses a suicidal threat as a weapon to force people to do as she wishes. The suicidal gesture is the ultimate threat to manipulate people to do what is desired. Janice's feelings are not the usually depressed ones found in a hopeless person who wants to die because she has given up efforts to meet her needs. Instead, her central feelings are anger and rage which she reflects by inflicting punishment in the form of guilt on other people. Manipulation involves trying to force another person to do something or be something other than what is spontaneous or desired on his part. In an immature way, no real concern about the other person is felt. This type of emotional blackmail usually arouses anger in other people after repetitions of the manipulating behavior.

It seems that Janice also has some confusion about her goals, needs, and values. Her sense of self-esteem is low. She appears to need a degree of limitation but also freedom to try out new patterns. It is difficult to help such an individual without a firm agreement. A realistic agreement could include a plan so that if the person did not show up for appointments or call to rearrange a scheduled time, therapy would end. This is not rejection but reality, and the individual makes the choice. Another way of contracting is to charge a fee for the service.

The most difficult problem in helping Janice will be her own feelings. Although things have not been going well for her, she is not really motivated to change her behavior. Only when she genuinely feels *she* wants to have help will any effort be successful. No outsider can persuade her, whether it be a friendly roommate or Chaplain Lee.

Chaplain Lee probably neither helped nor worsened this situation. By trying to clarify the sources of difficulty, he did more clearly identify the problem. Janice probably would have not accepted psychiatric help at this time any more than she would accept reality as reflected by Chaplain Lee. Although it is difficult, we all need to accept the fact that at times some people do not want to change. Janice may or may not get to a point where she wants to change. Such will probably depend upon the continuing success of her manipulative behavior.

Leslie

Leslie was seen by Chaplain Lee for only one visit after she called him one evening indicating that she needed to talk to someone right away. One of her girl friends had suggested that she call Chaplain Lee although Leslie was not a member of his church. The crisis which had prompted her to call had been precipitated by the breakup of her relationship with her boyfriend, Mike. Two weeks prior to the night she saw Chaplain Lee, Mike had informed her that he no longer loved her and wanted to date other girls. They had been going together for fourteen months and had talked at length of marriage when Mike graduated from college in nine months. Though she had at times experienced some doubt about the relationship, Leslie indicated that she was totally unprepared to hear Mike say that he no longer loved her or wanted to see her again.

Leslie, a twenty-year-old student attending business school in the city, had above average intelligence and was a most attractive and personable young lady who would have little difficulty in attracting males. In spite of this, it was Chaplain Lee's opinion that she had a low opinion of herself and blamed herself almost exclusively for the breakup of the relationship. During the hour, she cried for the first half of the session with her sobs gradually subsiding as the hour progressed. On several occasions, she indicated that she knew she was over-reacting to the situation, feeling that after two weeks she should be more in control of her emotions. She revealed not only that she had been crying a good bit since the breakup, but that she had difficulty sleeping and eating as well, and had spent considerable time ruminating about the mistakes she had made in the relationship. Toward the end of the hour, she indicated that she planned to go through with her plans, made several months earlier, to drop out of school for the winter quarter and work at a resort where she hoped to earn enough to pay her school expenses for the spring quarter.

Since Leslie appeared to be so upset, Chaplain Lee spent considerable time during the session discussing her grief and her plans for the future. When Chaplain Lee raised the question of suicide, Leslie informed him though she had given some thought to it earlier, she had no intention of killing herself. When Chaplain Lee attempted to arrange another appointment for the following day, Leslie indicated that she had final tests scheduled and would be unable to come in again before leaving for home at the end of the quarter.

By the end of the hour, Chaplain Lee was convinced that Leslie was not suicidal, and though upset, he perceived her as quite capable of coping with the situation. She appeared to be less depressed and indicated that talking with him had helped her considerably. Still concerned about her low self-esteem, Chaplain Lee encouraged her to return to see him when she arrived back in town. She refused to commit herself to any further appointments but did agree that she would arrange an appointment if she felt the need.

Though she made no effort to contact Chaplain Lee again, he saw her after her return to the city on several occasions during church services with her girl friend and once in the company of a young man. Interpreting this as an indication that things were going well, Chaplain Lee was shocked to learn from her girl friend later in the summer that Leslie had drowned while on an outing to the beach with several other girls from the school. Afraid that Leslie's depression had played some part in her death, Chaplain Lee inquired further as to the circumstances surrounding her death. He was able to learn that Leslie had continued to talk with sadness and regret of Mike and their relationship but had been seen by her associates as recovering from hurt and disappointment in an acceptable fashion. Though viewed as an excellent swimmer by her companions, they voiced the opinion that she had overestimated her strength and apparently drowned after swimming out too far from shore. Following a routine usually pursued in such situations, authorities ruled her death an accident.

Discussion

Leslie did not herself introduce the question of suicide in her sessions with Chaplain Lee as had the other individuals discussed in the cases presented above. Neither did Chaplain Lee, after talking with her and being assured that she would not harm herself, judge her to be a suicide risk. The investigating authorities apparently saw no reason to suggest that suicide was involved in Leslie's death and ruled accordingly.

Leslie's case is included in the chapter on suicide due to the consideration on the part of Chaplain Lee that her death might be other than accidental and in some way related to events which she had discussed earlier with him.

Deaths, which occur under circumstances similar to those related above in which there is reasonable cause to suspect that death might have been the result of planning on the part of the deceased, have recently come under close scrutiny by those interested in a more in-depth study of the possible relationship between many so-called "accidents" and suicide. It is difficult at best to substantiate such claims due to lack of any overt expression of such intent on the part of many who commit suicide and the reluctance of family and sympathetic officials to use the term "suicide" for obvious reasons. However, authorities are convinced that many deaths listed as accidental are in reality suicides. Although psychological autopsies, in cases where suicide is suspected, offer considerable promise in the study of suicide, they are not apt to increase significantly the reliability of statistics involving suicide. We do not intend to deal with the questionable nature of such figures, but we do regard suicide as one of the major causes of death in this country, particularly in certain age groups.

Whether Leslie's death was accidental or intentional on her part will in all probability remain unknown. However, in view of Leslie's overreaction to the breakup with Mike, her despondency, her low self-esteem and earlier thoughts of suicide, the possibility of suicide should not be ignored by those whose job it is to render some opinion or assessment of those individuals with self-destructive tendencies. Although the vast majority of those who intend to commit suicide communicate in some fashion their intentions, there will always be those who confound and deceive the ones who try to help as did Chaplain Lee. There are others who will openly defy any and all efforts on the part of those committed to help and eventually find some way to end their lives.

Most of the individuals who agree to some form of contract with their counselors as did Leslie are sincere and may be trusted to keep their promise not to hurt themselves. However, it should be emphasized that not all people who deny suicidal ideation or intent are sincere, or, as in the case of the more severely disturbed, capable of assuming responsibility for their thoughts or behavior. Although there is evidence to suggest that Leslie did not fall in either of these categories, it is within the realm of possibility that Leslie was such a person, who either deliberately or unintentionally failed to communicate the seriousness of her intent to Chaplain Lee. There is no reason to suggest that Chaplain Lee should have handled the situation differently. It appears that his discussion of her feelings and the precautions he took were adequate measures with no reason to believe that psychiatric referral was indicated.

Joan

Joan began her first session with Chaplain Lee by stating that she felt silly to be taking up someone's time with such an insignificant problem. She followed this statement, however, by crying. She said that she had been crying a lot lately and that things had gotten so bad that she decided to see Chaplain Lee when she began to think of suicide. On the way to his office, she had recurring thoughts of what it would be like to drive her car into a bridge abuttment. On other occasions, she had thought of throwing herself in front of a car. Joan quickly added that she did not believe she could ever do any of these things.

As the session progressed, it became apparent that Joan was experiencing considerable difficulty in her relationships with her parents and her boyfriend. She had also become involved in so many activities that she was sleeping only about five or six hours per night. Although she was always an excellent student, her grades were beginning to suffer her senior year due to her overinvolvement in extracurricular activities in school and church programs. For the first time she anticipated a grade of C.

Joan was an extremely attractive eighteen-year-old high school student who had maintained a 3.8 average throughout high school. She hoped to pursue a career as a physician. Not only was she attractive and intelligent, but she possessed considerable poise and social skills and was popular with both males and females on campus. Perceiving of herself as a sensitive person, concerned with other people and their problems, she found it difficult to say "no" to the many requests or demands placed on her by her fellow students and teachers. She was active in social clubs and in numerous other events and projects, both individually and collectively on campus. As a result, she found herself either unable or pushed to meet the unrealistic schedule and goals she had set for herself.

While insisting that she loved and was loved in return by her parents and sister, Joan described the family situation as one in which her parents obviously lacked trust in her ability to make decisions and assume responsibility for running her own life. Their view of Joan as a rather immature and irresponsible young girl conflicted greatly with Joan's perception of herself as a mature and responsible person, a person now demanding that she be permitted more freedom in becoming an individual.

In similar fashion, Joan had become involved with a college student, five years her senior, who had also assumed a somewhat possessive and authoritarian role in their relationship. This had reached the point that he was beginning to insist that he make many of the decisions which Joan believed to be her responsibility. He was also quite jealous of the time she spent with other females and had insisted that she not become involved with any other male in any way, romantically or otherwise.

Whenever Joan attempted to discuss her feelings with her family or her boyfriend, she complained that they tended to ignore her or else treat her as if she were a child. On the other hand, her peers in school, seeing her as a responsible and talented leader, looked to her as a person with whom they could share their concerns. Unfortunately from Joan's point of view they offered her little opportunity to share her problems in return. Consequently Joan felt a lack of meaningful two-way communication in her life with her parents, boyfriend, and peers. Resentful of such, she was nonetheless made to feel guilty, indicating to Chaplain Lee that she had failed to meet the expectations others had of her and had let people down who depended on her. Feeling somewhat helpless, trapped, and frustrated with no one to confide in, she had begun to have suicidal thoughts as a possible exit from the pressures of living.

Discussion

Despite her obvious unhappiness, Joan presents a situation which is more in accord with a normal developmental situation. She has well-developed interpersonal skills, a high achievement level, and is usually "successful." She appears to be a person who would respond quite favorably to counseling.

However, Joan does have some unrealistic goals. She is trying to do too much. Her idealism and perfectionism need modification. It is not difficult to understand her seeing Chaplain Lee as a person with whom she could talk. She has a need to redefine goals and to be given approval to say "no" to other's requests. She clearly wants support in her move toward self-identity and responsibility.

Having an opportunity to talk out some of her confused thoughts will probably be important to Joan. She has said that she is unable to share her feelings. This might be more complicated than she realizes as she has been struggling to win approval by being extremely conscientious, dependable, unselfish, and good. It might take some time to establish a relationship with Chaplain Lee before she can share other thoughts and feelings which she might consider "bad" for her. She will likely be able to clarify her own desires and to become more realistic as she does talk out her feelings.

Another expectation is that Joan will have considerable anger to express. Chaplain Lee might be able to help her acknowledge those "negative" feelings without thinking that she is a bad person. Encouragement in increased self-awareness and assertion of her needs will aid Joan in the development of a sense of identity which is so important to a person at this age.

Many times individuals seeking help are able to communicate quite accurately the severity of their problems. Although Joan said she had suicidal thoughts, she also made it clear that such thoughts were unacceptable to her. There is no need for Chaplain Lee to become unduly anxious over her statement. Joan has apparently been able to recognize her suicidal thoughts as warning to seek counsel instead of a signal to act.

In the case of Joan, though she referred to suicide, psychiatric referral does not seem to be indicated in light of other information presented. It is likely that sessions with Chaplain Lee would be as beneficial to Joan as seeing a psychiatrist.

Cathy

Cathy, a twenty-eight-year-old teacher, came in complaining of stomach aches, diarrhea, headaches, and tension, none of which had been relieved by frequent visits to numerous physicians over the years. She had recently been in the hospital for a series of tests and examinations in regard to her stomach disorders and had been told that nothing was wrong with her physically. On earlier occasions, she had been told by various physicians that her headaches were the result of tension.

In the initial session with Chaplain Lee, she seemed most concerned about her work in the school system where she taught, feeling that neither her students or supervisor appreciated the work she was doing. Things had become so bad, in her opinion, in recent months that she had begun to wonder if she was in the right profession. Following a session with her school principal, in which she had attempted to discuss some changes in the program she had initiated, she had returned home sad and depressed, when he had failed to agree with her thinking. Her attempts to discuss her feelings with her husband were met in the usual fashion, ending with his attention being diverted to a ballgame in progress on the television screen. Feeling rebuffed, not only by her principal but by her husband as well, Cathy began to think about suicide as she sat alone in her bed later that night. In was at that time that she decided to call Chaplain Lee and arrange an appointment for the following morning instead.

During the first session, it was apparent that Cathy was upset, not only by the problems and difficulties encountered in her job but by the fact that she had to work at all. Further discussion revealed that her husband, a second year medical student, had no source of income. Though they had agreed earlier that she would continue to work in order that her husband could get through medical school, Cathy had become increasingly discouraged by the long years ahead in which it appeared that she would be the chief breadwinner. Feeling that her husband could at least get a part-time job, Cathy's resentment had grown to the point that her earlier dreams of being the wife of a successful physician had diminished considerably. In spite of her complaints in this regard, Cathy hastened to add that she and her husband were still much in love and that their marriage was ideal in most aspects.

In subsequent sessions, she began to complain that her marriage was not the perfect relationship she had portrayed it to be to others. The sexual part of their marriage, which she had described as fantastic in the earlier counseling sessions, she now described as boring and uneventful to her. Although she had initially denied such intentions, she was eventually able to say that the withholding of sex when displeased and reward of sex for favors granted had become a rather potent weapon in her arsenal of tools which she used in an attempt to manipulate her husband into meeting her needs. Failure in her attempts to manipulate him in this or similar fashion usually resulted in depression on her part. On one earlier occasion, Cathy indicated that she had taken five aspirin tablets in an attempt to kill herself after her husband had refused to take her to a bridge party (something he had agreed to do several weeks earlier), choosing instead to referee a basketball game.

On other occasions similar to this when Cathy had felt neglected by her husband, she had turned to other men for the attention and recognition she felt due her. Although she often engaged in provocative and flirtatious fashion toward other men in an attempt to gain attention, even sitting on the laps of casual male acquaintances at social gatherings, Cathy denied any extramarital relationships or any intentions of becoming involved with any man other than her husband, insisting that such was totally against her morals.

In the fourth session with Chaplain Lee, Cathy discussed the depressing aspects of the upcoming Christmas season, a time she and her husband always spent with her family. In addition to her parents who were both still alive, Cathy had one older sister and two older brothers, the youngest of these being eight years older than Cathy. With this difference in ages, Cathy clearly indicated that she had been reared almost as if she were an only child and had become accustomed to being the focus of attention at Christmas time by her parents and older siblings. When Cathy was eleven years old, her sister had married, followed shortly by the marriage of her two older brothers. The arrival of their children and their presence in the home at Chistmas time had in Cathy's view deprived her of the attention usually bestowed on her as the youngest child in the family. Though she insisted that she loved her nieces and nephews dearly, even at this late date, Cathy stated that she still found it difficult to share the spotlight and resented strongly the attention they received from her parents and older brothers and sister. She was particularly jealous of the relationship which her father had enjoyed with his grandchildren and added that her father had always loved her sister best. Even now he sometimes called her by her sister's name or confused her name with that of her sister when introducing her to new people.

Discussion

Cathy's story reveals that she is in many ways like a little girl, wanting to be pampered and taken care of. She is angry, but as a "good girl" does not feel that she can express these feelings directly. Strongly needing the recognition of other people, she feels unappreciated. Her physical symptoms and suicidal thoughts are indicative of her need for better ways to communicate her frustrations and anger. Her immaturity further complicates her striving toward more direct communication. She apparently has considerable difficulty in delaying her gratification, wanting instead to have the best of all things now as do most small children.

For Chaplain Lee, work with Cathy will be challenging. Continuing to manipulate people as she has in the past with some success, Cathy seems to have some rather unrealistic needs for attention and goes to rather extreme lengths to get these needs met. Although it may be difficult for Chaplain Lee not to respond to Cathy's pleas, threats, or demands, to do so would only serve to reinforce the undesirable pattern established through the years.

One of the first steps in working with Cathy should be that of defining a set of conditions for appointments. Once a schedule for meetings is arranged, the plan must be adhered to with firmness lest Cathy become a constant caller whenever things do not go as she desires. The demands of the real world must be acknowledged and Chaplain Lee can be of considerable help to Cathy in the establishment of a realistic program provided he does not succumb to her attempts to manipulate him as she has with other significant people in the past. Cathy might also be encouraged to seek out areas in which she can contribute and be made to feel that she is important—coordinating some church program or other activity which is separate from her job and her husband. The encouragement of diversified interests to better meet her needs as opposed to putting all her hopes for success and self-esteem in one basket is also important. The major goal is to provide Cathy with the opportunity to talk to an interested listener about her feelings so that she may learn better ways to express her feelings.

Chaplain Lee will probably find working with Cathy difficult but not hopeless. Clinging stubbornly to a childlike, selfish set of expectations, Cathy will need help in sorting out those goals and needs in her life which are realistically obtainable and desirable. Once defined, healthier and more mature ways of moving in this direction must be found if Cathy is to escape the morass of physical and emotional symptoms which spurred her to seek help initially.

Chaplain Lee can probably work with Cathy. However, he should be alert to the possibility that she might need psychiatric care at a later date. If he does begin to feel too uncomfortable in the face of her threats of suicide or attempts to seduce him into responding through sexual ploys which are almost certain to come up sooner or later, then a referral for psychiatric evaluation might be in order. In any respect, Cathy will be difficult to work with; exhibitionistic, demanding, and manipulative, she will possibly evoke feelings of inadequacy and frustration at times in anyone who agrees to work with her. In a situation such as this Chaplain Lee can probably benefit from ongoing communication with another colleague.

Mrs. Baker

Mrs. Baker was viewed by Chaplain Lee as one of the most dependable and well-adjusted women in his church. Therefore, he was surprised that she had scheduled an appointment for the purpose of discussing personal problems with him.

A college graduate, Mrs. Baker was married to a successful professional man in the community. Though the mother of two teenagers herself, Mrs. Baker maintained a busy schedule, participating in numerous civic projects as well as being involved in church groups and activities.

As she entered his office, Mrs. Baker immediately indicated to Chaplain Lee that she felt somewhat embarrassed about coming to see him with personal problems. In an agitated manner, Mrs. Baker then began to discuss a small scar, barely visible over her right eye, which she described as the source of considerable anxiety and shame to her.

Since the scar was so tiny that only the closest observer would have noticed its existence, Chaplain Lee was surprised to hear that Mrs. Baker, who had always concerned herself with the more weighty matters of life, would be so upset about something so insignificant. When he tried to assure her that her scar was practically invisible and detracted not at all from her physical appearance, Mrs. Baker ignored Chaplain Lee, continuing to insist that it was at the root of her discomfort and anxiety. Indicating that it had resulted after a fall on some gravel some years ago when she was a child, she insisted that it had been changing in recent weeks and bothered her more and more. Though she perceived it as being a small thing to other people, she stated that it was of such concern to her that she had visited several surgeons in recent months. In each case she had been told that treatment was unnecessary, an opinion she refused to accept. At this point she asked that Chaplain Lee supply her with the names of other surgeons with whom she might consult about her need for an operation to relieve the discomfort caused by the scar. Upon receiving the name of a surgeon with whom Chaplain Lee was acquainted, she thanked him and left the office.

Thinking the matter closed, Chaplain Lee was surprised when Mrs. Baker returned two weeks later to inform him that once again she had been told that surgery was unnecessary. Stating that no one understood just how bad things were, she began to discuss the scar again, saying that it seemed to be pulling her eye tight and that she could not continue to live with her eye this way. Describing herself as sensitive and repulsed by the way it must look to others, she related that she had curtailed many of her activities and had become depressed.

Convinced that Mrs. Baker was over-reacting to something of relatively insignificant proportions, Chaplain Lee again attempted to convince Mrs. Baker that a return to her religious and civic work would in time prove to be the best course for her to pursue in combatting her depression and worry.

Seeming to heed Chaplain Lee's advice, Mrs. Baker resumed some of her former activities in the church and community. Appearing to be her old self again, she scheduled no further appointments with Chaplain Lee. Remaining friendly when she saw him, no other reference to her eye was made, nor did she indicate in any way that she was upset.

Six weeks later, after leaving a note for her husband and driving her children to the home of relatives, she drove her car into an oncoming train, killing herself instantly.

Discussion

There are times when mental illness is expressed as a distortion or change in an individual's perception of his physical body. The incident with Mrs. Baker is an example of this kind of disturbance. What appeared to be a case of overreaction, and passed over by Chaplain Lee as insignificant, was in fact a much more serious and pervasive response to life on the part of Mrs. Baker.

More specifically in Mrs. Baker's life, a small blemish suddenly became a symbol of each and every stress she had experienced. Since Mrs. Baker could not deal with her real feelings in a direct fashion, tending to deny them instead, she had to communicate indirectly. While most people learn to accept variation in their emotions and adapt to these feelings, Mrs. Baker had never learned to tolerate feelings. She could either be rigid, intellectualized, and objective, doing the "right" thing always or else become overwhelmed by feelings which she could not tolerate.

Chaplain Lee apparently failed to realize the seriousness of Mrs. Baker's problem and her need for psychiatric referral. His advice to continue her good works ignored the more basic and underlying pathology in her. Following his advice, Mrs. Baker did experience a brief, but temporary, flight into health. To assume that a return to her former busy work schedule would make things right was unrealistic. In all probability such had been Mrs. Baker's defense in the past to protect herself from fear and loss of self-control. When such failed to serve as a defense, she switched to concerns over her physical appearance. Mrs. Baker, already sick in a serious way, becoming overwhelmed, began to distort reality. Her focus on her scar, a symptom of her distortion, was a cry for help, though an indirect one. Unfortunately, Chaplain Lee failed to hear her confusion and panic. Stereotyping Mrs. Baker as an achieving, adequate person he failed to see the changes, only her past. This pseudoadequacy masked a frightened and confused individual. Such gross distortions of physical appearance or bodily functions should be considered bases for psychiatric referral.

Summary

Suicide. The very use of the word gets attention as few other words in the English language can. The emotional impact of the word is exceedingly strong and is one of the most anxiety-arousing subjects with which the clergyman or mental health worker has to deal. However disturbing it may be to do so, one of the most essential steps in dealing with the potential suicide is the direct confrontation of one's desires or intentions to kill one's self. Before such is possible it may be helpful, even necessary, for some clergymen to re-explore and clarify their own attitudes and feelings about suicide so that they may deal with the topic without undue personal stress.

Almost everyone at one time or another thinks of suicide. However, thoughts are quite different from actions or plans for action. Most suicidal attempts (acting on suicidal thoughts) are made by people who are depressed. Causes of the depression may be unknown or may be attributed to more obvious happenings such as the loss of a significant person through death, separation, or divorce. The elderly are particularly susceptible to such losses. Often there is anger directed at another person with retaliation toward some specific person often involved. Although attempts might be made, it is somewhat unusual for a person to commit suicide while involved in counseling or therapy. When attempts are made, they are rarely successful.

Since suicidal persons are often depressed, clergymen should familiarize themselves with the warning signals of severe depression as discussed in chapter 3. Sadness, outbursts of crying, and thoughts of suicide, particularly if accompanied by signs of abject hopelessness and total lack of meaning or purpose in one's existence, should be interpreted to mean that the need exists to protect a person from himself with immediate psychiatric referral indicated. Clergymen should also be alerted to the possibility of suicide if the patient suddenly changes his attitude and becomes calm after discussing suicide. This closing of the subject may mean that a decision to die has been made. Other symptoms such as decreased appetite, loss of sexual interest or other pleasure seeking behavior, weight loss, and sleep disturbance should not be ignored. A high suicidal risk is also often involved whenever psychotherapy, medication, and/or electroshock therapy have failed in bringing about a change in the mood or depression. Other situations, which may also signal a high risk of suicide include those individuals who may be extremely anxious, even panicky, as a result of homosexual thoughts or behavior which they find unacceptable. Likewise the individual who is too confused or disturbed to recognize the full consequences of his action is a good candidate for suicide.

Further danger signals in any assessment of suicidal potential include fascination with suicide, a specific plan to carry it out, and a lack of any good reason to continue living. Rather than a direct statement that the person intends to kill himself statements may be of a more subtle nature, such as "I won't be around much longer for people to kick around" or "My family would be better off without me." The rejection of the "no suicide contract" is another significant indication that the person may be in danger of harm to himself.

Finally, it should be reiterated that in rare cases the desire to kill one's self is so intense and pervasive and the sufferer so lacking in both internal and external resources that death results despite the combined efforts of friends, family, clergymen, and mental health professionals. Even if locked in a padded cell, the person intent on self-destruction will eventually manage to find some way to end his life. In such a case, those involved in trying to help should derive some comfort from their concern and efforts rather than engage in self-flagellation over something in which they had little or no control.

Chapter 5
Sex

For certain individuals sex may be the viewing of some badly produced sex film in an uptown movie theater or a peep show in a curtained cubicle, usually found in the backroom of some sleezy, rundown building located in almost any town throughout this country. For others, sex is the ultimate expression of love and human emotion which is permissible only after marriage. For still others engaged in the quest for fun, pleasure, and excitement, sex offers the greatest promise of fulfillment and release from tension. For a small number of individuals, sex is seen for purposes of procreation only.

Whatever it represents, sex brings with it myriad other related problems as anyone engaged in counseling well knows. For reasons which remain unclear, more people are being seen in the offices of clergymen, psychiatrists, and psychologists, as well as in sex clinics, than ever before for sexual problems. While some authorities insist that sexual problems are on the rise, others claim that people are just more open in their discussion of sexual matters than in previous generations. Whatever the reason it is rare to find a case in which sex does not enter the picture in some form or other whenever individuals come in for counseling. Despite the efforts of various individuals and groups through the years who have insisted that human sexuality be ignored or suppressed, sex is here to stay.

In any discussion of sex there are many issues involved, morally, socially, physically, and emotionally. Our purpose, however, remains that of dealing with cases in which sexual behavior may be indicative of emotional disturbance. While many interpret sexual stimulation through the viewing of movies or magazines classified as pornographic as being sinful, such is not sufficient reason to label the person engaged in such activities as mentally ill. If so most of the males in this country would be classified as emotionally disturbed at some time or other in their lives. On the other hand, there are situations in which sexual practices, combined with other symptoms, can be indicative of psychopathology and it is with those that we are concerned in the following cases.

Millie

Millie, a twenty-two-year-old college student, in an agitated fashion, indicated to Chaplain Lee that she had a sexual problem. Describing herself as having been to bed with thirty-four men in the last year she was beginning to wonder if she could ever settle down to marriage with only one person. Seeing herself as ugly, lacking in social skills and stupid, she stated that sex was the only thing she had to offer. Again and again in the sessions she would refer to herself as socially inferior. Revealing that she had no close friends she attributed this to the fact that she had been an "army brat" who had never stayed anywhere long enough to put down roots. Her feelings of social and intellectual inferiority had not been lessened by her mother who made no attempt to conceal her opinion of her daughter as too stupid to make it through college or too ugly to have a steady boyfriend. Attempting to compensate for these perceived inadequacies, Millie saw herself as an adequate performer in bed, but one who was confused by the briefness of her relationships with males.

In succeeding sessions Millie spoke of her up and down performance in school, often making A's and F's in the same subject in succeeding weeks. At times she would find herself so excited and turned on by a school project that she would go for two days and nights without sleep, producing work of a superior quality. At other times she would be depressed and so lacking in energy and initiative that she could do nothing at all. Working part time as a waitress she would sometimes work two or three shifts in succession without feeling tired. In other areas of her life she saw herself as being disorganized, going about her activities in a frantic fashion but with little visible results. In recent weeks she had been plagued by many problems with bills piling up and checks bouncing on two occasions. Though she was active and involved in many activities, most were short lived and seldom pursued to the finish. She described herself as getting upset over little things and felt that she was the butt of many jokes or singled out for ridicule by teachers and acquaintances. At times she had difficulty in distinguishing between dreams and reality. In the sessions themselves she might be bubbly, moving about a lot, speaking rapidly, jumping from one subject to another. While appearing to be exuberant and speaking in an animated fashion, she would often reveal that she had been depressed several hours earlier. Without any obvious reason she would snap back and find herself with boundless energy, walking about campus or performing chores far into the night.

After several sessions with Millie, Chaplain Lee suggested that she see a psychiatrist. Placed on medication and psychotherapy begun, Millie dropped by several months later to inform Chaplain Lee that she felt much better with things on a more even keel than ever before.

Discussion

There are a number of indications in the first session that Millie is a rather disturbed person whose sexual problems are not in themselves as much cause for concern as is her total psychological makeup. While it is not uncommon at this age to experience wide swings in moods, from depression to elation, Millie's rapid and extreme mood changes suggest the need for psychiatric evaluation. In all probability Millie will need medication before any form of psychotherapy can be effective. Her opening statement, in which she reveals that sex is the only thing she has to offer, tells us something of her low self-esteem and image. When a person sees himself as having only one trait which can be appreciated, such is usually suggestive of more severe disturbance. Her random and disorganized ways of living, sleeping, and working are also cause for concern along with her inability to sustain close relationships for any period of time or to complete tasks once started. Her poor relationship with her mother is not encouraging and considerable work will need to be done here also. While we no longer see too many cases like Millie's, experience has shown that counseling alone is not enough but when used in conjunction with recent advances in medication can be effective.

George

George, a twenty-eight-year-old truck driver, came to see Chaplain Lee in partial fulfillment of a court order which had been handed down after he had been arrested for exposing himself in the nude to females in an adjoining apartment complex. While never apprehended before, he reported that in earlier years he had an overwhelming desire to look in windows at nude women. In recent years this had changed to the point that he now felt more inclined toward self-exposure. Even though engaging in such behavior he stated that he received no sexual satisfaction or even sexual stimulation from the act and did not know why he did it.

Married for five years and the father of two small boys, he indicated that his sexual relationship with his wife was unsatisfactory since she permitted sex but was never really involved. Her major complaint was that her husband never showed any emotion or affection but treated her like one of the trucks he drove each day. Describing himself as having a violent temper he kept it under tight control with others, usually venting his anger on his wife. He described his relationship with his two boys as excellent, and he spent large amounts of time each evening with them in play and games. Toward his wife, however, and other people in general, he freely admitted that he was pretty insensitive and uncaring in regard to their needs.

Further discussion revealed that his parents had separated when he was six. George continued to live with his mother who described George's father as a perfectionist, always demanding that his son do everything just right. A brilliant man, he frequently pushed his son far beyond his age level and insisted that he perform tasks which the child was not able to perform. When George failed, the father's response was one of anger. He also developed asthma about this time and was told by his doctor that it was probably psychological. After two sessions with George, Chaplain Lee suggested that he talk with a psychiatrist about the sexual aspect of his problem and come in with his wife to discuss problems in their marriage. While agreeing to both suggestions George arranged an appointment with a psychiatrist, but he failed to keep his appointment for marriage counseling with Chaplain Lee.

Discussion

George's sexual complaints point to a generalized sort of emotional problem. He apparently does not know how to relate in a warm and caring way to females. It would be important to learn from George how he feels about his parents' separation and if he considers himself to blame. George could probably be helped through a program designed to improve his social skills and in finding ways to get outside himself. The suggestion that George and his wife be seen for conjoint therapy was appropriate. However, there is some question as to whether George is motivated to seek change or if he is only following a court order. This is another situation in which it is demonstrated that individuals cannot be sentenced to psychotherapy.

Contrary to what many believe, exhibitionists and "peeping toms" are not apt to harm anyone physically. Such practices are usually not engaged in by females but by males who generally feel insecure about their masculinity. Their behavior is believed by many to be an attempt to prove to others through exposure of their sex organs that they are not sexually deficient as they believe themselves to be.

To change one's sexual orientation or practices is usually highly dependent on the desire to change and the willingness to exert the time and effort to bring about such change. Even if the desire is present, the change is more apt to occur through long-term therapy or through newer techniques employed by psychiatrists and psychologists in the field of behavior modification.

Eve and Derek

Eve and Derek came to see Chaplain Lee with Eve opening the session revealing that she had spent the previous night with a girl friend after Derek had knocked her down in their apartment. She stated that she was afraid to return home with Derek even though he assured her that he had no intention of hitting her again. Both freely admitted that they had had many fights in the six months of marriage. Derek indicated that they were usually the result of sexual insults hurled at him by his wife.

Further discussion revealed that both Eve and Derek were divorced and had married after having known each other for only two weeks. Eve had two small daughters by her previous marriage but revealed that her husband had obtained custody when the court ruled that she was an unfit mother. She volunteered the information in front of Derek that she had been involved with other males in her first marriage and had continued the practice after marriage to Derek, due to a lack of sexual satisfaction with him. Insisting that they had a great sex life, Derek stated that Eve would taunt him with the criticism that her other lovers were much better in bed than he was. Appearing to go to great lengths to flaunt her promiscuity before Derek in an attempt to provoke him, Eve seemed to have no qualms about her sexual behavior.

In discussing his first marriage, Derek revealed that his wife had divorced him after he had lost his temper and beat her on several occasions. Even after the divorce, she had called the police after Derek had broken down her door one night in an attempt to talk to her about a reconciliation.

During the initial session, Derek appeared contrite and apologetic, insisting that he loved Eve enough to take her back in spite of her many infidelities. Giving in to Derek's pleas, Eve agreed to return home with him with an appointment arranged to see Chaplain Lee the following week. However, Eve called Chaplain Lee three days later to inform him that she had had to call the police and had moved out after Derek had again lost his temper and knocked her across the bed. She still wanted to keep the appointment as scheduled, insisting that she wanted to salvage her marriage if possible. Arriving for the appointment thirty minutes early, Derek was infuriated when his wife failed to show up. Insisting that he be permitted to call her, Derek was informed by Eve that she had forgotten the appointment. When she did arrive, she remained quiet most of the session, refusing to respond to her husband's attempts to get her to talk. This infuriated Derek even more. After twenty minutes, Derek walked out, stating that his wife had no interest in working to save the marriage and that he was through. However, he called the next week insisting that Chaplain Lee see them together again. In the following weeks, Derek would show up for the appointment early while Eve would either fail to show up altogether or come in late. By the time she did arrive, Derek was usually in such a rage that communication was impossible. Eve seemed to go out of her way to taunt her husband into saying and doing things which she insisted she could not tolerate. Leaving the session in rage and frustration, Derek would often attempt to talk to his wife outside the office, in the parking lot, or call her at home. On several occasions, Eve had asked Chaplain Lee's secretary to walk with her to her car due to her fear that Derek would be waiting outside to harm her.

After several sessions in which Eve failed to show up, Derek returned to inform Chaplain Lee that Eve had instigated divorce proceedings. He also revealed that he had been following her around town without her knowledge and that she was involved with several other men. Continuing to see Derek for several more sessions individually in which he tried unsuccessfully to deal with his anger and resentment, Chaplain Lee suggested that Derek seek the help of a psychiatrist. Indicating that he had no money available for such, Derek did agree to seek help through the Community Health Program. Failing to follow through with his promise, Chaplain Lee learned that Derek had instead surprised his wife and her lover embracing in a parked automobile on the outskirts of town where, according to police reports, he had apparently killed them both and then committed suicide.

Discussion

This marriage was obviously not "made in Heaven." Although divorce is a touchy moral issue for many, it is our opinion that such relationships should be "put asunder" as rapidly as possible. Two people relating to each other in such a pathological fashion can only result in heartache and tragedy for all involved. Both apparently had serious problems apart from the marriage itself which only seemed to worsen the already explosive situation. No matter how strongly one feels about divorce the best that one can hope for in such destructive relationships is that it will be terminated before permanent damage or death results for either or both. It is unrealistic to expect that any therapist could help this couple when their motivation to change is so totally lacking. Both appear, at best, to have wanted change in the other, if at all.

From the information given above, immediate referral of each to a psychiatrist would have been the best policy. Chaplain Lee's continuation of appointments, when things seemed to get worse rather than improve, probably encouraged both to continue their destructive ways of relating to each other. The potential for violence was apparent in Derek's lack of control as evidenced, not only in his relationship with Eve, but with his former girl friend as well. Adding to this Eve's taunting and insulting sexual remarks, we have a potentially explosive situation. Background information is sufficient to suggest that both were seriously disturbed individuals and in need of more intensive care than most clergymen are inclined to offer. Even with psychiatric help the prognosis for change would have been a guarded one.

Mimi

Mimi, a lovely twenty-three-year-old artist, after considerable talk of trivial matters, revealed to Chaplain Lee that she had really come in to see him because she had fallen in love with another girl. Although she believed her behavior to be sinful and abnormal, she indicated that she had no desire to change since she knew for the first time in her life what it was like to really love someone else. Describing herself as having been turned on recently by her encounter with Freda she stated that she had had several relationships with a number of men in the past but never with any feeling or enjoyment. She described these men as usually rough, crude, and aggressive men who were usually in trouble of some sort, one even having been in prison for armed robbery. She also revealed that she had been pregnant on two occasions and had had abortions each time.

In her several sessions with Chaplain Lee, she began to discuss calmly her sexual involvement with her father, beginning at age nine and continuing until she entered college at nineteen. Though they had never had sexual intercourse, her father would enter her room while she was asleep and place her hand on his penis and masturbate. Though this always awakened her, Mimi pretended to remain asleep. On other occasions she would walk past her father's open bedroom and see him in a state of undress, sometimes masturbating. He would always get up and close the door as if it were an accident even though it had been obvious to Mimi that he made no attempt to keep her from seeing him. In the nine or ten years such went on, no mention was ever made by either Mimi or her father of their involvement. Though she felt guilty about her conduct with her father, Mimi stated that she never offered any resistance.

With other males she usually permitted them to do anything they wanted, indicating that she would do anything to avoid conflict or argument. Describing herself as having been reared by a religious mother, she would often despair of her behavior to the point that she had made one suicide attempt at seventeen and thought about it often on other occasions. Asking God's forgiveness after her sexual encounters, she would vow not to have sexual relations again until marriage. However, usually after drinking heavily, she would find herself the next morning in some man's bedroom with only vague memories of what had transpired the night before. At no time did she ever use any method of birth control even after becoming pregnant on two occasions. She explained her refusal to use birth control pills as a fear of the negative side effects she had read so much about. When questioned further about her drinking, Mimi stated that she could not handle liquor but at such times it was as if something outside herself told her to go ahead and drink and to engage in sexual relationships, which she usually did with the feeling that she had no control over her behavior.

Referring again and again to her current relationship with Freda, Mimi insisted that she could think of little else, with thoughts of Freda so strong that her studies were suffering. Though possessive of each other, to the point that they fought frequently, Mimi said that she had been so content in the relationship that she had not thought of suicide in several months and could not bear the thought of life without Freda even though they were living in sin. In the fourth session with Chaplain Lee Mimi stated that she and Freda were moving to another state because her mother suspected that something was wrong with their relationship.

Discussion

"Coming out" can be a period of great stress for homosexuals. For some it is almost a panic stage. Others approach it with relief that a decision has been made. Clergymen will sometimes see homosexuals first, even before psychiatrists or psychologists. Each clergyman will have to decide for himself how he feels about homosexuality as an alternate lifestyle but remember that sermonizing is most often not appropriate. With homosexuality becoming more open, clergymen can expect to see increasing numbers of individuals wrestling with the frustration of homosexuality, and they should not hesitate to refer if they feel uncomfortable or ill prepared to deal with the situation.

In Mimi's case, there appears to be much more chaos than just the matter of dealing with her immediate sexual desires. Her long history of sexual behavior, going back to her relationship with her father, is one for concern. As unpalatable as such may be to most, experience has suggested that cases involving incest are more numerous than we would expect. Since sexual relationships with close relatives are almost universally taboo, such behavior usually causes immeasurable guilt, a low opinion of self, with poor sexual adjustment in later years, as demonstrated by Mimi. With such a long history of sexual maladjustment, long-term therapy would probably be involved even if Mimi expressed a desire to change. At this point in her life, however, she is quite adamant that she has no such desire. In view of her previous relationships with men this would not be unexpected.

In addition to the behavior we have discussed, Mimi is also engaging in a lot of self-destructive behavior. For example, she has been pregnant twice but still refuses to take any precautions against future pregnancies, citing as her reason the bad side effects of birth control pills. It is surprising that many individuals will refuse to take birth control pills or medications prescribed by a physician for their nerves, but will use LSD or pep pills, given to them by a total stranger, or risk pregnancy and abortion, all of which involve risks far greater than the prescribed medication. This, in itself, should be looked at with concern that such may be indicative of mental confusion or instability.

As for working with individuals who have reached the decision to go the homosexual route, the major emphasis may be that of working with their guilt feelings or the problems usually associated with such a lifestyle. While working with a homosexual who wants to change is usually a task for mental health professionals trained in such areas, clergymen can often counsel individuals like Mimi just as effectively as psychiatrists or psychologists, provided they can accept the person's decision to lead a homosexual life. Regardless of one's feelings about "right" or "wrong" where homosexuality is concerned, each individual should be treated as a worthwhile human being, deserving of the best care we can provide.

Vic

Vic, a twenty-nine-year-old tall, slender male, ascetic in appearance, opened his session with Chaplain Lee with the announcement that he had decided that morning to kill himself. He had rented a car which he planned to use that afternoon to kill himself by attaching a hose to the exhaust pipe. When queried by Chaplain Lee as to why he wanted to kill himself, Vic indicated that he had had sexual problems for as long as he could remember and that numerous sessions with psychologists and psychiatrists had been of no help to him. He described his problem as one of impotence in which he had found it impossible to have a full erection even when masturbating. He had only one date with a girl in his life in which he had attempted sexual intercourse. This had occurred two years ago on a hiking trip and he had been unsuccessful. The girl's attempts to reassure him that it was nothing to worry about had been of little comfort. He had visited several prostitutes over the years which had likewise resulted in failure and embarrassment for him. He had at one time become so discouraged that he had decided on a life of celibacy as a priest. However, he had soon tired of his studies and withdrew from school. A brilliant person, he was currently working as a draftsman, a job which he found unsatisfactory and beneath him.

He revealed that he had begun masturbating around eleven years of age and had been seriously punished by his mother on several occasions when she caught him in the act. Although he felt extremely guilty, he continued to masturbate as often as two or three times a day for years. Even now, he stated that he masturbated daily to ejaculation but always had a weak erection. He indicated that he received the greatest satisfaction sexually when he inflicted pain on himself and often used cigarettes to burn himself. When he initially began masturbating, he revealed that his fantasies had been of girls. However, in recent years, these had begun to fade with either thoughts or acts of inflicting pain becoming more prominent.

In discussing his social relationships, he stated that he liked men better than women but hastened to add that he was not homosexual. He had made one serious suicide attempt in his freshman year in college. During the session he was glib and sarcastic, not only about himself but toward others, including Chaplain Lee. He indicated that he had reached the end of his rope after an appointment with a physician in which he had sarcastically requested that the doctor supply him with some aphrodisiac which would solve his problems. Becoming more serious, he stated that he had on numerous occasions asked for medicine which would enable him to become more sexually potent. His most recent disappointment had involved an inquiry regarding a new drug he had read about which had listed increased sexual drive as a side effect. When told by the doctor that he did not think it would be of benefit to him, Vic had concluded that his situation was hopeless. He then decided to kill himself.

After two hours with Vic, convinced that he needed to be hospitalized for his own safety, Chaplain Lee persuaded Vic to accompany him to the hospital where he was admitted overnight. With appointments set up on a regular basis with a therapist at the hospital, Vic returned to see Chaplain Lee several weeks later. He confessed that while he had been depressed, his talk of suicide had been his way of making sure that he received immediate attention for the problem he found so distressing.

Discussion

Vic's problems indicate a need for prolonged psychotherapy. His long history of masochistic behavior, impotence, and low self-esteem combine to present a problem of such magnitude that most clergymen would feel a need for psychiatric referral. Though of primary concern to Vic, the problem is more than just a sexual one. Vic's demands that Chaplain Lee help him with his sexual problem or else he would kill himself, while most unrealistic, were apparently Vic's way of calling attention to his desperate plight.

While Vic is probably not ready for them at the moment, different approaches have been developed in recent years in the treatment of such problems as premature ejaculation, impotence, and frigidity. Clinics dealing with sexual problems have also sprung up throughout the country in recent years. While many such sex clinics are legitimate and report success in working with the problem of sexual dysfunctioning, caution should be exercised in referring unless one is familiar with the agency and the reputation of the people involved.

In addition to the sex clinics as such, more traditional treatment facilities have adopted other behavior modification techniques in the treatment of sexual disorders. Since Vic had been seen previously, with little success, by several psychiatrists and psychologists, he might possibly be a candidate for one of the newer approaches. It is highly probable however, that due to the severity of the problem described above that long-term psychotherapy will be needed first for Vic, with referral for sex therapy a future consideration.

Alex

Alex, a twenty-eight-year-old ministerial student, came to see Chaplain Lee complaining that he was unable to sleep or concentrate on his studies. He saw his major problem as one of depression and anxiety. Though obviously intelligent and creative, he had been in and out of school for the past ten years with a poor academic record. Now enrolled in a seminary he was still uncertain as to which direction he would move in regard to his career. He had in the past taught school and worked in a boy's club. Unmarried, he still lived at home with his parents, apparently unable to break away from a domineering mother who had made most of his decisions for him.

He dated quite frequently but usually after the girl had taken the initiative in arranging and planning the date. Even then he usually dated girls perceived beneath him socially and intellectually. His sexual fantasies about females involved girls who were in his thinking immoral.

During the sessions, Alex was suspicious, hostile, and at times belligerent in his attitude toward Chaplain Lee. When the hour was over, he attempted in numerous ways to prolong the session, demanding that something be done or asking that decisions be made for him. In the fourth session, for the first time, he began to discuss his fears of being homosexual, indicating that he never became interested or aroused in his relationships with females. In the seventh session with considerable reluctance he disclosed that he had been involved sexually with a ten-year-old boy in one of the churches he had worked in several years earlier and had been asked to resign. Though he had not been involved in a sexual relationship of any sort since, he expressed concern that it was on his record for all to see. Of even greater concern, however, he had continued to experience feelings similar to those which had caused him to seduce the young boy. These feelings had become more prominent in recent months when he again began working with young boys as part of a course he was taking at the seminary. He described his desire to touch and caress young boys at times as almost overwhelming. Rather than guilt or desire for change Alex seemed more concerned with the fact that he had been caught, appearing to be interested in seeing society change its ways of viewing his sexual conduct as deviant.

After several additional sessions Alex informed Chaplain Lee that he was apparently not qualified to help him with his problem and that he intended to see a psychiatrist. Following through with his stated intentions, Alex saw a psychiatrist for four sessions before returning to see Chaplain Lee again. Over the next year Alex saw several psychiatrists, psychologists, and pastoral counselors and became involved in two groups. One minister had suggested in the course of counseling that if Alex would live three days without sin and pray for one hour each day that he would no longer be a homosexual. When this failed, he had scheduled his most recent appointment with Chaplain Lee who he continued to see sporadically for the next few months. Leaving the seminary after two years where he took a job as music director in a large church, he appeared not to have changed in his condition although he had refrained from further sexual involvement of a homosexual nature.

Discussion

Due to an increase in permissiveness in general and to a wider acceptance of varying sexual lifestyles in particular, sexual practices which were once considered deviant are no longer viewed as such by many in our society today. As evidence of this trend, homosexuality is no longer classified as mental illness by the American Psychiatric Association. While still a controversial issue for many, homosexuality between consenting adults is now more widely accepted than ever before.

Despite this more liberal trend, however, sexual involvement with a child, whether homosexual or heterosexual, is considered a criminal act. Child molestation arouses anger and concern in most people quicker than any other crime short of murder. Not only is such behavior considered criminal, it indicates, in most cases, that the individual is limited in his interpersonal development and unable to formulate meaningful adult relationships. As in other cases discussed, Alex's sexual behavior suggests more generalized personality disorder and the need for psychiatric referral. As with many other sexual problems including exhibitionism, voyeurism, transvestism, fetishism, and sadomasochism, the treatment of homosexuality is usually not a problem which most clergymen are inclined to treat.

Clergymen should be aware, however, that certain treatment methods can result in change for many homosexuals who sincerely want to change. Since many therapists are not so optimistic about change, it is important that clergymen who wish to refer know something of the therapist's attitude and methods of treatment regarding homosexuality and refer clients to those therapists who have experienced success in working with homosexuals.

For homosexuals who have no desire to change, clergymen can play an important role as they attempt to deal with the moral issues and guilt usually involved. For most homosexuals, sermons, in lieu of counseling, accomplish little. Despite Alex's numerous visits to see Chaplain Lee and other counselors, he showed little evidence of any real desire to change his sexual behavior or even to deal with other feelings usually associated with being homosexual. Since he does appear to be such a troubled individual however, the effort should be continued to get him involved in psychotherapy with the hope that he might eventually profit from counseling or other treatment methods.

Doug

Doug, a seventeen-year-old high school senior, reluctantly opened the session by saying he was impotent. Physically well developed and an excellent athlete, he had received a football scholarship to a major university. Recent events, however, convinced him that he might have homosexual tendencies, a way of life he insisted he could not endure. Though he had experienced successful sexual intercourse with several girls for extended periods of time over the past two years, he had on occasion fantasies in which he was involved in sexual relationships with another male. Having read several novels in which considerable emphasis had been placed on the size of the penis during intercourse he had become obsessed with the idea that his penis was too small and that he would be the object of ridicule by girls with whom he had become involved sexually. So concerned had he become with such matters that he had recently experienced difficulty, even while masturbating, in obtaining an erection. His last two attempts at sexual intercourse had ended in failure. As a result of his distress he dredged up events from the distant past in which he had engaged in sex play with young boys his own age as further proof that he was homosexual. So fearful had he become of failure that he had not dated a girl in two months.

Outwardly appearing to be a sophisticated young man who had been around, it soon became apparent that Doug was unaware of even the most rudimentary details of knowledge regarding sexual matters. During the first hour Chaplain Lee attempted to convince Doug that occurrence of homosexual thoughts did not mean by any stretch of the imagination that he was a homosexual. Chaplain Lee concluded the hour by suggesting that Doug read a sexual manual which he often recommended in premarital counseling, which contained basic information about those matters Doug had so distorted. Expecting that Doug's problem would require counseling Chaplain Lee was surprised to hear Doug say, in the second session, that he was now convinced that he was normal and that he anticipated no further difficulties.

Discussion

Many situations exist in which problems can be solved if certain information is provided to the individual seeking help. Due to the vast amount of ignorance and incorrect information in sexual spheres, some sexual problems are subject to verbal cures. With Doug, however, his "cure" is perhaps premature or the result of wishful thinking to say the least. Doug's reaction might more appropriately be termed a "flight into health" which will in all probability be a temporary one because of more pervasive problems. Doug did not show much willingness to deal with the problem in depth. Chaplain Lee's reassurance and the information presented in the sex manual seemed to enable him to suppress some of his more complex feelings temporarily.

While counselors should not immediately assume that all problems brought before them are the result of serious emotional conflicts, evidence suggests that Doug's concerns about his masculinity and homosexuality need to be explored more in depth.

Adolescence and young adulthood are for most young people a period of many concerns about their sexuality. It is important that Doug be presented with certain factual information about male and female sexual equipment and its functioning. It is also important that he realize that sexuality is on a continuum with no individual completely free of homosexual or heterosexual thoughts or desires. It is quite common for some young men and women to become convinced that they are homosexual if they have occasional homosexual fantasies. Some even experience a homosexual panic, occasionally doing drastic things as a result of fears, often unjustified. Most individuals experience some concern about breast or penis size. Others become obsessed with the fear that they are inferior or inadequate. All males will at some time or other experience situations in which they will be impotent.

Despite the recent torrent of articles dealing with female sexuality and orgasm, many females, both young and old, do not enjoy sex or experience orgasm. Whether male or female, the need exists for more responsible sexual education. This, among other things, would allow individuals to evaluate their sexual performance and feelings in a more realistic light without the sense of failure and loss of confidence, often inherent, when things do not always go as they have been led to believe they should. Clergymen, teachers, and others in the business of educating and helping people have not only the opportunity but the responsibility to provide guidance in this most important area of human sexual behavior.

With Doug however, more than just sexual information seems lacking. While Chaplain Lee or a psychiatrist could probably be of help, Doug does not seem to be ready for additional counseling at this point. It is possible that Chaplain Lee did him a disservice in attempting to reassure him that he was "normal" in that a rather pervasive problem seemed to disappear overnight.

Sarah

Sarah, a thirty-two-year-old Sunday School teacher and mother of a twelve-year-old boy, made an appointment with Chaplain Lee to discuss her fears that something was wrong sexually with her son, Tommy. She had noticed that as a baby he seemed to delight in fondling his genitals. When she bathed him, he often had an erection. Later in his eighth year she had discovered him in the garage with a seven-year-old girl playing "doctor." Both prior to and following this episode, he had been known to display curiosity and interest concerning his mother's and dad's sexual organs. Much to his mother's horror, he had on occasion touched her breasts. Of even greater embarrassment to her, as a five-year-old he had grabbed the breast of a teenage girl who had been employed as his babysitter. On another occasion, he had been a member of a Sunday School class in which the teacher had stated that masturbation, under any circumstances, was sinful and physically harmful. Physical punishment along with frequent warnings that such behavior was sinful and harmful had, in Sarah's opinion, served to put an end to such behavior until recently. However, the week before she had entered his bedroom where she found Tommy and another twelve-year-old boy engaged in mutual masturbation. Convinced that he was by now perverted and well on the way to becoming a homosexual, she had confided in her husband that she intended to seek professional help for her son. With her husband's approval, she made an appointment with Chaplain Lee.

After two sessions alone with Sarah, Chaplain Lee, at her insistance, agreed to see Tommy. Greatly embarrassed by the whole thing, Tommy sheepishly began the first of several sessions in which Chaplain Lee attempted to deal with the confusion, distortion, and guilt which had become a part of Tommy's thinking as a result of his parents' lack of knowledge regarding sexual behavior in children. Separate sessions were also held with Tommy's parents in which Chaplain Lee, with some difficulty but to the great relief of the parents, managed to communicate that Tommy's behavior was not that of a sexual deviate but was in fact quite normal for a boy his age.

Thinking that Sarah's reaction to Tommy's sexual behavior might be indicative of sexual conflicts in her own life, Chaplain Lee suggested that Sarah resume her individual sessions with him. Though she did so with great difficulty, Sarah informed Chaplain Lee that her husband had had an affair with a younger woman several years earlier. Convinced that the affair was ended, Sarah, however, had been unable to forgive or forget. Though she insisted that she had tried, she found sexual intercourse with her husband upsetting since the affair. Further discussions revealed that she had never really found sex exciting or desirable which she viewed as just the opposite of her husband who wanted sex several times each week.

Over a period of months, Chaplain Lee saw Sarah individually and later in joint sessions with her husband. Though not experiencing radical changes, Sarah was able gradually to trust her husband more and to enjoy sex somewhat, though she still failed to find it as appealing as did her husband.

Discussion

Sexual curiosity is a normal aspect of growing up. There is nothing sinful about such curiosity. Sarah is obviously unduly concerned and uptight as evidenced in her overreaction to what is usually perceived to be normal sexual behavior in her son. Since she was so overly concerned, it was appropriate for Chaplain Lee to suggest working with Sarah in regard to her personal feelings about sex. As with Sarah, many parents unconsciously pass on to their children their own sexual problems and frustrations. Many children and adults suffer for a lifetime as the result of well meaning but poorly informed Sunday School teachers, clergymen, or others in positions of authority who manage to convey their distorted beliefs that sex is sinful or harmful. Nowhere is this more true than with masturbation which is engaged in by most human beings at various times in their lives.

Though masturbation has been blamed for many physical, mental, and spiritual ills through the centuries, most authorities now agree that masturbation is quite normal and harmless unless it results in guilt feelings which the individual cannot handle, or is engaged in extensively to the exclusion of contact with other human beings. In regard to Sarah's fear that her son might be homosexual, it is also not uncommon for children to engage in sex play with members of the same sex. If there is other evidence that the child is confused or not accepting of his sexual role as a male or female, then counseling is in order.

As for the sexual problems which were experienced between Sarah and her husband, Sarah should not be made to feel she is a failure as a woman due to her lack of orgasm and sexual enjoyment. As stated earlier, there are many females, both young and old, who have been convinced that they are abnormal and beyond help when they do not experience instant and total sexual gratification in the first few weeks of sexual intercourse. The truth is that in many cases it takes years to overcome the earlier conditioning which has made sex unenjoyable for millions, both male and female. With patience, understanding, and skillful counseling most people can realize their potential for a more satisfying sexual relationship. It should also be stressed that sexual differences do exist in which one partner may have a stronger sex drive than does the other. Again, with patience, cooperation, and a willingness to work on the problem, adjustment is possible.

Jena

Jena, a thirty-seven-year-old married woman with two teenage daughters, came to see Chaplain Lee complaining of recurring sexual fantasies with males other than her husband. Though the men in her fantasy life changed, they usually involved a guest at some social event she had attended. On several occasions, she found herself fantasizing that she was being raped by a strong, rugged, handsome male with whom she was completely helpless, unable to resist. On occasions, even while having sexual intercourse with her husband, similar thoughts invaded her consciousness. Reared in a home where sexual involvement with any male other than her husband had been viewed as sinful, she found herself feeling increasingly more guilty. With great embarrassment, she indicated that in recent months she had resorted to masturbation, something in itself which had previously repulsed her as being abnormal and unladylike. Despite her guilt, she had on infrequent occasions continued to masturbate while thinking of sexual relationships with other men. Unable to discuss her feelings with her husband, she had become so upset by such thoughts that she called in a state of great anxiety and arranged an appointment with Chaplain Lee. Insisting that she would never have sexual intercourse with any man other than her husband and that their sex life was great, Jena nonetheless felt perverted.

In the several sessions that followed Jena, with Chaplain Lee's help, became less critical of herself when told that similar thoughts were experienced by most women at various times in their lives.

Discussion

Sexual problems, as well as sexual successes, are for the most part psychological. While some lead a more active fantasy life than others, sexual fantasizing is an important part of any sexual act. Most, if not all, individuals have thoughts of sexual involvement with males or females other than their spouses. What one does with these desires or thoughts is largely determined by his religious or moral convictions. Not wishing to become involved in a discussion of whether pre-marital or extra-marital sex is right or wrong, we think it is important, for psychological reasons, that a distinction be made between "thinking" and "behaving."

Experience has shown that the failure to make such a distinction has probably generated more guilt and ill feelings about one's self than any other single act or event through the centuries. To equate sinful or unacceptable thoughts with sinful or unacceptable behavior is tantamount to placing a burden on the shoulders of every human being which is, in our opinion, unforgivable. To label any woman who has sexual thoughts toward a man other than her husband as an adulteress, but who, for moral reasons, refuses to engage in extra-marital sex, is analogous to the labeling of a man as a murderer who ever entertains the idea of wanting to kill someone. While such thinking may be theologically acceptable, it is psychologically untenable for the simple reason that all people entertain such thoughts at some time or other. However, relatively few people ever murder anyone. It is therefore commendable that Chaplain Lee was able to help Jena realize that she was not seriously disturbed as a result of her fantasies about other males or her masturbation.

On the other hand, while sexual fantasies about other males are not inherently evil or abnormal, it is possible that Jena's were an indication of some dissatisfaction on her part with her husband and their relationship. It is also not uncommon for some females to fantasize about being raped since under these circumstances they can entertain sexual desires which they find unacceptable without accepting the responsibility for sexual involvement. In any event, it would be appropriate to explore, at some depth, Jena's feelings about herself sexually and the possibility of broader inter-personal difficulties involving her husband.

Ella and Ralph

Ella, a forty-nine-year-old housewife, complained of de-pression and a sense of worthlessness in her first session with Chaplain Lee. Never having really enjoyed sexual relation-ships, Ella stated that she had never had an orgasm through sexual intercourse with her husband. She had on occasion been able to through masturbation or oral sex. As if being a frigid woman (as she referred to herself) was not enough, she was now going through the change of life. This she interpreted as the end of any faint hope she might have entertained that she could ever have a better sex life.

Although she was obviously embarrassed, Ella's response to Chaplain Lee's carefully worded inquiries revealed that sexual intercourse between Ella and Ralph usually lasted less than ten minutes. Seeing Ralph as a man with a voracious sexual appetite, Ella saw herself as undersexed by comparison. In describing their relationship, Ella indicated that Ralph might want to have sex three or four times each week. Follow-ing no particular time pattern, he would often approach her while she was cooking dinner or cleaning house. With no pre-liminaries, he would persuade her to follow him to the bed-room or sofa with the entire act over in a matter of minutes. Although a loyal husband and responsible family man, he had little time for romance or affection in his relationship with his wife. Ella revealed that she especially disliked sex in the daytime due to the fear that her children might interrupt their lovemaking.

In the following weeks, Chaplain Lee was able to help Ella understand, with proper medical supervision, that meno-pause did not have to be the emotional and physical trauma envisioned by many females. Following Chaplain Lee's sug-gestion that she discuss her fears in detail with her doctor, Ella returned in a different frame of mind to see Chaplain Lee for the purpose of discussing ways in which sexual inter-course with her husband could become more rewarding for her. After several joint sessions with Ella and Ralph in which Ella's needs as a woman, sexual techniques, and other relevant matters were discussed, Ella informed Chaplain Lee that things were improving and that she no longer viewed herself as frigid. Although she still had not had an orgasm through sexual intercourse with her husband, she had begun to enjoy sex for the first time and had been close to orgasm on several occasions.

Discussion

The problems presented by Ella are shared by many middle-aged women who have rather prudish ideas as well as considerable misinformation about sexuality and menopause. In view of Chaplain Lee's expertise in dealing with sexual problems of this sort, there seems to be no reason to suggest psychiatric referral. Referral to a physician instead, for the purpose of enlightment in regard to menopause, was most appropriate.

At least part of the problem appears to be Ralph's lack of knowledge in regard to the sexual needs of women. While the importance of sex manuals has perhaps been over emphasized in recent years, they can make a significant contribution in the area of sexual adjustment for both males and females. Unfortunately, many individuals, especially males, do not appreciate being told that their sexual techniques leave something to be desired and often balk at the thought of reading a sex manual or seeing a counselor in regard to sexual problems. Since there is an abundance of good books on the subject available today, no attempt will be made to offer suggestions in regard to Ralph's rather striking lack of sensitivity to Ella's needs as a woman other than to say that for most women, love, affection, and romance are part of the total relationship and a meaningful sexual encounter is seen as more than just a hurried ten minute copulation. Apparently Chaplain Lee was successful in communicating such to Ella and Ralph.

Jill

Jill, a twenty-eight-year-old statuesque former beauty contestant, opened her session with Chaplain Lee with the statement that life for her was empty and meaningless, with something vital missing. Before the first session was over, however, Jill had begun to focus on sexual problems in her marriage, complaining that she had never experienced orgasm in seven years of marriage. Most of the difficulty she attributed to her husband who never spent enough time with her but was always playing golf or immersed in his work.

In the beginning session, Jill had appeared dressed in a rather expensive but conservative fashion. After the first few sessions, however, Jill seemed to develop a penchant for brevity in dress and appeared in mini skirts with low cut blouses. Spending a major portion of each hour discussing sex, she often engaged in coy and seductive behavior toward Chaplain Lee, frequently interspersing her conversations with comments such as: "You are the only person who has ever understood me," "I wish my husband could be more like you," "Tell me something about yourself," "I wish I could come in more often."

Although still attractive physically, Jill expressed great concern about growing fat and wrinkled. Popular in high school and college, involved in many sorority functions, cheerleading, dating, she revealed that she found marriage depressing and boring. She resented the loss of attention she had enjoyed prior to marriage. Even though she complained that she missed the attention bestowed on her by men in the past, she described several incidents in which it appeared that she suffered from no lack of attention from men at the present time. Denying that she made any effort to attract men, she complained to Chaplain Lee that she was always being approached by some aggressive and unscrupulous male wanting to get her in bed. As an example, Jill related an experience with a football player she met while on a tour of a foreign country with a group of college students. Although not married at the time, she was engaged. Despite the young man's attractive qualities, Jill indicated that she found him to be a bother and a nuisance in that he continued to make sexual advances though she had told him repeatedly that she was engaged and had no interest in him as a lover. She did admit that they were alone together on many occasions and even embraced on several occasions. Even when her seductive behavior became so obvious to other members in the group that the tour director called her in on one occasion and chastised her for her conduct, even suggesting that she send her engagement ring back to her fiancé, Jill continued to insist that she was doing nothing to encourage the young man's attentions. With great conviction, she said that she was the victim of people who just could not understand the situation. She did admit that she found his attentions flattering.

After using the major portion of the first hour to discuss her behavior and feelings in regard to the young man, Jill spent the succeeding session relating a series of events which culminated in her being raped. Further questioning revealed, however, that Jill had been alone with the man in his hotel room at 2 A.M. and later saw him on other occasions after the alleged rape for purposes of intercourse. Even after such an admission, Jill continued to insist that she had been entirely innocent, attributing all the blame to the insensitivity and aggressiveness of the young man who would not take no for an answer.

Jill told of other similar incidents in which she had been the victim of acts committed by sexually aggressive males, each entirely unsolicited on her part. These incidents, both before and after marriage, involved advances and propositions from doctors, clergymen, and lawyers whom she visited professionally. In most of these encounters, Jill would allow herself to become involved to a limited degree after which she would, in great anger and surprise, beat a hasty retreat.

While seeing Chaplain Lee, Jill took a job in a large company as a receptionist. In the following weeks, she described her job as satisfying, finding herself once again the center of attention in a large office staffed by admiring males who showered her with compliments and attention. Several weeks later she returned, once again in low spirits, indicating that her supervisor had called her into his office that morning concerning her involvement with one of the young married executive trainees which had resulted in considerable gossip. Once again, Jill insisted that she had done nothing but was the victim of gossiping and jealous women who had nothing better to do with their time. Before the hour was over, however, Jill acknowledged that in fact they had spent large blocks of time with each other and talked on the phone after work many evenings about their feelings for one another.

Told on numerous occasions by Jill that he had been of great help to her, Chaplain Lee was surprised when she cancelled two appointments informing his secretary that she would not return.

Discussion

Jill's case is representative of one of the more common types of problems encountered by clergymen and others working in the helping professions. Although such cases are common, it is with this sort of individual that counselors frequently permit themselves to be lulled into a false sense of therapeutic accomplishment or on occasion themselves become a participant in the counselee's seductive pattern of relating to people. Often they insist that they are being helped by the counselor, but their behavior for the most part remains unchanged.

Of even greater significance to those attempting to work in a counseling relationship with individuals such as this, gossip or scandal is a common result. Although Jill initially came in for marriage counseling, she almost immediately began to relate to Chaplain Lee in much the same sexually manipulative way she related to other males.

All human beings have needs to be recognized and to be the center of attention at times, and thus they display many of the same behaviors and symptoms as did Jill. The case presented above, however, involves the description of a person who had adopted such a way of thinking and behaving as a lifestyle rather than as a temporary manner of coping with her environment. Jill goes far beyond that which is considered to be a normal, healthy need to be recognized and loved to the point that her behavior may be described as narcissistic and exhibitionistic.

Although a significant number of individuals do visit mental health agencies describing feelings and behaviors similar to those discussed above, the prognosis for change in individuals such as these is usually not good. Lack of success in working with such individuals results from the fact that these individuals are often quite shallow, engaging in superficial ways of thinking and behaving, refusing to recognize any cause and effect relationship in their lives or to look at themselves in any depth. They have instead adopted avoidance and denial of responsibility for their behavior as their modus operandi. They are usually immature and engage in infantile behavior and thinking, particularly where sex is concerned, often using sexual provocation and flattery as a means of obtaining the attention they so desperately crave. They play games in which their behavior is largely incongruent with what they profess to be doing or thinking.

Such people are not only insincere and immature, but usually vain, narcissistic, histrionic, and dependent with much of their behavior self-dramatizing. Denial and projection are the tools most often used by these individuals as evidenced by Jill's refusal to accept the responsibility for her sexual involvement, insisting instead that she had done nothing wrong or else placing the blame on others. They often have low self-esteem and feel insecure and inadequate as a person. Much of their behavior is motivated by the need to prove to themselves that they are still attractive and desirable. Consequently they may depend on such external trappings as elaborate wardrobes or hairstyles, feeling that such will cover up or compensate for their perceived inadequacies as a person.

In regard to their past, a large number of these individuals are extremely attractive, having been cheerleaders, winners of beauty pageants, and members of socially elite clubs or sororities. Though now adults, they may still dress as cheerleaders, often in a revealing fashion, still seeking the plaudits of their peers. They tend to do quite well so long as they receive the recognition and applause of the crowd. Once the secondary gains diminish, however, they may become depressed as did Jill, feeling that she had become old and unattractive. When faced with the more serious aspects of the present and of growing up and becoming a wife and mother, they may feel threatened.

Even though they are sending out sexual messages, they often fail to follow through and may become disturbed or even panic when the male responds to their sexual cues. As with Jill, they may holler "rape" or else become righteously indignant, accusing the male of making passes which were totally unsolicited. Their attitude, indicative of immature and irresponsible sexual behavior, must inevitably lead to frustration. Though they become incensed by the seductive attempts of males, they are the seducers rather than the seduced. They are often unable to receive sexual gratification for the simple reason that they are "getters" rather than "sharers." Their entire lifestyle is patterned in a fashion to get attention for the soul purpose of getting attention rather than for the purpose of establishing meaningful relationships involving the giving of one's self to another.

As for psychiatric referral, Chaplain Lee will probably be able to work as effectively with Jill as a psychiatrist would, provided that he is aware of the personality dynamics involved and refuses to allow himself to be manipulated by an expert.

Summary

Sexual problems, like the tip of the proverbial iceberg, may be the only visible sign that more serious and pervasive emotional problems lie undetected beneath the surface for many individuals. On the other hand, not everyone who engages in socially unacceptable sexual activities or who experiences sexual difficulties is mentally ill. True, there have been those in the past (and there are still some) who insist that individuals who masturbate, look at sex magazines, or have sex with persons other than their spouses with the male in the dominant position be declared mentally ill.

Although the church is not the cause of all the sexual problems in the world today, it is not blameless. While unrestricted sex will not solve all the problems in interpersonal relationships, an enlightened clergy could do more than most to dispel much that is not only taboo but also emotionally harmful in the area of sex. While we would not be so presumptuous as to claim that we know what the Creator had in mind when males and females were equipped sexually, we do not believe that it included the multitude of problems which has turned sex, for many, into a battle-ground on which many human conflicts and aberrations are acted out.

Fully aware that the so-called "new morality" has made it more difficult to classify, on the basis of sex, those individuals who were at one time labeled "deviant," "abnormal," "perverted," or "sick," some clues still signal that all is not well. These include those individuals who

- find it difficult or impossible to engage in not only satisfactory sexual relationships, but any sort of intimate relationship with another human being;
- always turn to activities such as masturbation or the viewing of sex movies or magazines as a substitute for more meaningful contacts with other human beings;
- have a need to inflict or be inflicted with pain in order to enjoy sex;
- are restricted to any sole sexual practice or activity in order to receive gratification;
- are unduly inhibited or prudish in sexual matters;
- are sexually promiscuous but unable to achieve any sense of satisfaction;
- resort to voyeurism or exhibitionism;
- are homosexual;
- are frequently impotent or frigid;
- are in other ways noticeably disturbed emotionally;
- are attracted to or attempt to engage young children in a sexual relationship.

Clergymen are reminded that while any one or combination of the above may signify the existence of mental illness, there is by no means a consensus of opinion as to whether or not any one of the above is indicative of mental illness.

Chapter 6
Problem Pregnancies and Abortion

For the typical woman, no other news is so anxiously awaited as the results of her pregnancy test. Somewhat stunned and in awe of the greatest of all miracles, the conception of a child, most women respond with joy and exuberance when the results are positive. For others, however, the awareness of pregnancy can be devastating. The initial response may involve humiliation, hatred, anger, guilt, shame, even thoughts of suicide. Once the shock has subsided however, most begin to consider the alternatives available. For a large number in our society, abortion seems to be an increasingly acceptable alternative.

Despite the view held by many clergymen and other professionals that abortion is immoral, we cannot escape the fact that abortion is now legal. Only a short time ago viewed as a criminal act, abortions are now being legally performed at an astounding rate in reputable hospitals and clinics throughout the country. There is also reason to suspect that many other abortions are still being performed outside the law and without benefit of proper medical care. While we do not choose to become involved in the discussion of premarital sex, contraception, pregnancy, or abortion as moral issues, we can state that most clergymen will find themselves involved in counseling situations with individuals struggling with these problems and issues at some time or other during their ministries. Although premarital sex, pregnancy, and abortion are not necessarily symptoms of mental illness, they are sometimes the result of emotional stress or instability. In four of the five cases we are presenting, the pregnancy and abortion are probably symptomatic of emotional problems. The fifth case was selected for purposes of comparison—A young woman engages in premarital intercourse and experiences pregnancy and other unfavorable results, but there is little reason to suspect that she is emotionally ill.

Edith

Edith, a seventeen-year-old high school senior came to see Chaplain Lee in March complaining of being despondent, crying uncontrollably, and having nightmares to the point that she had slept little for several weeks. She launched almost immediately into a discussion of an abortion she had had three months earlier. At her boyfriend's insistence and with the help of a girl friend, she had arranged to contact a former midwife who had performed the illegal abortion without benefit of any sedative and with minimal concern for her patient's welfare. As a result, Edith remembered in full detail the pain she suffered as well as having witnessed the procedure in its entirety. Leaving the house the same day, she had thought of herself as a murderer. Several weeks later, after experiencing difficulty, she had consulted a gynecologist who informed her after thorough examination that she needed further surgery which would render her incapable of ever having children. The surgery was delayed until Edith graduated in June.

Two days after being told the news, Edith had gone to her pastor for advice. After listening for a brief period, he began to lecture Edith on the error of her ways and her need to repent. Already overwhelmed with feelings of guilt, with visions of herself as only half a woman once the surgery was completed, Edith was discovered by her parents later that night near death from an overdose of her mother's sleeping pills. Rushed to the hospital, Edith lived but remained in the hospital for several weeks for psychiatric treatment. Once she was discharged, things had gone well for a time. However, as time for the surgery drew nearer she again became depressed and less sure of her decision. A devoutly religious person and still deeply concerned regarding the moral implications of her behavior, she had decided to see Chaplain Lee whom a friend had recommended.

In the first two sessions, Chaplain Lee was able to learn that Edith had been reared in a home where premarital sex was considered "an unpardonable sin." Her older brother had been forced to marry a girl he did not love after she became pregnant. In Edith's words, this situation "broke her mother's heart" and made her even more determined that Edith approach her wedding night untouched by any man. Although she had managed to keep her pregnancy and abortion a secret from her mother, she felt herself now compelled to tell her mother the full story. Edith informed Chaplain Lee that she did not believe that her mother would be able to survive the shock of her only daughter's behavior since she had suffered a nervous breakdown some years earlier.

In the third session, at Chaplain Lee's suggestion, Edith for the first time began to discuss her feelings toward Rick, the man with whom she had been involved sexually. As with other matters discussed, Edith talked in a soft and pleasant manner, with a smile on her face, of her anger and resentment toward Rick. Although she had avoided any reference to him in previous sessions, she now indicated that she was consumed with hatred for Rick and a driving need to get even with him for all the suffering she had endured while he got off scot-free. Edith revealed to Chaplain Lee that her nightmares and dreams involved the hurting or punishment of Rick. Describing herself as an easy going person who never lost her temper, she stated that she was not sure what she might do if she ever saw Rick again. This she saw as unlikely, however, since he had resigned his position as a teacher in the high school which she attended and moved to another state shortly after her abortion—even though he had told her many times of his love for her and desire to stand by her in her time of need. As a result of his betrayal, Edith stated that she had grown to distrust all men. Although she had never enjoyed the sexual part of the relationship and saw herself as abnormal because she did not experience orgasm, Edith had continued to participate since she was convinced that she could never attract or hold Rick any other way. Even though a pretty girl, she viewed herself as unattractive to men, concluding that closeness to another human being through sex was worth any price she might have to pay now or later. Rick's leaving and her upcoming surgery had proved to be too much however. Edith concluded that she could not make it through the summer.

With Chaplain Lee's encouragement, Edith agreed to return to the hospital on an outpatient basis where psychiatric help was again provided. In addition to the psychiatrist who prescribed medication to help Edith sleep at night, she also saw a female social worker with considerable experience in counseling young girls, before and after abortion. Joint sessions were held at the hospital with both Edith and her parents. In the following weeks, before and after her surgery, Edith and her parents had a number of sessions with Chaplain Lee as well. The parents, while hurt and resentful, were able to offer some support to Edith. For several months Edith continued to see Chaplain Lee and the social worker on a regular basis. As she improved, she began to date again. After some months, she dropped by to inform Chaplain Lee that she was in love and wanted to be married. Though she had told her boyfriend of her previous experience, he still insisted that he loved her and wanted to marry her. They discussed at some length plans to adopt children in the future. Although she found it difficult to believe, with the aid of the social worker and Chaplain Lee, Edith was gradually able to accept the love offered her. After several sessions together, they were married in his church two years after her first visit to see Chaplain Lee.

Discussion

Despite the apparent complications surrounding Edith's initial attempts to deal with the emotional aspects of abortion, she reflected some basic trust in people by going to see Chaplain Lee. Fortunately, he allowed her to express her feelings toward Rick and her fears, which enabled her to face herself and her anger toward men. Chaplain Lee again showed his basic good judgment in dealing with the entire family. The parents' involvement was essential with the complications of this abortion.

An important aspect was the sensitivity Chaplain Lee reflected. He met with Edith to let her pour out her feelings, giving her a right to be angry. Not until she had changed her focus to surgery did Chaplain Lee suggest a return to psychiatric outpatient services. Chaplain Lee's acceptance of Edith enabled her to begin the long, uphill journey back to self-respect. Since the need for surgery and medication could not be met by Chaplain Lee, his greatest contribution was helping Edith to accept herself as a worthy person who could still love and be loved in return. He was also able to help her understand that she could still be a mother even though she could no longer bear children of her own.

The ability to reestablish her dating patterns and her decision to be married suggest that Edith is basically an emotionally sound young person, who could adapt to stress and move on with the process of developing a full life for herself. The critical incidents were left in the past.

Vicki

Vicki, a twenty-two-year-old secretary and a member of Chaplain Lee's congregation, opened her first session with Chaplain Lee with the statement that she was extremely lonely and withdrawing more and more from people. She had decided to see Chaplain Lee the previous day after she had sat alone all day in a chair moving only when the position became unbearable. Describing herself as wanting to spend more and more time alone, locked in her room, fearful of seeing or talking with anyone, Vicki said that she had only one friend with whom she could relate or trust. Resenting Vicki's possessiveness and dependency on her to the point that relationships with other males and females were for the most part curtailed, her friend had insisted that she see Chaplain Lee. Fearful that she was about to lose her only friend, Vicki consented to an appointment.

For approximately fifteen minutes of the first session Vicki talked sparingly of her feelings of loneliness and alienation, responding for the most part only when Chaplain Lee asked a direct question. Explaining her difficulty in talking, Vicki indicated that there were things which were too painful to talk about and that she found it much easier just to avoid them. Without further explanation she jumped from her seat, pausing only long enough to inform Chaplain Lee that she was leaving.

Approximately two weeks later, she returned and, without reference to her previous behavior, she began to discuss her low self-esteem and lack of motivation to do anything. Somewhat incidentally and without any change in expression, she began to discuss calmly events of the previous week in which she had been raped after leaving work late one evening. Although she indicated in response to Chaplain Lee's inquiries that it had been a terrifying experience, she soon moved to another topic displaying no real feelings or emotion. Chaplain Lee was able to learn that Vicki had been seen by a psychiatrist two years earlier on an irregular basis for approximately six months and that she had been pregnant on two different occasions over a three year period. In the first of these she had had the baby but placed it up for adoption. The last time she had an abortion. She talked a great deal about suicide and revealed that she made several attempts to kill herself as a teenager. In spite of Vicki's promises to Chaplain Lee that she would not harm herself, her girl friend called Chaplain Lee on several occasions concerned that Vicki was about to kill herself. On one occasion, she had rushed her to the hospital by ambulance after Vicki had drank a large quantity of liquor in a two hour period and failed to respond to her friend's frantic attempts to revive her. On another occasion, she had been injured slightly while driving a friend's car with little regard for her safety or that of others.

In later sessions, Vicki began to talk more freely of her fear that people were talking about her and to refer to a big blackness in her life which seemed to dominate a lot of her thinking. She complained of chest pains, headaches, difficulty in breathing, insomnia, and depression which had become so bad that she found it difficult to get up in the morning. When Chaplain Lee suggested that she see a psychiatrist, she refused saying that she had not received any help in her earlier sessions with a psychiatrist.

In the seventh visit, Vicki began the session in a calm manner with an occasional smile. Shortly, however, she began to discuss the nightmares she had begun to experience which were so disturbing to her that she dreaded going to sleep at night. When she did fall asleep she usually woke up during the night and found herself unable to return to sleep. At one point in the session she interrupted her train of thought to say, "Incidentally, I think I'm pregnant." After a brief discussion in which she said that she had no intention of having the baby, she turned to other matters. Acknowledging that she was reluctant to reveal such for fear of being locked up, she began to discuss a knocking on her bedroom wall at night and the feeling that someone was in her bedroom. Always sensitive to smells, she had begun to notice new smells, particularly at night which she viewed as further evidence that some person was in her room. She described her depression and situation as being so overwhelming and hopeless that thoughts of suicide were recurring with increasing frequency. There were moments in which she felt almost hypnotized by the sight of a razor blade or running water. Referring again to her pregnancy, she indicated that she had been relieved to discover that she was pregnant, feeling that such was the basis of her depression and discomfort in recent weeks. Consequently the termination of her pregnancy, which she had arranged for, was seen as a cure for the discomfort she was now experiencing. Her only dread seemed to be that of breaking the news to her parents.

Possessing certain convictions and doubts regarding the matter of abortion and yet concerned with Vicki's emotional state, Chaplain Lee requested again that she seek psychiatric help. Much to his surprise, his suggestion was this time met with approval and an appointment arranged. Through her friend, Chaplain Lee was later informed that Vicki had received an abortion in a nearby hospital and later admitted to the psychiatric ward for further treatment.

Discussion

This is a situation dealt with in an effective manner by Chaplain Lee and proof that clergymen can be of great assistance in getting disturbed people to accept the type of treatment needed. Chaplain Lee helped Vicki to reach out to someone other than her roommate, to acknowledge her experiences, and to prepare her for further psychiatric help. It was good that Chaplain Lee did not attempt to detain Vicki when she fled from his office but showed in other ways his interest and desire to help. However, he might have explored in more detail Vicki's feelings about being raped. As with abortion, there are many crisis lines and centers set up to deal quite effectively with rape. Clergymen should be aware of these resources in the community and not hesitate to utilize them when the need arises.

There are a number of indications that Vicki needs psychiatric care. Three unwanted pregnancies in three years suggests that Vicki is unable or unwilling to learn from past experiences as she continues to engage in behavior which is destructive and demeaning. While one unwanted pregnancy is difficult enough, the repetition of such, along with her cavalier attitude toward pregnancy and abortion, is indeed disturbing. For many reasons there are women who unconsciously want to get pregnant even though they deny such intentions vehemently. These self-destructive acts, combined with her over indulgence in alcohol, reckless driving, previous attempts at suicide, and her current preoccupation with suicide are warning signals that her life may be in jeopardy. Her depression, impulsivity, insomnia, and strong sense of alienation are also signs which should not be ignored. Finally, her fears and unfounded beliefs that someone was in her room at night, her reasoning that her pregnancy is the basis of her difficulties, her impoverishment of social relationships, her extreme dependence on her roommate, her jumping from one subject to another, her bland and irrational way of talking and thinking suggest that she is a seriously disturbed person with immediate need for psychiatric care.

Judy

Calling Chaplain Lee's secretary, Judy, a twenty-two-year-old legal secretary, arranged an appointment for the following week. However, she showed up unexpectantly two days early indicating that she could not wait and had to see Chaplain Lee immediately. Attempting to explain her sense of urgency she was, in her words, terrified that she was about to have a nervous breakdown. She described her feelings of being all quivery inside as panic and depression with the fear of falling apart. These sensations had begun three weeks earlier, precipitated, in her opinion by an abortion she had undergone. Prior to this she had thought herself a normal, sensible, young woman with no history of emotional unrest.

Further discussion revealed that Judy was engaged to an engineering student in a nearby state. Describing herself as a moral and religious person, Judy had always believed that she would be a virgin when she married. However, after going with her boyfriend for three years "something had happened," and on their first and only attempt at sexual intercourse, Judy had become pregnant. Neither Judy nor her boyfriend had taken any precautions against pregnancy since both had been led to believe that a girl could not become pregnant in her first attempt at sexual intercourse. Upon discovering that Judy was pregnant, her fiancé had agreed to go along with any decision Judy made. Without seeking counseling, though they had considered such, Judy reached the decision to obtain an abortion. This decision had been strengthened by the fear that the child might be abnormal because Judy had been involved in an auto accident during the first week of pregnancy. She had also been in the process of recuperating from a bout with mononucleosis which she thought might cause damage to the fetus. Her lack of readiness to become a mother, she cited as the final reason for her decision.

Experiencing no physical problems, with the abortion performed by a physician in a large city hospital, Judy initially felt relieved. For several weeks she had no regrets, convinced that she had made the right decision. In recent weeks, however, she had begun to have second thoughts about the abortion and while in Chaplain Lee's office, referred to herself as a killer who had no right to stop the process of birth. When alone in particular, she became depressed and concerned that she would be unable to handle it emotionally. Experiencing difficulty in sleeping she had been drinking rather heavily in an attempt to forget. Despite this, when alone and sober, she cried uncontrollably with her feelings of guilt increasing to the point of obsession that she had done wrong. Though complaining of depression, she denied any intent of suicide and she gave no indication that she was in reality approaching a state of insanity.

In the second session, Judy focused primarily on her stupidity for not using contraceptives and on her disappointment to her father who had such great faith in her. At the same time, she remained adamant in her decision not to share information concerning her pregnancy and abortion with him or anyone else. Concerned about the level of Judy's anxiety, Chaplain Lee suggested that she see a physician for tranquilizers. Judy agreed to do so and while in the physician's office discussed at some length the abortion and her reasons for having it. Her physician confirmed the possibility of damage to the fetus as a result of the illness and accident. Returning to see Chaplain Lee, Judy appeared to be more accepting of her situation, feeling that her decision had been supported by medical opinion.

However, Judy later returned for several sessions in which she tended to vacilate between feelings of guilt and acceptance, at times convinced that she would never get over it and would eventually have a nervous breakdown. In her worst moments, she saw the depression and guilt as becoming more severe rather than lessening. Her boyfriend's attempts to convince her that she had done the right thing, along with the physician's opinion, were ignored at these times.

Possessing a number of reservations about abortion Chaplain Lee was more immediately concerned with Judy's well-being and focused on her feelings rather than on moral judgments. Chaplain Lee was convinced after several more sessions that Judy had become more accepting of her abortion, though in principle opposed to abortion herself. Shortly afterward, she accepted a job in another city.

Discussion

Judy, responding in a more traditional fashion to abortion than did either Edith or Vicki, seems fairly representative of the less disturbed, naive, young unmarried female with high moral values experiencing an unwanted pregnancy. She engaged in a lot of agonizing with considerable rationalizing, regret, and remorse. Chaplain Lee is a good example of a compassionate and sensitive clergyman who was able to help Judy in her time of need though he did not approve of abortion himself. Had he approached counseling with Judy in an unforgiving manner he could easily have convinced her that her life was over, with self-destruction possibly the end result. Instead, in a more productive fashion, Chaplain Lee encouraged Judy to express and explore her mixture of feelings. With Chaplain Lee's help, Judy was able to view human error as forgiveable and subsequently to judge herself less harshly. It is not our purpose to deal with theological matters involving the ethics of premarital sex or abortion. However, we are of the opinion, when counseling with individuals already overwhelmed with guilt and self-recrimination, that moralizing or sermonettes are most inappropriate, even dangerous. Judy, as did Edith, in an impulsive fashion, decided to terminate her pregnancy without benefit of any sort of counseling. All of the sermonizing in the world cannot change her action. It could serve to push an already upset or disturbed individual over the brink into suicide, or other forms of self-punitive behavior. Unfortunately, we do still have many young women who, lacking information, find themselves pregnant at an undesirable time in their lives. Clergymen often have unique opportunities to disseminate sexual information to those who need it. This includes seminars and discussions involving topics such as marriage and the family, pre-marital sex, pre-marriage and marriage counseling.

If an unwanted pregnancy does occur, individuals should seek pre-abortion counseling before rushing into an abortion. Again many do not, failing to realize that once done the act is irreversible. Regardless of pre-abortion counseling, counseling should always be strongly emphasized after termination of pregnancy. Unfortunately, many doctors, counselors, clergymen, and others faced with the matter of abortion do not stress the need for post-abortion counseling. And yet it is at this time that many individuals need help the most. Chaplain Lee was able to recognize the need and responded skillfully to Judy's plea for help.

Angie

Angie, a thirty-one-year-old waitress, called Chaplain Lee the day after her fourteen-year-old son, Cliff, had been sent home from school for cursing a teacher. Unable to cope with her son's recent behavior, she arranged an appointment to see Chaplain Lee. In the first session, Angie revealed that she had been divorced for nine years. She had married Lou at seventeen with her son being born six months later. Questioning revealed that Angie and Lou had been dating only three weeks when she became pregnant. Not at all interested in having a child, Angie was afraid to confront her parents with her pregnancy or desire for an abortion. Although Lou had demanded that Angie have an abortion, she insisted on marriage even though she confessed that she knew that Lou did not love her.

After several weeks of agonizing delay, Lou had reluctantly given in. From the beginning, it was obvious that he resented being married to Angie. Shortly after Cliff's fourth birthday, he moved out of the house. Although Angie insisted that she loved both her husband and her son, she stated that she had also resented being tied down and felt that she had been cheated out of the things a young woman should be entitled to. Forced to take a job as a waitress to supplement her husband's salary after Cliff's birth, she had depended on her mother to take care of Cliff. However, due to her mother's ill health, Cliff received minimal care, often going for days without a bath or sleeping whenever or wherever he happened to fall asleep for the night. In his first two years, though his parents made an adequate salary, he was never well dressed, properly fed, or given the attention and care that his peers received. Although she was a hard worker, Angie switched jobs a number of times, never seeming to find a job that really suited her.

A bright child, Cliff was the last in his class to learn to read. Although aware that he was behind in his school work, Angie confessed that she had neither the time nor inclination to help him with his homework.

Insisting that Angie bring her son to the second session, Chaplain Lee learned that beginning with his first grade, Cliff would frequently be left alone in the house during the day for long periods of time while his mother worked or visited with male and female friends. By the end of the fifth grade, he was left alone at night with his mother being gone on numerous occasions for the entire day and night. In her absence Cliff would have to get up, fix his own meals, and get to and from school as best he could. He could still recall the panic he experienced in the first and second grades upon arriving home from school to find his mother away and the doors locked. When the neighbors complained, Angie saw them as nosy busybodies who had no right to tell her how to raise her son. When it was suggested to her that she place her son in a foster home, Angie refused to do so since child support payments would then cease. Because of his mother's attitudes, Cliff found that most parents would not let their children play with him. In his tenth and eleventh years, lonely and unattended, he had begun to associate with boys considerably older, some already using drugs and alcohol. Shortly after his thirteenth birthday Cliff had been brought home by the police for drinking in a poolroom with older boys. Undaunted, Angie had bragged to her date for the evening how quickly her son had grown up. She defended her absence and Cliff's having to fend for himself, as good training for adulthood in a world in which everyone had to look out for themselves. She saw nothing wrong with his smoking or drinking at his young age.

Already spending a minimum of time with her son, Angie revealed that she looked forward to the two weeks Cliff spent during Christmas and the summer with his father. Apparently unconcerned about her own mother's bad health she would insist that Cliff visit his grandmother at least once each week so that she might have some time to herself. Always complaining about the critical lack of money to buy food and clothes whenever Cliff asked for something, she never seemed to lack for clothes herself, and she spent considerable sums on cars and personal pleasures.

Ignoring the complaints of neighbors, who continued to complain to community officials, Angie had turned in desperation to Chaplain Lee when Cliff's principal had told her that Cliff would not be permitted to return to school unless she was willing to come back with him and promise school officials that she would assume more responsibility for his conduct in the future.

In the two sessions with Cliff and his mother, Cliff remained for the most part sullen, withdrawn, and suspicious, replying in monosyllables whenever Chaplain Lee directed a question to him. Communication between Cliff and his mother appeared to be nonexistent. No love or affection was displayed. Although he extracted a promise from Angie to return the next week, Cliff refused to agree to another appointment saying only that he might come back. When neither appeared, Chaplain Lee discovered that Angie had quit her job and left town, taking Cliff with her.

Discussion

While there is no simple answer in the case of an unwanted pregnancy there is also no simple answer for an unwanted baby. Cliff is a good example of the damage which can result when a child is born in a home where parents are unready or emotionally unstable to the point that parenthood should have never been considered. While insisting that she loved her son, Angie resented his presence and in many ways, both consciously and unconsciously, displayed her resentment. Angie appears to be a fairly disturbed individual who has the potential for even more serious emotional problems but who has managed to function at a minimal level for years without confinement to a hospital. Her neglect of Cliff borders on child abuse and is obviously behavior which a responsible mother would never consider. The pleasure she derived from seeing her son engage in drinking and smoking at such an early age is symptomatic of the sick pattern she finds gratifying for some strange reason. Her view of his having to fend for himself in a hostile world as good training is in all probability symptomatic of her own hostility and distrust toward society. In cases such as this, social intervention is indicated with placement in a foster home a consideration. However, at Cliff's age this is difficult to accomplish. Rather than trying to see both of them together, Chaplain Lee might have suggested that Cliff see another therapist. In most communities there are Children and Family Services available to which clergymen can refer when such is needed. Lacking the support that youngsters need in childhood, Cliff will probably continue to have difficulty in the future unless drastic measures and remedial therapy are undertaken.

Nora

Nora, a beautiful twenty-seven-year-old ex-fashion model, came to see Chaplain Lee when she could no longer sleep without recurring nightmares involving the child she had conceived out of wedlock and subsequently placed up for adoption. Although the decision had occurred five years before, she stated that she could not get it off her mind. It was the first thing she thought about in the morning and the last thing on her mind before sleep. She explained in dramatic fashion how she had become involved sexually for the first time at twenty-two. After learning that she was pregnant, her boyfriend Hank had insisted on an abortion. Believing that a child could help her hold on to a relationship which had been deteriorating for some time, Nora decided to have the baby. Informing Nora that he wanted no part of a child which would only tie him down to a marriage he was not ready for, Hank left town. Failing to hear from Hank again, Nora agreed to the suggestion of her parents that the baby be adopted.

Nora expressed her anger and regret that Hank had not married her or wanted her to keep the baby. She would look at dresses for toddlers and at large dolls, imagining what her daughter might look like had she stayed with her mother. She bought a giant sized doll to dress and care for. This lasted about a year. She grew tried of the expense. She wondered if her daughter had curly hair, what she might have done with dance lessons, and how cute she would have been.

For the several sessions which Nora attended Chaplain Lee attempted to deal with her feelings concerning the adoption of her baby. Despite his efforts, Nora seemed unable to accept herself and rebuffed any attempts on the part of Chaplain Lee to help her deal with her feelings. Convinced that Nora needed more intensive therapy than he could provide Chaplain Lee suggested that she see a psychiatrist.

Discussion

It does sound as if Nora is a "spoiled child" who wants to have the rest of the world do as she wishes. She appears to have a strong need for more attention and for better feelings of self-worth.

Nora's obsession with her "lost" child suggests that psychiatric referral is needed. Seemingly a rather narcissistic type of individual Nora possibly desires a "toy" to control or an object to increase her self-esteem. Her "poor me" attitude is suggestive of those individuals who go to great lengths to attract the attention they so desperately crave. Work with this type of individual is difficult since it is so easy for clergymen and counselors to become entrapped in the morass of self-pity which Nora is striving to reinforce rather than trying to deal with her problem in a more mature fashion. Though it is questionable as to whether Nora will respond to psychiatric treatment positively, the attempt should be made.

Although there are those mothers who elect to keep the baby born out of wedlock and rear the child alone, it is often questionable as to whether such is good for either the mother or child. Many social workers who have worked closely with those individuals in which adoption is an issue have suggested that the decision to keep the child is often an attempt on the part of the mother to atone for the sin of having an illegitimate child. Others keep the baby, as did Nora, with the hope that the father will someday return. A large number of those women who become pregnant before marriage are "children" themselves, either emotionally or physically, and not prepared to assume the responsibilities of parenthood. In such cases they often grow to resent the child and the restrictions placed on them as mothers. While it may be a difficult decision to make, clergymen and others in this position should work with unwed mothers and consider what is best for all involved. In many cases this might well be adoption.

Summary

There is no simple or painless solution for the woman who finds herself pregnant when she does not want to be. Regardless of the decision, pain and suffering are usually inevitable. Our purpose is not to condone or condemn abortion. It is, however, our hope that the preceding cases have served to make the reader more aware of abortion and pregnancy as crucial issues with which most clergymen will be confronted at some time or other. Whether one approves or not, the attitudes toward abortion have undergone drastic changes in recent years. If for personal and moral reasons, some clergymen find themselves unable to counsel objectively with females who are pregnant and considering abortion or who have already had an abortion, then they should not hesitate to refer them to some reputable person or agency who can and will. Since abortion is for most individuals a serious moral issue, clergymen may be in a better position to offer assistance in the decision-making process and in the handling of guilt than psychiatrists or other mental health professionals.

For the woman considering abortion, the various alternatives should be explored with every attempt made to consider possible repercussions, emotional, physical, and moral. For the woman who decides to continue the pregnancy the question of marriage, the future, support, and adoption, should be looked into thoroughly. For the woman in whom pregnancy has already been terminated through abortion, moralizing or attempts to make her feel guilty and less worthwhile are most inappropriate and may be detrimental to her well-being. In most cases, she has already suffered untold guilt and anguish.

If referral is decided on, clergymen should be reminded that agencies specializing in abortion and abortion counseling have mushroomed in recent years. Undoubtedly many of these are reputable and professionally run, while others are concerned only with a fast and easy dollar. Counseling before and after the abortion, if such is the decision, should be strongly emphasized. If at all possible, the male should be a responsible participant in the counseling sessions and in the decision making. While it is the female who usually occupies center stage in situations involving pregnancy and abortion, the male should not be ignored. Many males also undergo great stress when their partners become pregnant or have an abortion. Surprisingly enough, many want to become involved in the counseling sessions and to assume partial responsibility for what has happened. While such involvement should be encouraged, it is usually detrimental to all involved to pressure a reluctant and irresponsible male into coming in for counseling or into marrying when he has no desire to do so.

Although such is not usually the case pregnancy can be pathologically motivated. With this in mind clergymen might want to consider referral to a psychiatrist if the woman is depressed for a long period of time, either before or after the abortion. If she is unable to cope with guilt feelings engendered as a result of the abortion, has had two or more abortions, or displays other signs of mental illness and emotional stress referral is also recommended.

Finally, it should be emphasized that while an unwanted pregnancy and abortion are a painful experience for most women, not all suffer the serious consequences dwelled on by those opposed to abortion in any form. While we do not condone abortion, experience in counseling with females who have had an abortion, leads us to the conclusion that many women who have abortions do make a good adjustment. This seems most probable in our opinion when the woman has high self-esteem and a positive concept of herself as a person. As a result, such a woman is able to forgive herself for having done something stupid. A woman with a poor self-image is inclined to view the unwanted pregnancy and abortion as further proof that she is worthless. A more tolerant view of abortion in recent years also seems to have enabled women to look at themselves in a different light. While abortion remains a serious problem, it is not a new one. Many authorities are doubtful if it is increasing as much as one is sometimes led to believe. They suggest instead that women are more prone to discuss abortion openly now that it is being performed in clinical settings.

Chapter 7
Loneliness and Alienation

The proliferation and popularity of condominiums, high rise dormitories, and sprawling apartment complexes in this country in the latter half of the twentieth century are beyond imagination. Colleges and universities, as well as industries and businesses, have increased in size and enrollment to the point that officials have turned to computerization to keep track of their students and employees. Our expressways are clogged with traffic, and even hikers and campers do not always find the solitude they seek. The situation has become so critical that one is now hard put to find a spot where he can ride, walk, or sit with any measure of privacy.

Although we are fast on the way to overpopulating this country, feelings of loneliness, alienation, and isolation are increasingly being heard as major complaints in mental health clinics and counseling centers. We do not wish to imply that loneliness is a symptom of mental illness. Everyone, at times, experiences feelings of being alienated, even in the midst of a large crowd. To be human is to know loneliness. For most, such feelings are usually mild and temporary. For a significant number, however, feelings of loneliness, isolation, and boredom, and an absence of meaningful relationships with other human beings have become a way of life. When such feelings are pervasive and overwhelming, one is led to suspect that mental illness is already existent or at least to be anticipated unless something is done. The following cases are examples.

Glenn

While driving to deliver the commencement address at a high school some 200 miles from his home, Chaplain Lee found himself, with mechanical difficulties, stranded on a little traveled highway still seventy-five miles from his destination. His meager knowledge of mechanics soon exhausted, he attempted unsuccessfully to stop several cars before a man, looking much older than the fifty-five years he professed, stopped to offer assistance. Upon learning that the stranded motorist was a clergyman, Glenn volunteered to drive Chaplain Lee to the nearest garage. After a brief exchange Glenn began to discuss, without any prompting from Chaplain Lee, his retirement fourteen months earlier and the death of his wife seven months later. Though not of retirement age, Glenn, a rural mail carrier, revealed that he had been forced into early retirement due to emphysema which had become so severe that he could no longer walk up the slightest incline without sitting down. Always an active man in his church and community, Glenn had gradually reduced his activities to the point that he seldom left the house anymore. After retirement, he reported that he had lost interest in his wife sexually and on several occasions had been impotent when he did attempt sexual intercourse. Suffering from a loss of appetite, he began to lose weight. He spent a major portion of his day in a chair on his front porch. An avid football fan, he was no longer interested in football games even on television. Seven months later after his retirement, his wife had been killed in an auto accident. Despite his family's demands that he quit crying and snap out of it, he became even more depressed. Never a heavy drinker he had, since the death of his wife, turned more and more to alcohol. The alcohol, along with tranquilizers prescribed by his family physician, now enabled him to sleep a major portion of his time. Expressing the opinion that he had nothing to live for anymore, he rejected the attempts of his family and friends to get him involved again.

Concerned over the length and depth of depression as described by Glenn, Chaplain Lee asked that he be permitted to drop in on Glenn on his way back home the following day. Availing himself of the opportunity to speak alone with Glenn's daughter during the brief stopover the next day, Chaplain Lee encouraged her to seek immediate psychiatric intervention for her father.

Several months after the encounter with Glenn, Chaplain Lee received a letter from Glenn informing him that he had agreed to see a psychiatrist at the insistance of his daughter. Hospitalized, with treatment for his depression undertaken, Glenn had slowly begun to recover and to take interest in life again.

Discussion

For many individuals, retirement alone is enough to cause depression and feelings of worthlessness and loneliness. In Glenn's case this was compounded by the limitations placed on him by his chronic physical illness and the death of his wife. These events resulted in a classic display of signs of depression—loss of appetite, weight, and interest in sex as well as other activities previously enjoyed. His increased use of alcohol only served as an escape and probably made his depression worse. Tranquilizers, sometimes indiscriminately prescribed by physicians, in all probability increased his depressed feelings also. Tranquilizers alone are not usually effective in treating depression, and their combination with alcohol not only serves to increase depression but can be lethal as well. For this reason it is wise for any person taking drugs to inquire of his doctor if the consumption of alcohol along with the drug is permissible. Antidepressant medication sometimes in combination with tranquilizers is usually the most acceptable mode of treating the severely depressed person.

Chaplain Lee's response is to be commended. Glenn's depression has lasted much too long to attempt to alleviate by counseling alone. Immediate psychiatric referral should be stressed in cases such as this.

The situation with Glenn demonstrated the unique position clergymen occupy as opposed to psychiatrists and other professionals who cannot intervene without being requested to do so by the patient or his family. Even though they are not asked to do so specifically, sensitive and interested clergymen can often detect signs of emotional problems and encourage the individual to obtain the help he needs.

Gwen

During her initial session with Chaplain Lee, Gwen, a twenty-one-year-old college student, focused on her loneliness and concern that she was about to crack up. She followed this up by saying that she saw this at times as a desirable alternative to her present situation. When thinking of insanity in moments such as this, she compared it to a long vacation in which she would be free from the overwhelming loneliness and neglect which caused her such great concern. During the session, she described herself as alienated and not close to anyone. Failure on the part of her fellow students on occasion to invite her to lunch made her feel slighted and was seen as proof that she was not welcome in her small circle of friends. She was particularly distrustful of her grandparents whom she saw as engaged in a plot to deprive her of her rightful inheritance as a result of her father's death several years earlier. She was also quite vocal in her criticism of her professors who were going to great lengths to give her a hard time. Attempting to live with her boyfriend the previous quarter, Gwen had found the situation intolerable and moved back into the dormitory though she insisted that they were still going together and that she was unable to imagine a life without him. During the sessions Gwen appeared to be angry, irritable, and hypercritical of those who disagreed with others. Despite her criticism of others, she found criticism of herself intolerable and labeled her critics as stupid or wrong. Though her hostility and anger continued to be manifested throughout the sessions, Gwen appeared to be unaware of such feelings on her part and responded to Chaplain Lee's attempts to reflect such to her with disdain. Reluctant to answer questions posed by Chaplain Lee, she glanced uneasily around the room during the session and questioned him at length concerning confidentiality and his qualifications for counseling. Though not in use, a tape recorder in the room was viewed by Gwen as evidence that Chaplain Lee could not completely be trusted.

In the second session Gwen continued to reveal her distrust and fear of involvement with others. Obviously intelligent and possessing a high academic average, Gwen was concerned that she would not be permitted to graduate by her professors, and she was considering dropping out of school. After two more sessions with Chaplain Lee in which he found himself unable to establish any sort of relationship with Gwen, she informed him that she was leaving school and would not schedule any more appointments.

Discussion

Most people fear a loss of control. A sense of responsibility for one's welfare is usually a valued aspect of living for healthy people. The severity of Gwen's condition is suggested by her statement that a period of insanity would be like a long vacation, freeing her from the things which caused her such great concern.

The level of anger, suspicion, and distrust in Gwen was so severe that she could not deal with the mildest of comments by Chaplain Lee. In response to a reflection of her apparent unawareness of those feelings, Gwen questioned Chaplain Lee's qualifications and safeguards of confidentiality. While often difficult with people like Gwen who are unable to trust, psychiatric referral is indicated. Sometimes it is helpful to admit to the patient that you do not feel qualified to help in his case and that you would like to have him seen by someone else who is.

Gwen's anger and suspicion are outer layers covering a more central and severe emotional problem in which she is unable to handle interpersonal relationships. At this point, Gwen backed away from the entire situation, including Chaplain Lee and school itself.

Although Gwen does show evidence of extreme psychopathology, she was able to overcome her distrust enough to see Chaplain Lee and discuss her problems to some degree with him. However, as her barriers came down, she became more frightened but she might have accepted professional help at this time.

Without help, it is probable that Gwen will be a person without close relationships. She will probably remain distrustful and upset much of the time and move around a lot to contain her behavior. Whether or not she actually does develop a delusional system and require hospitalization is probably dependent upon the degree of fright she feels in relationships with other people and events.

Babs

Babs, a twenty-six-year-old sales clerk, came to see Chaplain Lee complaining of loneliness and despression. She indicated that she was so despondent and the future so bleak that she had been considering suicide for two days. Sobbing softly, she stated that no one knew just how lonely she was or how much she hurt inside. Having suffered a broken wrist several days earlier, she informed Chaplain Lee that the pain was nothing compared to the hurt and misery she had to live with constantly from within. Weighing over 200 pounds, with acne on her face and shoulders, Babs had been discharged from a mental hospital six months earlier after undergoing treatment for three months. Describing her lack of friends, she revealed that not one person had been to her apartment to see her in over two years. Her cat, which she described as the most important thing in her life, had died two weeks before and left her with a profound sense of loss. At times she became so lonely that she had been to see a number of ministers in the community, as well as community mental health workers, just to have someone to talk with. At times she would be seeing as many as three or four people for counseling at one time. She had been seeing one psychiatrist on an outpatient basis weekly since her discharge from the hospital and volunteered the information that she had seen in her chart that he had diagnosed her as schizophrenic. In the last year, she had for the first time begun to have sexual relations with a number of males. Most of these were men she picked up in bars where she went to escape the loneliness of her apartment. Babs indicated that she seldom saw any of the men again after the first date. Her current boyfriend, whom she described as an alcoholic, had been seeing her on an infrequent basis for two months. However, he never took the initiative in arranging a date nor did he ever take her out. Their time spent together usually involved sexual intercourse after which he would often ask her to leave. Feeling rejected, she usually called and begged him to let her come over or else showed up at his apartment unannounced where she sometimes found him with other women. It was after one of these occasions that she decided to see Chaplain Lee. Never having any lasting relationships with males, she described most of the men she dated as unhealthy sort of individuals who only added to her despair and feelings of worthlessness as a woman.

As a result of her unhappiness, she had two days earlier resigned her job and informed Chaplain Lee that she just wanted to get away from everything and that if she could not be happy, then life was just not worth living. Wanting to contact her parents, Chaplain Lee learned that her parents were both dead and that her only sister refused to have anything to do with her. Even the mental health workers and clergymen in the area had tired of her frequent visits and phone calls at all hours of the night. This seemed, in Bab's opinion, to be the final proof that no one wanted to see her or could help her.

Thinking that Babs was indeed desperate enough to harm herself Chaplain Lee suggested that she enter the hospital for psychiatric evaluation. Agreeing to do so Babs requested that he accompany her to the hospital where she was admitted as a patient.

Discussion

Babs seems to be an example of a borderline personality who has for years alternated between the need for hospitalization and the ability to function minimally outside the hospital. At the time seen by Chaplain Lee, overwhelmed by stress, she was no longer able to function at even a marginal level and had to be hospitalized. Obviously an unhealthy person, Babs seems to be also lacking in the skills needed for change. Extremely lonely she continues to shop around for love and affection with little success. Babs' extensive need for personality restructuring, and her long history of emotional difficulties, her lack of social skills, and the fact that several therapists have previously struck out in treating her lead to a rather dismal prognosis.

Her peeking at her chart, in which she was described as schizophrenic, emphasizes the danger or harm which can be done in labeling individuals expressing emotional difficulties. The word "schizophrenic," for example, carries with it, for most people, a connotation of something shameful and frightening and does little to encourage optimism on the patient's part.

While most people do not need to be escorted to a hospital or mental health agency, Chaplain Lee's willingness to walk the "second mile" was perhaps indicated in this case due to Babs's lack of family or friends and her extreme feelings of loneliness and desperation. With people such as Babs, it is usually necessary to set limits in regard to their expectations of counselors, clergymen, or psychiatrists. While communicating to the disturbed person that you do care and are available, you must teach them not to place unrealistic demands upon you by calling at all hours of the day or night whenever they feel lonely.

Howard

Howard, a forty-three-year-old school principal who had returned to school for the summer to work on an advanced degree, came to see Chaplain Lee complaining of loneliness, hopelessness, and depression. Having few friends, Howard spent most of his time in class or in his room studying. Obviously a bright student, he was concerned that he was going to flunk out of school though he had an A average. Always fearful that he might leave something important out on a test, he could never respond to his professor's instructions to discuss briefly any subject. No matter how much he studied he never felt prepared, nor was any grade ever high enough. Never satisfied with anything less, his goal was to be the top teacher in the state. In spite of his goals to exceed, Howard felt inadequate and insecure. As a result, he pushed himself every minute of the day, feeling that he was being driven by some force over which he had no control. As the sessions progressed, Chaplain Lee was able to learn that even as a young boy at home, Howard had never been able to accept things as they were and to relax. He felt his parents and siblings never lived up to their potential, educationally, vocationally, morally, or otherwise. He viewed his older sister now married and the mother of three children as a poor parent. Her children failed to live up to Howard's ideals and expectations also. Even his parents' marriage failed to satisfy Howard and in his thinking had been a failure. Though he admitted he had no power to change or alter the circumstances, he continued to return again and again in the sessions to a discussion of his parents' marriage and his sister's failure as a mother. Chaplain Lee's attempts to persuade Howard that his sense of obligation and responsibility to do something about his parents' and his sister's situation was unrealistic met with failure. Though agreeing verbally, Howard continued to insist that he had no control over his feelings and could not change. Resistant to any talk of change, Howard would say "Yes, I agree, but . . ." followed by a long and detailed list of reasons he could not change. Academically he became more dissatisfied with himself as the weeks passed. He often found himself unable to complete class assignments as a result of becoming sidetracked on issues of interest to him. In his reading assignments he felt compelled to explore in great detail the meaning of every word in a sentence and to analyze the philosophical implications of any given text. As a result he was often far afield from the task assigned and unprepared when assignments were due. Contentious, eager to disagree and debate with Chaplain Lee on every sentence, he adhered rigidly to the way he believed things should be. Despite his unhappiness and complaints of loneliness, Howard argued against any suggestion Chaplain Lee made to involve himself in groups in the church or elsewhere, giving a number of reasons as to why he could not. Two months after the initial session, frustrated by Howard's hopelessness and helplessness in regard to change in his life, Chaplain Lee suggested that he see a psychiatrist.

Discussion

A perfectionist who is rigid and inflexible, Howard may never be able to change much in his attitudes and behavior. He has developed a pessimistic style and avoids dealing with feelings by logical and judgmental pronouncements. Never expecting anything good to happen, he is rarely disappointed.

Understandably, Chaplain Lee experienced great frustration in attempting to work with Howard. With people like Howard, the counselor must recognize that he has rights also and that all people cannot profit from therapy. It might be helpful in the initial session to define the goals which clients want to accomplish in counseling. Then, if the individual is uncooperative, constantly arguing and disagreeing, with nothing being accomplished, the counselor has every right to terminate the sessions or suggest referral.

Ruth

Ruth, a sixty-four-year-old housewife, came to see Chaplain Lee complaining that she had suddenly and without reason lost interest in everything and stayed at home most of the time. Always a devoted wife and mother and a conscientious housewife, she described herself as now having difficulty getting started in the morning. Also, having difficulty in going to sleep, she usually woke early in the morning finding it impossible to go back to sleep. Relating that she had always had a hearty appetite she had recently lost any desire to eat and had lost weight to the point that she could no longer wear her clothes comfortably. One of Chaplain Lee's most dedicated church members, she still appeared for each service but had discontinued the many duties she had assumed through the years. This sudden and inexplicable change in Ruth's behavior and attitudes had convinced her that she was losing her mind. Even prayer and Bible reading, formerly a source of great inspiration to her, seemed to be futile. Visits from her children and grandchildren tended to aggravate rather than help her condition though she insisted they were still the greatest source of meaning in her life. Having led an active life physically, Ruth had in addition been forced to slow her pace considerably in recent months, due to arthritis. Her work in the house and yard, which had been done meticulously in the past, had been sharply curtailed with the result that Ruth viewed her home with considerable dismay, expressing the feeling that she found it difficult to live in such a mess. Now finding it difficult to complete the tasks which she had accomplished before with ease, Ruth had lost confidence in herself, feeling unworthy and guilty, with considerable difficulty in making decisions.

After several sessions with Ruth in which she continued to complain of physical and emotional fatigue, with feelings of emptiness, sadness, and hopelessness, with no sign that she was improving, Chaplain Lee suggested that she see her family physican. Reassured by Chaplain Lee that she was not going crazy, Ruth agreed to do so. She returned to see Chaplain Lee the following week indicating that she had been given antidepressants along with medication for her arthritis. The physician recommended that she see a psychologist or continue to see Chaplain Lee on a weekly basis. Still dependent and distressed because the medication had not helped her depression, Ruth continued to see Chaplain Lee for several weeks before she began to notice any significant change in her moods. Encouraged by both Chaplain Lee and her physician after four months, Ruth felt her depression lifting to the point that she discontinued the medication and counseling sessions.

Discussion

In working with older people it is important to determine if their depression is a reaction to some specific event, change, or loss in their lives or to the more general experience of growing older. The physical causes of depression must be dealt with. Chaplain Lee's alertness in recommending that Ruth see a physician opened the door for cooperation between clergyman and physician. Such a practice can be of immeasurable benefit for many individuals in which counseling can be an adjunct to the drug program specified by the physician. Counseling can be especially helpful when a drastic change in lifestyle is necessitated by chronic illnesses such as arthritis or emphysema. Physicians are themselves quite often uninformed as to the qualifications and training clergymen possess which can make them a valuable member in the treatment of patients.

In Ruth's case, referral to a psychiatrist was not necessary due to this cooperation between clergyman and physician. Churches, through their various programs, are also in the unique position of having much to offer to individuals like Ruth. While unable to perform many of the functions previously engaged in, older people and those suffering from chronic physical disabilities should not be put on the shelf to stagnate and waste away. Instead, there are many functions and responsibilities which they should be encouraged to perform. Their insight and knowledge gained through years of experience can be a storehouse of resources from which clergymen and other church members can profit. Having his wisdom accepted can cause the aged individual to feel useful again.

Dawn

Dawn, a twenty-four-year-old graduate student in pharmacy, came to see Chaplain Lee complaining of loneliness, severe insomnia, depression, emptiness, and inability to concentrate on her studies. Though she was attractive, her appearance was one of neglect. During the hour she remained aloof and appeared to be extremely uncomfortable, going for long periods without speaking or eye contact. She discussed numerous physical complaints though she had seen several physicians and had been pronounced in good health. She had first seen a psychiatrist at age sixteen after telling her parents that she felt different from her peers and wanted to kill herself. At age eighteen she had again visited a psychiatrist after her parents had discovered that she was smoking marijuana rather frequently. In each case she had ceased treatment, feeling that she could not relate to her doctor and convinced they were not helping her. Her parents, a domineering mother and a passive father, had also seen a psychiatrist several months before, after her younger brother had made an attempt at suicide. Another brother, a senior medical student, had dropped out of school and taken up the life of a hippie.

In the first session Dawn revealed that her major professor had suggested she see someone when she had become upset in his office after being told that she did not possess the ability to do the work required of a grad student in pharmacy. Insisting that she had placed all her hopes in obtaining a graduate degree, she refused to drop out of school though her professor strongly encouraged her to forget her plans to continue. In the second session she focused on her inability to relate to people in social relationships. The previous weekend she had invited a male acquaintance to her apartment for a swim and then found herself unable to talk to him and ended up viewing the evening as a miserable failure. Though disappointed she indicated that she always sensed that relationships would end this way even before they began. Though attractive to males she seldom had a date, but she occassionally allowed herself to be picked up for an evening in which sexual intercourse usually took place. However she failed to experience any feeling of satisfaction or sense of closeness in such a relationship. If she did begin to feel involved emotionally she would immediately take steps to terminate the relationship. Though she denied any desire for involvement, she indicated that she was always being approached by homosexual females and that one in particular had been persistent in recent weeks.

In the third session she related that unpleasant events of years past kept cropping up in her thoughts, consuming her attention to the point that she was unable to complete the tasks at hand. Most of the remembered events had occurred five to ten years earlier and would be considered by most people to be insignificant and forgotten in a day or two. They might involve such incidents as a slip of the tongue while reciting before a class which had resulted in laughter on the part of her classmates.

As she continued to display signs of withdrawal and seclusion it soon became apparent that Dawn's insistence on remaining in school could be interpreted as an attempt to maintain the only contact she could endure with any comfort with other people. As a result she had thrown herself completely into her work, indicating on several occasions that school was her entire life and only hope for the future. Experiencing recurring thoughts of suicide, she did not see it as a probability in the immediate future but a distinct possibility in the distant future if things did not improve.

Despite her discomfort and unhappiness Dawn called Chaplain Lee after four sessions to indicate that she would not return as she did not feel the sessions were of benefit to her.

Discussion

Several indicators suggest psychiatric referral in Dawn's case. Her suicidal ideation, depression, feelings of isolation and emptiness, as well as her lack of social skills should be considered. In addition, her rather chaotic family situation is not encouraging. Being told that she could not continue in graduate school seems to have closed the major avenue she had maintained for a meaningful existence. A person so deprived that he puts all his eggs in one basket can find himself in a desperate state if, and when, this is taken away.

She seems typical of the large group of unhappy individuals who spend a lifetime shopping around for some magic cure or remedy for their discomfort and lack of satisfaction in living. Her repeated failures to find relief through her visits to several psychiatrists previously along with the termination of her sessions with Chaplain Lee are not reasons for optimism. While she is unhappy enough with her isolated style of living to seek help, she is apparently not so discontent that any extensive altering of basic personality patterns seems likely. If she were ready for such then a group approach to counseling might help her in the acquisition of more adequate social skills. The repetitive and circular patterns which she seems locked into would suggest that her present way of relating to life will probably continue until she becomes desperate or else flips out entirely. The only other alternative considered by Dawn at the moment, suicide, is even more disturbing. Her lack of trust in psychiatrists based on previous encounters, makes psychiatric referral questionable, though indicated. With people such as Dawn about the only thing that clergymen or mental health workers can do is to show interest and concern, leaving the door open for future sessions if they are desired.

Summary

While there are many and varied symptoms of mental illness, the impoverishment of social relationships should be a warning signal to clergymen that all is not well. Although we live in an age where people may live for years without knowing the name of their next door neighbor, most individuals manage to establish and maintain relationships with a significant number of other individuals. For sure there are those who elect to isolate themselves more than others, communing with nature or their dogs or cats. Though sometimes labeled as eccentrics, many apparently seem to be satisfied with such a lifestyle. For most individuals, however, there is a strong desire for companionship. For most, the absence of close relationships with others is cause for unhappiness and concern to the point that many seek counseling in order to develop more adequate ways of relating to other human beings.

While even the best adjusted among us feels neglected and miserably alone at times, the cases presented above are examples in which loneliness is presented as the major problem. In reality it was only one of several symptoms indicating more serious emotional problems. Clergymen should be

alert to the possibility of more serious problems if complaints of loneliness are accompanied by:
- insomnia or sleeping too much.
- crying and feelings of despair, hopelessness, helplessness, worthlessness, and lack of meaning or purpose in life.
- withdrawal to the point that one isolates one's self, feeling that he is completely cut off in communicating with others.
- excessive drinking or use of drugs, whether prescribed by physician or not.
- drastic or sudden changes in behavior.
- morbidity, depression, talk of harming self or others.
- inability to establish and maintain relationships with others even when tried.
- willingness to do anything or go to any length not to be alone and to be accepted.
- repeated involvement with others who take advantage of him or who are themselves unable to establish healthy relationships with others.
- refusal to get involved with others and resorts to phone calls, visits, etc. in which he appears to be desperately seeking to establish some sort of relationship with others.

While loneliness is not necessarily symptomatic of mental illness, special attention should be given to those complaining of it if they have experienced the loss of a loved one through death or separation. The aged are especially apt to feel alienated and uninvolved due to the loss of a significant person in their lives or to retirement or some chronic disease which has disabled them, curtailing many of their previous activities.

While the church cannot be expected to be all things to all people, no other institution has more potential to provide comfort and assistance to the multitudes plagued with feelings of alienation and loneliness. Of the many contributions made by the church through the centuries perhaps none is so unique or fundamental as the concept of the church as a community or brotherhood, in which human beings come together to help one another. Unfortunately, in too many instances, this has remained a concept only. Despite the progress made in recent years there seems to be considerable room for growth when it comes to making the church a community in the real sense of the word, whereby all people are involved, including the lonely, the old, and those experiencing emotional problems. Well aware that not everyone in the church is prepared, or inclined, to be a counselor or junior psychiatrist, there are without question many opportunities to make the ex-mental patient, the lonely, and the aged feel welcome and a part of something vibrant and worthwhile.

Chapter 8
Alcohol and Drugs

Pill popping has become such a part of our lives that in many homes tranquilizers occupy a space on the kitchen table beside the salt and pepper shakers or in the bathroom where they may be used as casually as the toothpaste. As shocking as it may be to parents, most children are now exposed to marijuana, or even harder drugs, at least by the time they are fifteen years of age. We all know someone who takes a pill to go to sleep at night, something to get going in the morning, and tranquilizers to calm down during the day. In addition, he may take something to stay awake during the evening or have a few drinks to relax on the way home. In recent years many individuals have turned to the use of mind altering drugs to escape the sometimes humdrum, sometimes frightening, day-by-day matter of living.

For many years such practices, falling under the broad umbrella of morals, were primarily subjects for those concerned with spiritual matters and the development of good moral character. In recent years, however, the use of drugs has become so rampant, that many social and physical scientists have also become alarmed.

Not wishing to become embroiled in the controversy between those who extol the good points of the moderate usage of alcohol and marijuana as opposed to those who insist that the harmful effects should be evident to even the most casual observer, we hope in this chapter to deal with the use of alcohol and drugs as symptoms of mental illness.

Most people who drink moderately are not mentally ill. Neither are the vast majority of those who smoke pot occasionally. While usage of either remains for many a moral issue, the occasional use of alcohol, marijuana, or even stronger drugs does not qualify one for the label of "emotionally disturbed" unless other symptoms are present. The following cases will hopefully provide some insight in those cases in which the use of alcohol and drugs appears to be the major problem when in reality the usage of such is symptomatic of more severe psychopathology.

Mark

Mark had been seventeen when he first came to see Chaplain Lee almost ten years ago. At the time he had just been placed on probation after being arrested while under the influence of alcohol and being involved in a minor traffic accident. His parents, prominent in social, civic, and religious affairs in the community, had urged him to see Chaplain Lee for counseling. His two older brothers had finished college with one becoming a pharmacist and the other a minister. The month following his arrest, much to his parent's joy, Mark had appeared for his sessions with Chaplain Lee apparently contrite and repentant, insisting that he had seen the light and that his life would now be different. After five sessions however and without any notification, he failed to keep his appointment with Chaplain Lee. Later during the same week the church custodian hearing a noise in the church found Mark and a young woman having sexual intercourse on one of the church pews. When confronted by Chaplain Lee, Mark succeeded in persuading Chaplain Lee not to report him and to give him another chance.

During the sessions with Mark and his parents, Chaplain Lee learned that Mark had been a problem throughout his school years, frequently playing hooky from school or being involved in trouble often serious enough to warrant suspension. On other occasions when in trouble, he would use the many charms and skills for which he was noted to persuade school officials that he was innocent of any wrong doing. Though intelligent and gifted, Mark's grades were never good due to the absence of any real effort or involvement with studies on his part.

Mark continued to see Chaplain Lee occasionally until he withdrew from school in his senior year, taking a job as an electrician's helper. During the next several years, Mark continued to become involved in numerous escapades which brought him to the attention of legal authorities in the community. On three occasions his father, a respected business leader, managed to use his influence to keep his son out of prison. As in school Mark refused to take his work seriously and drifted from job to job. Despite his poor work record and difficulties with the law he never had any problems getting a new job. Viewed as a gifted person by his employers, he was frequently rehired two or three times by the same employer even after having been fired or having quit his job, evidence again of his powers of persuasion. In the five years following his leaving school Mark married twice. His first marriage, taking place after five dates with a seventeen-year-old girl, ended in divorce after two months. His second marriage, three years later, survived a stormy ten months during which his wife gave birth to a son. Shortly after the birth of his son, Mark separated from his wife and despite his efforts and promises to provide financial assistance he failed to live up to his word once again. On more than one occasion he beat his wife physically. His use of alcohol continued to be a problem with his relationships with females a close second. Never becoming deeply involved in any relationship, he had a number of affairs, both during and after marriage. He was also involved in passing bad checks. Again and again his father came to his rescue, convincing all involved to drop the charges against his son.

Over the years Chaplain Lee refused to give up on Mark and on a number of occasions visited Mark in his home in an attempt to help him with his drinking problems. At infrequent intervals he saw Mark in his office for counseling whenever he became involved in new difficulties. On each occasion, with glibness of tongue, Mark managed to convey the impression that he was innocent or ready to reform, not only to Chaplain Lee but to the host of people who had fallen under his spell. In spite of their help and his promises he continued to return again and again to his old patterns of behavior which above all else appeared to be characterized by a lack of conscience and the inability to learn from previous experiences. Acts resulting in considerable shame and guilt when engaged in by others seemed to bother Mark not at all.

In one last effort Chaplain Lee found Mark a job with

considerable promise which Mark acknowledged with some gratitude. When he failed to show up for his first day on the new job Chaplain Lee found him in jail on a drunk charge. When released, Mark left town. For the next several years he wandered around the country writing home only when in trouble or in need of funds. With the help of police Mark's mother located him when his father died. Mark with little evidence of grief failed to show up for the funeral. Several months later Chaplain Lee learned that Mark had been arrested for armed robbery. Sentenced to prison, he wrote Chaplain Lee informing him that he had decided to enter the ministry after his prison sentence had been completed.

Discussion

Drinking, along with other forms of socially unacceptable behavior, seems to be symptomatic rather than the primary illness in Mark's case. Mark is typical of those who turn out to be chronic juvenile delinquents or adult criminals. They are different from other delinquents or criminals, however, in that they never seem to feel guilty and usually succeed in rationalizing away their responsibility for the criminal deed. Though they sometimes appear remorseful in order to escape punishment, they do not seem to learn from experience and go out and repeat similar acts again and again. They are usually impulsive, irresponsible, immature individuals, seemingly lacking in conscience or ability to postpone gratification. They want everything right now with little concern for how it may affect others.

While psychiatric referral is indicated in Mark's case, success in therapy is relatively rare when the patient fails to realize that anything is wrong with him or that he needs help. While many such individuals are sentenced by the courts to receive counseling, the results are usually minimal for the simple reason that compelling one to seek therapy is most often not conducive to psychotherapy. Mark gives no evidence that he really wants to change his behavior. So there is little that Chaplain Lee or any psychiatrist could do under these circumstances to alter his way of living. Further imprisonment is highly probable in Mark's case. While

Chaplain Lee's persistence in working with Mark is to be commended, his failure, along with that of Mark's father and others, to confront Mark or either come to his rescue, did little to encourage Mark to change.

Fred

Fred, a seventeen-year-old high school student, first came to see Chaplain Lee due to a fear on the part of his parents that he was behaving in a crazy fashion. His parents, prominent in both church and community, had become extremely upset when Fred was arrested for illegal possession of drugs. At the time seen by Chaplain Lee he was awaiting trial in the local courts. Fred readily admitted the use of drugs including marijuana, amphetamines, LSD, and cocaine on occasion. He also stressed to Chaplain Lee that he had come only at his parent's insistence, though he had the previous year asked that he be permitted to see a psychiatrist which his parents refused. Using the word "paranoid" to describe himself, he was concerned about his inability to relate to people with a fear on his part that he was about to go crazy. He was especially angry with his parents, insisting that they were only interested in turning him into a carbon copy of his father. Any deviation from what they expected resulted in disciplinary measures on their part. Further discussion revealed that Fred's feelings of depression and paranoia had become greatly intensified shortly after he began taking amphetamines. Despite Chaplain Lee's suggestion that there might be some correlation between his depression and paranoid feelings Fred refused to consider that such might be possible. Throughout the session he remained adamant in his claims that drugs not only helped him to understand himself better but others as well.

Perplexed by Fred's attitude and lack of trust in him, Chaplain Lee after several sessions agreed with Fred that the sessions did not appear to be accomplishing much in the way of improvement. Fred continued to be unable to relate to or share with Chaplain Lee his feelings and responded for the most part only when asked a direct question. Chaplain Lee's suggestion that he consider group therapy also met with a negative response. When Fred learned that the drug charges against him had been dismissed he refused to return for further sessions. Through Fred's parents Chaplain Lee learned that Fred remained in school and though they suspected he was still using drugs they were unable to verify such since he came home infrequently. When he did, he remained for the most part uncommunicative, spending a major portion of the time in his room.

Sixteen months later Fred again scheduled an appointment with Chaplain Lee. Much to Chaplain Lee's surprise Fred appeared to be a different person, indicating that he had fallen in love with an eighteen-year-old girl who was herself heavy into drugs. Shocked by the change in her after she began drugs, Fred had begun to see some of the negative effects which drugs had had on him as well and had stopped the use of drugs altogether. Moving from his home to an apartment he no longer came into conflict with his parents so often. While still not agreeing in all their values, they were now able to sit and discuss differences more intelligently. With Chaplain Lee's help Fred was encouraged to bring his girl friend with him for joint sessions. Several months later they terminated. His girl friend was no longer using drugs, and they had plans to marry in the near future.

Discussion

It is hard to tell in the earlier sessions if Fred is seriously disturbed or if his use of drugs is a typical form of teenage rebellion against parents. He does appear at first to be an egocentric, immature, and irresponsible person with problems in conforming and self-control. While such antisocial attitudes and behavior are not uncommon in adolescence, if continued in later years, they are indicative of a more serious disorder. Trying to cope with the problem of emancipation from parents and the establishment of one's own identity, adolescents have through the centuries selected ways of setting themselves apart from their parents. Attempts to do so may result in nothing more serious than a drastic departure from what has been acceptable by the preceding generations and may involve changes in hair styles, types of clothing, work, or dances. The more permissive attitudes on the part of parents in recent years have prompted more widespread acceptance of behavior which was once sociably unacceptable (i.e. premarital sex, teenage drinking, smoking). As a result young people have turned to more "far out" sorts of behavior in an attempt to prove their separateness. Unfortunately, for many this has involved the use of drugs which may be harmful, both physically and psychologically.

Where the use of drugs is involved, it is often difficult to distinguish between cause and effect. Many individuals begin using alcohol or drugs in an attempt to cope with existing, serious emotional problems. For those already experiencing emotional illness or those on the borderline, the use of drugs can be likened to Russian roulette. On the other hand, there are those who seem to be quite stable who suffer serious consequences emotionally after using drugs. On the basis of the information provided Fred does not seem to fall in either of these categories as he did appear to make a good adjustment without any serious or permanent damage done. With young people going through the throes of adolescence, counseling sessions with the entire family can often help and could be suggested by Chaplain Lee. Attempts to lecture young people involved with drugs who come in for counseling usually meets with resistance and failure. Though Chaplain Lee suggested that there might be a correlation between Fred's use of drugs and his emotional reactions, he apparently did not alienate Fred with a sermon on the effects of drugs. As a consequence, Fred returned to see Chaplain Lee when he was more receptive to change.

Perry

Perry, a thirty-seven-year-old Navy Commander, came to see Chaplain Lee after his wife threatened to leave him unless he did something about his drinking problem. While admitting that he had a drinking problem, Perry did not believe that he should give in to his wife's demands that he stop drinking altogether. He viewed total abstinence as a sign of weakness on his part and believed that he should, and could, learn to drink socially, able to stop after one or two drinks. A career officer in the Navy, he stated that he had begun drinking at social functions where attendance by junior officers was usually expected. In discussing his earlier years in the Navy, Perry described himself as a person who, after a few drinks, would become belligerent and aggressive, and on several occasions he had hurt people rather severely while drunk. When not drinking, he saw himself as a rather passive, unaggressive person who hated the competiveness of military life. Discussing his life with his wife, Perry described her as a nagging woman who was constantly badgering him about something, particularly his drinking. He felt that she derived great pleasure from berating him and she seldom offered praise when he did something which he was proud of. In his opinion, using sex as a weapon or reward, she would permit sex only when he did as she wanted. Confessing that he was not the perfect husband Perry stated that his wife had bailed him out of many hot spots in their time together. He was prone to run up bills beyond his means to pay. His wife, after severely chastising him, would usually come to his rescue and help with the payments.

Their most recent conflict had developed after his wife had extracted from her husband several weeks earlier the promise that he would not drink anymore. Upon learning that he had been passed over for promotion, however, he had come home drunk. After another argument he had again promised that he would not drink. His wife had been furious several nights later when she discovered that he had deceived her by claiming to be in a training class when in truth he had been at the officer's club drinking until a friend had to bring him home. Citing reasons for his failure to receive a promotion as favoritism on the part of his Commanding Officer, Perry admitted that he had a tendency to let his work pile up, completing it only after pressure was exerted from above. He viewed this pattern as having begun in elementary school when he would refuse to complete his assignments until forced to by his mother. Again emphasizing his dislike of having to compete, he revealed that he would prefer to go to the club and have a few drinks or go to the golf course as opposed to studying or preparing himself for promotion. Though seeing himself as bright he perceived of himself as a disappointment and a failure to his parents and his wife.

In the following weeks, Chaplain Lee saw both Perry and his wife for a number of sessions. Convinced that his wife meant business this time, Perry agreed to attend an AA meeting. Though depressed by the environment, he returned the following week to inform Chaplain Lee that he had been impressed enough by the visit to continue going.

Discussion

Despite the recent emphasis on the drug crises in this country, alcohol is by far the most misused and potentially dangerous drug in our society today. Though exact figures are hard to come by, it seems safe to say that the number of addicts hooked on drugs other than alcohol is miniscule by comparison with the number of alcoholics. Perry seems to be fairly typical of individuals who have been described as possessing alcoholic personalities: passive-aggressive, dependent, clingy, and demanding. Due to their long standing pattern of passivity and dependence, alcoholics can be difficult to work with. Clergymen, family, and friends who try to help often see them as individuals to whom you can never give enough. Though most would deny it, nonalcoholic spouses often unconsciously seek out and encourage those who drink to excess. Someone has said that for every alcoholic there is a husband, wife, child, or parent who supports him and on whom he can depend to bail him out when trouble appears. Though Perry's wife would deny such, she seems fairly typical of the women who marry alcoholic males. She nags, scolds, manipulates, picks him up when he falls, and is always there for him to lean on. It is possible that if Perry stopped drinking and became self-sufficient that she would be a most unhappy wife.

Since the spouse and family of an alcoholic are victims, whether voluntarily or otherwise, Chaplain Lee's attempts to work with them together are most appropriate. His efforts to get Perry to join Alcoholics Anonymous is also in keeping with the most successful means of treatment for the alcoholic willing to seek help. Involvement in AA would seem to suggest that the alcoholic is at least willing to assume some responsibility for himself as opposed to many who see a psychiatrist or clergyman with almost messianic expectations that someone else can save him from his drinking.

Mickey

Mickey was a handsome, muscular, twenty-two-year-old, baseball player in his senior year in college who had had several offers to play professional baseball. He came to see Chaplain Lee complaining of being depressed and feeling guilty. He attributed his state to his use of drugs begun the quarter before when he had been unable to cope with the pressures exerted on him by sports writers, pro scouts, and others who deprived him of any opportunity to relax and be alone. After signing a contract, although much of the pressure had been lifted, he continued to smoke pot daily, enjoying the relaxed feeling he experienced as a result. At the urging of his friends, he tried LSD while attending a concert on the university campus. Describing the experience, Mickey stated that the people in the audience suddenly looked like machines surrounding him. He felt that he was dying and was being judged by God. He was having such severe chest pains and he was convinced that he was dying and lay down on the floor to await the inevitable. Realizing later that he was not dead, he threatened to kill his closest friend unless he helped him from the auditorium. Unclear words were being repeated fifty to sixty times each. Panicked with the thought of dying, he was determined that he would die at home and began walking the sixty miles to his home. Discovered by a friend who recognized him walking along the highway, Mickey was carried to the hospital where he remained overnight. Although he had been released the next morning and had not used drugs of any kind again, Mickey stated that he had on several occasions experienced the same sensations, although of less intensity, in the following weeks. Although he had perceived of himself as an emotionally stable person prior to his episode with drugs, Mickey now believed that he might be losing his mind. Prior to his last quarter in college, he had been not only a star athlete but a leader in school, president of his junior class, a B+ student, and well-adjusted socially. For the first time in his life this quarter he anticipated failing grades. A religious person, he had considered entering the ministry at some time in the future and felt guilty that he had let his parents and God down by his use of drugs. Denying any history of depression, he indicated that things had gotten out of hand temporarily and that he could not handle drugs.

Due to his concern about the recurring episodes which Mickey experienced, Chaplain Lee suggested that Mickey see a psychiatrist. Agreeing to do so he returned to see Chaplain Lee four weeks later to say that he felt he had reoriented himself again but that he still needed guidance in working through feelings of guilt that he had commited some great sin. With Chaplain Lee's help, Mickey was able to forgive himself and gradually resumed a position of leadership both on and off the baseball field.

Discussion

While the use of drugs can be indicative of psychopathology, Mickey seems to be typical of the all-American boy with high morals who is introduced to drugs through curiosity or peer pressure. Unfortunately, his trip was a bad one. Though relatively few experience such fearsome results, the number who do and the potential for doing so in others are cause for great concern. Prior to the ingestion of LSD, Mickey considered himself to be an emotionally healthy person, and from the information given above, he seems to have returned to a state of normalcy, though he did have to seek medical treatment first. Despite Mickey's sound emotional state, however, he was temporarily psychotic. For reasons which we do not yet understand, certain individuals under the influence of LSD or other hallucinogenic drugs experience a form of chemical psychosis. Though such a state is usually temporary, Mickey continued to have flashbacks several weeks after the initial episode. During such episodes, in which the person is literally psychotic, the danger exists that he might do all sorts of crazy things, even killing himself or others. At such times some individuals have been convinced that they could fly and have jumped from great heights or performed some other equally destructive act. With those individuals experiencing a psychotic reaction, medical help should be sought immediately. In most cases tranquilizing medication helps. It is also important that the person, both during the episode and afterwards if necessary, be reassured that he is not losing his mind.

In addition to the physical problems encountered, Mickey also seems to be experiencing considerable guilt and regret. In such cases clergymen should perhaps be the primary therapist with psychiatrists serving in the role of consultants who provide medications if needed. Chaplain Lee seems to have been able, in collaboration with the psychiatrist, to provide the guidance needed.

Amy

Amy, a beautiful but slightly overweight twenty-eight-year-old female, came to see Chaplain Lee about her inability to control her desire to eat. She also complained of being nervous, tense, and jumpy. She attributed her eating problems in part to her depression and lack of purpose in life and expressed the hope that Chaplain Lee would be able to provide her with the inspiration necessary to give some meaning to her existence. Having had a weight problem since a teenager, Amy had been taking diet pills off and on for several years, but had recently increased the dosage. Bored a good portion of the time, she indicated that when she became anxious and depressed she would go on eating binges, at times consuming as many as fifteen or twenty candy bars in one night. When depressed, which she described as occurring about every eight days, she had no interest in anything but eating. At these times she would increase the number of diet pills taken. Though having slacked off in recent months she stated that she drank a lot also, getting drunk as often as two or three times a week. If she had a task to perform she would then take pills to keep her awake. Though she denied making any suicide attempts she indicated that she thought of it often. Married for one year to Phil, a sensitive and caring sort of person, Amy stated that her marriage was the only thing that held her together. Before her relationship with Phil, she had never been able to trust any male, which she attributed to a poor relationship with her father who had never understood or accepted her. Even with Phil she lived in constant fear of losing him due to her dependency on him and often accused him of not loving her and running around with other women, which he denied. She had never been able to enjoy sex with Phil even though she insisted that she loved him dearly and found him attractive physically. Amy described herself as having a low opinion of herself as a person and did not feel that anyone liked or respected her. Having held a number of jobs in the past, she had never found any of them to be of interest or challenging to her. Much of the time she admitted that she dreamed of great accomplishments and successes and set high goals for herself which she could never meet. She would then berate and degrade herself as a failure for not doing so.

In the following weeks Amy would appear for the sessions with Chaplain Lee in a depressed state or so anxious that she felt that she had to scream. On several occasions she said that she felt as if she were about to splatter all over the room. These feelings began to increase more and more as she perceived her marriage to be slipping away. Accompanying her on several visits, Phil attempted to reassure his wife that he still loved her and had no intention of leaving her. His efforts were ignored by Amy, however. As a result Amy began to eat and drink more heavily than ever. After Amy refused to follow Chaplain Lee's suggestion that she see a psychiatrist, Phil called several days later to say that he had taken Amy to the hospital the night before when she became so upset that he could no longer handle her.

Discussion

Amy appears to be another case in which weight, overeating, frigidity, or some other difficulty is focused on as the major problem when, in fact, such is only an expression of more pervasive personality disturbance. Her depression, low self-esteem, lack of purpose, eating, drinking, pill popping, lack of trust, sexual difficulties, and fear of losing control combined are cause for concern with psychiatric referral indicated. Her use of diet medication along with alcohol is alarming and presents a medical problem which should not be ignored. The use of amphetamines and alcohol together is exceedingly risky. Though the fad of weight reduction through medication seems to be declining, for many it still poses a problem of drug abuse.

While a physician would be able to advise Amy about the improper use of drugs, her problem seems to go far beyond that of diet and drugs alone. Her unhealthy ways of meeting her needs for love suggest that she needs a more comprehensive restructuring of personality. While Chaplain Lee might be of help, in all probability a long-range therapy program will be necessary for any significant improvement.

Mrs. Wilkes

Mrs. Wilkes, a seventy-two-year-old widow, received a visit from Chaplain Lee after he had been asked by her children to do so. Remembering her as an active and devout member of his church, who had, due to arthritis, ceased to attend services nine months earlier, Chaplain Lee was astounded by the change in her appearance. Sitting in a chair by the window, she took little notice of his presence staring into the side yard for the larger portion of his visit. Conversation with her daughter, who had moved in to care for her mother, revealed that her condition had deteriorated to the point that she had to be fed most of the time. An excellent cook and avid reader she had seemed to lose all interest in both. When first restricted due to her arthritis she had become a dedicated fan of afternoon television programs. However, she now showed no interest at all in such. Sleeping a good portion of the time, she ignored the many visitors who dropped by to see her. When she did try to talk, her words were slurred and her thoughts unclear. On several occasions while trying to walk she had fallen and at other times appeared to be drunk. Desperate as to what to do next her daughter informed Chaplain Lee that she was seeing two doctors; both were prescribing medication for her nerves and sleeping difficulty, and pain killers for arthritis. Further inquiry on the part of Chaplain Lee revealed that she was also taking over-the-counter medication suggested by well-intentioned friends for ailments of which she complained.

Following Chaplain Lee's suggestion that she tell her family physician of the various medications being taken by her mother, Mrs. Wilke's daughter called Chaplain Lee several weeks later with the good news that her mother seemed much improved. Surprised when he learned that Mrs. Wilkes was taking eight different drugs, her doctor had immediately reviewed her case and eliminated those which he believed uncalled for.

Discussion

Chaplain Lee's response to the request made by Mrs. Wilkes' daughter is another example of ways in which clergymen can become involved in helping those experiencing emotional problems when they have not been directly asked to do so by the patient. Chaplain Lee's alertness helped to uncover a not too uncommon problem of older people or those suffering from chronic physical disorders—too much or ill-prescribed medications. It is amazing how many patients are placed on tranquilizers by physicians too busy to diagnose depression. Unfortunately, tranquilizers in the case of the more depressed patient often tend to make the depression worse. It is also common to see patients on multiple drug programs who are completely bombed out. In such cases a review of all medication should be undertaken. In some chronic disorders such as arthritis making the patient completely symptom free may require the use of more drugs than the patient can tolerate. In still other cases it is not unusual for medication to mask the sort of depression often suffered as one grows older. Fortunately, such depression is usually treatable through medication supervised by a physician who knows of the other medication being taken by the patient. For the chronically disabled and for those suffering from pain which cannot be entirely alleviated, clergymen can often help them to accept their condition and to live with a certain amount of discomfort. It should again be emphasized that the patient suffering from a chronic illness such as arthritis not be put on the shelf but encouraged to maintain his interests whenever possible.

Deanna

Returning home from a speaking engagement late one evening, Chaplain Lee answered the phone to learn that Mr. and Mrs. Dawson had been trying to reach him for over two hours. Frantic with worry they poured forth their concern that Denna, a twenty-nine-year-old woman they had known for less than a year, was about to kill herself. Discussion revealed that in an attempt to make Deanna, a new church member, feel welcome they had invited her several months earlier to their home. Much to their surprise she had attached herself to them to such a degree that she was a visitor to their home several nights a week. Not wanting to be rude they had refused to answer the door at night, pretending to be away or asleep. Confessing to Caplain Lee that they felt guilty about doing so, they admitted that they knew of no other way to handle it. After not hearing from Deanna in several weeks, they had assumed that she found other relationships. However, this evening they had returned from a movie to find her sitting in her car in front of their house drunk and mumbling threats of suicide. Afraid that she might kill herself, either intentionally or accidentally if she attempted to drive, they took her inside and called Chaplain Lee.

Agreeing to see her the next morning, Chaplain Lee discovered that Deanna worked as a counselor in an employment agency. However, in recent months she stated that she had been unable to do her work and frequently stayed out from work. Describing herself as bored, lonely, and afraid she had isolated herself in her room only leaving to go to the store or to work. Though unhappy in her work she could think of nothing she wanted to do more and indicated that she had no desire to do anything. Describing herself as listless and tired all the time she found it a real effort to make it to Chaplain Lee's office. Finding it difficult to go to sleep at night, she would drink and take sleeping pills while watching television until she could no longer stay awake. Once asleep she would stay in bed until noon or later. Sometimes dressing to go to work, she would drive downtown but find it impossible to enter the door of her office. Indicating that she did not trust people she had had no social contacts in almost a year. Though an attractive woman, she could not believe that anyone would like her enough to date her and when they tried she managed to find some excuse not to go out. As for sex she said that she could not even talk to people much less get close enough to go to bed with them. She described going out and talking to people as the most difficult thing in the world for her. She attributed her distrust of males to the fact that her father was an alcoholic who had always been distant in his relationship with her, even when sober. Seeing him as a weak person who had caused much anguish in her life, she talked at some length of her resentment toward her father. She stated that she had not done anything she had enjoyed in so long that she would not know how it felt and was seriously considering suicide and had not done so simply because she did not have a gun. In an unfeeling fashion, Deanna revealed that she had been lying in bed for the last two days without even getting up, with the feeling that she was suffocating. She had made two attempts at suicide earlier in her life. Not only did she see herself as having a drinking problem but confessed that three years earlier she had been using other drugs as well including speed, LSD, mescaline, and others. However, in the last two years she had turned primarily to alcohol and sleeping pills. Describing herself as a perfectionist, she stated that she wished that she could clear from her head all the old thoughts and memories and start again. She saw the future as bleak and hopeless with little chance that things would ever change for her. Feeling lonely and isolated, lacking in motivation and purpose in life, she could not understand or believe that anyone could care for her despite Chaplain Lee's attempts to reassure her that she had much to offer.

Failing in his attempts to break through Deanna's pervasive feelings of worthlessness and despair, Chaplain Lee managed, after some time, to get her to visit a mental health agency. That afternoon she was admitted as a patient.

Discussion

Deanna is still another example in which drug use is symptomatic of more severe emotional problems. Her excessive use of alcohol, much like the suicidal gesture, is perhaps a desperate cry for help. Her latching on to people in an effort to cure her isolation is another signal of desperation. Though well-meaning in their intentions, Mr. and Mrs. Dawson are examples of those sincere and compassionate individuals who want to help but end up being taken advantage of. It might have been helpful had they been able to say to Deanna, "We cannot meet the needs and demands you are placing on us." Had they been more open, Deanna might have sought the help she needed earlier. Chaplain Lee's referral to a hospital was appropriate in this case. Drinking does not appear to be the primary problem here but only part of a larger problem demanding more intensive care than Chaplain Lee could provide.

Summary

Not too long ago the use of illegal drugs was usually associated with criminals and the poor living in slum areas of our largest cities. Drugs have now "moved uptown" to include individuals, young and old, from all economic and social levels. This recent, widespread use of drugs has been cited as a major factor in the increase of mental illness, suicide, homicides, crime, and broken homes. While we hear more about illegal drugs and the emotional and physical havoc created by drug pushers in the lives of millions, the rampant prescribing of drugs by physicians is also partially responsible for the "drug culture" in which we live. And alcohol, despite its widespread acceptance, is still the number one drug problem in this country.

While it is fairly easy in some cases to spot the person with severe drug or emotional problems, it is often difficult to ascertain which comes first. Is the person who comes in, obviously disturbed emotionally and heavy into drugs, experiencing difficulty because he has turned to the use of drugs? Or has he turned to drugs because he was emotionally disturbed to begin with? It should be emphasized again that most individuals who drink alcohol or use other drugs are not emotionally disturbed individuals. Unfortunately with a sizeable number of individuals there appears to be a strong correlation between their use of drugs and emotional instability. In some cases, even when the individual is emotionally stable, he can become addicted or dependent on drugs, thus creating a serious mental problem which might have had its origin in curiosity or desire to experiment. Whenever a person does become psychologically dependent or physically addicted to any drug, he usually requires treatment by a professional equipped to deal with such problems. Despite the dramatization on television and in movies, withdrawal or detoxification can usually be accomplished without undue problems in a hospital setting. The real difficulty is in the return to the use of drugs at a future date. While detoxification and medical care are jobs for the physician, clergymen can be valuable members of the treatment team in helping drug abusers decide to seek medical help and in providing therapy and support after withdrawal.

While large numbers use drugs and alcohol without any apparent damage, we should remember that the jury is still out in regard to both the short- and long-term harmful effects certain drugs can have on physical and emotional health. While it has been proved that some drugs do result in emotional and physical damage, we are flooded with contradictory research studies which some people do not hesitate to use to defend their particular beliefs. Despite the fact that use of alcohol, marijuana, and other drugs may or may not be a sign of pathology, these chemicals do possess great potential for abuse and heavy usage or reliance does suggest emotional problems. If, for example, an individual has to smoke pot to have fun or be relaxed or if he has to drink alcohol to be sociable, it is probable that psychological problems also exist.

Chapter 9
Problems in Courtship and Marriage

We are told that over one-third of the marriages in this country now end in divorce with the number fast approaching 50 percent. Often seen as the only way out of a frustrating relationship, divorce is apparently not the panacea it is perceived to be by many, if certain authorities are correct in their assessment. There are those with considerable experience in working with divorced individuals who maintain, for example, that divorce seldom solves problems for the simple reason that divorced people are often attracted again and again to individuals similar to their former spouses. While some would disagree, this is, in all probability, due to the role which the unconscious plays in the decision of two people to marry in the first place.

As human beings, we like to think of ourselves as logical, thinking creatures with our decisions and behavior generally based on sound reasoning. Such is not always true. The truth is that most people are attracted to each other, in large part, for unconscious reasons. While many couples, as a result of this attraction, refer to themselves as "being in love," they are often attracted to each other for reasons which have nothing to do with love in any realistic or healthy sense of the word. For purposes of our discussion, we would like to suggest that love is closely correlated with need satisfaction. Men and women are attracted to each other if certain needs are satisfied and uninterested if an adequate number of needs go unmet.

If sufficient needs are met, then marriage may follow. Unfortunately, the needs attracting individuals to each other may be healthy or unhealthy. If healthy, the relationship may endure with reasonable success. If unhealthy, the relationship may still endure or end in unhappiness or tragedy for all concerned. The following cases are examples of individuals who were apparently attracted to each other for unhealthy reasons. In several cases, either one or both of the individuals was disturbed to the point that the marriage had little chance for success without outside help.

Lisa and Dan

Lisa and Dan came to see Chaplain Lee at the insistence of Dan's father who had become concerned on learning that things were not going well with his son's marriage. Both Lisa and Dan were twenty-three-year-old graduate students in psychology. Both appeared to be of superior intelligence and quite attractive physically. They were quite open in the discussion of their problems which they perceived to be due to differences in their views about sexual practices in marriage. Dan readily admitted to both homosexual and heterosexual relations prior to and since his marriage to Lisa. He expounded at some length on his philosophy of the "good life" which included as one of its basic tenets the license to have sexual relations with anyone at anytime, male or female, so long as the participating parties were in favor of such. His concept of the ideal society was one in which people were free of all sexual restraints and though he included other prerequisites, he was primarily concerned with sex. In spite of his glibness and eloquence in discussing such a society, he freely admitted that he had many sexual hangups himself, with fears of sexual inadequacy of paramount concern in his life.

Lisa, on the other hand, indicated that she had entered the marriage with a monogamous concept of the relationship and had been repelled initially by her husband's sexual attitudes and behavior. However, she had eventually given in to his requests that she not only permit him the sexual freedom he desired, but also to his demands that she engage in extra-marital sexual relationships as well. Though she stated that she did so with great reluctance, she had become involved with several men and had grown fond of one in particular. To her surprise, Dan insisted on hearing each and every intimate detail of her sexual encounters with other males. In spite of his philosophy of sexual freedom and sharing of adventures, apparently he resented his wife's involvement with other men and saw it as further proof that he was inadequate as a male. On several occasions he found some excuse to interrupt his wife and her lover before or during the course of their lovemaking, even though he had joined his wife in plotting the seduction, frequently of a close friend. On another occasion, he had become so upset that he began taking a weight lifting course to get in shape to punish one of his wife's lovers.

Lisa interpreted her husband's numerous sexual escapades as a reaction against his homosexual tendencies and as an attempt to prove that he was the man that he so desperately wanted to be. Though he had been successful on a number of occasions in heterosexual encounters, he had occasionally been impotent when he had attempted sexual relations. This only served to make him more depressed and to question his masculinity even further.

Although Lisa described their sexual way of life as most unsatisfactory to her, she continued to join her husband in plotting and arranging sexual affairs in which both had sexual relations with others outside marriage. Even though Dan insisted that he had to have sex with a different person each day and masturbated three or four times a day, Lisa revealed that they engaged in sexual intercourse as man and wife on the average of once every two weeks or so. He insisted even then that his wife make up stories in which she would be involved sexually with another female which he found sexually stimulating.

Dan and Lisa had visited a psychologist prior to their marriage after Dan had become upset when Lisa informed him that she could not marry him. Due to Dan's persistence and Lisa's feelings that he needed her and that she could not let him down when he needed her so desperately, Lisa agreed to the marriage.

Though she had hoped that things could work out, Lisa indicated that things had not improved and that her needs, sexually, emotionally, socially, or otherwise were not being met to her satisfaction. Rather than a wife, she had come to see herself as more of a mother to an exceedingly immature and insecure young child governed by unhealthy and unrealistic desires.

Three weeks after the initial session, Lisa called Chaplain Lee in a state of panic, insisting that she needed to see him that night. When she arrived, she indicated that her husband had been depressed for two days. She had called Chaplain Lee when he began earlier that evening to cry, throw furniture about, stomping and raging about the apartment, and threatening suicide. Similar episodes had occurred before, and in each instance she had fled in fear only to return the next day. On these occasions she indicated that she could never predict her husband's condition. He might be completely subdued and profusely apologetic on her return or she might find the apartment a shambles with Dan missing. On several occasions she had returned to find him in bed with one of the female students he tutored. He would usually insist that his wife join them in bed which she did on occasion. On such occasions they might engage in sexual intercourse in her presence or else spend the night talking about school or philosophy. Though Lisa stated that she felt uncomfortable under these circumstances, she usually conceded to her husband's wishes. He also had her write letters to people who advertised in magazines for interested partners to have various types of sexual experiences.

In the following sessions, Chaplain Lee was able to learn that, in spite of Dan's obsession with sex and his insistence on different partners, he often found some way to retreat from the situation even after he had gone to great lengths to arrange such a meeting for sexual purposes.

Dan also discussed freely in the presence of his wife sexual fantasies which he enjoyed during intercourse and while masturbating. In some fashion, these usually involved the inflicting of pain, sometimes to the point of death, and frequently involved the act of urination, usually on himself. Lisa, though steadfastly maintaining that she believed such thinking to be weird, admitted that she continued to permit herself to become involved and often served as the object on which Dan inflicted pain, though usually of a mild nature in her case.

As the sessions continued, Dan appeared to become more and more obsessed with sex and subsequently more and more depressed as he experienced failure as well as success in his attempts. Though his successes outnumbered his failures, he concentrated far more on his failures than on his successes. In the later sessions he began to leave Chaplain Lee with the impression that he was in the presence of some great mystic or philosopher who spoke in general and glowing terms of loving "everybody" but in real life unable to love "anyone."

Dan saw his mental health improving as he moved more and more in the direction of his "ideal society," which included among other things, an ever increasing number of people with whom he could relate sexually, emotionally, or otherwise. He defined true love as the willingness and desire to share this love for other people, male and female, with his wife, which he saw as a way of improving their relationship. Though he continued to speak in this fashion of his love for all mankind, it became apparent that he was removing himself more and more from actual contact with people. According to both Lisa and Dan, he involved himself less and less in his school work as well as in other extra curricular activities in which he had achieved considerable success. Though he continued to talk of his love for his wife and his need for and dependence on her, even here he alienated himself from her in any real fashion. Lisa, becoming more and more frustrated and disillusioned with marriage, turned to other men with whom she had become involved, spending considerable time with them in preference to her husband.

As this trend continued, for the first time in the sessions with Chaplain Lee, Lisa began to consider divorce. Though Dan had earlier voiced the opinion that marriage to any one person did not fit his scheme of living, the thought of losing Lisa terrified him.

Before the discussion of divorce could be pursued further, Dan and Lisa finished their graduate work at the university and moved to another state. Both expressed the opinion and hope that things would improve in a new environment where they could begin anew.

Discussion

While there has been much talk in recent years about "open marriages," few individuals or marriages can tolerate well any such arrangement. This seems fairly obvious in the case of Lisa and Dan. Despite Dan's liberal sexual philosophy, neither he nor his wife could handle extra marital encounters. Among other things, Dan seems to have some real sexual problems. Rather than dealing with his problems and sexual feelings, however, Dan has resorted to intellectualizing as a defense, erecting an elaborate and complicated philosophical system to justify his way of thinking and behaving. Since he has gone to great lengths to erect such colossal defenses against sexual thoughts and impulses which he finds intolerable, he would probably suffer severe consequences if they were torn down by Chaplain Lee at this time. As disturbing as his thinking is, it might well be preventing him from a more serious psychiatric episode.

Unfortunately, Dan's distorted thinking has apparently affected his wife. Although initially opposed to such, she gave in to her husband's demands with some rather unhealthy repercussions on her part. Both Lisa and Dan seem to have difficulty in defining themselves as individuals and sexual beings. As a result of their behavior, their frustrations and confusion seem to have increased.

Not only does Dan appear to have sexual problems, but also there is evidence of other severe psychopathology as evidenced by his mood swings, uncontrollable rages, masochistic and sadistic fantasies, depression, threats of suicide, and his increasing withdrawal from contacts with school and people into mystical and philosophical matters. There is also the possibility that he might harm his wife in one of his rages. While a change in environment can, in some cases, help to alleviate stress causing problems, it is probable that Lisa and Dan are altogether too optimistic that their move to another university will change things for the better. Psychiatric referral is definitely recommended in this case for both husband and wife.

Ann and Richard

Ann and Richard began their first session with Chaplain Lee with Ann insisting that she wanted a divorce which her husband opposed. Ann was a twenty-six-year-old graduate student in psychology. Richard, twenty-seven years of age, had been on an overseas assignment with an oil company for which he worked as a geologist. He had just returned home when his wife informed him that she had been seeing other men in his absence and wanted a divorce. He had retaliated by voicing the opinion that his wife was mentally unstable and insisted that they see a counselor together. Ann agreed provided Richard would give her a divorce after the sessions.

She readily admitted to Chaplain Lee that she had no interest in marriage counseling and had come only to prove to Richard that she was sane and knew what she was doing in asking for a divorce. However, she did indicate that she had on two previous occasions in their six year marriage been to a psychologist. On one of those visits, she had peeked at her chart and read the diagnosis which she described as "antisocial schizoid personality." Prior to her marriage, she had become pregnant on two occasions. The first pregnancy ended with an illegal abortion. She entered a home for unwed mothers on the second occasion where her baby was immediately placed for adoption.

In discussing these events, Ann did so with no visible signs of remorse or regret, although she did indicate during the time of pregnancy that she did become rather depressed and saw a psychiatrist while in the home where her child was born. She indicated that she married Richard because she again thought she was pregnant. However, after marriage, she learned she was not. At this juncture, she stated to both Chaplain Lee and Richard that she did not love Richard, never did, and only married him out of desperation to escape an unhappy home life and fear of being pregnant. She described Richard as smothering her with his possessiveness and jealousy. She had stayed married to him while he was away for long periods of time but, now that he was home again, she was feeling pressure and a renewed desire for her independence.

During the session, both Ann and Richard indicated that they had both been involved in numerous affairs since their marriage. Ann described her sexual relationships as beginning in the ninth grade, involving a number of different males. However, she stated that she had received little in the way of sexual satisfaction in any of these relationships, including the one with Richard.

In the second session, Richard appeared to be more reconciled to the divorce although he still cried at intervals during the session insisting that he still loved Ann but wanted what was best for her. Ann then asked to speak with Chaplain Lee alone at which time she informed him that she found life unbearable with Richard and wanted to be rid of him as soon as possible so that she might return to her lover and resume their sexual relationship. Richard remained while his wife spoke to

Chaplain Lee and then asked to speak alone with Chaplain Lee also. During this period he referred again to his concern for Ann's mental health revealing that she was a frequent user of drugs including pot, LSD, mescaline, and opium. He also described her as a person who lied frequently, a statement with which Ann later agreed. The session closed with Richard's agreeing to Ann's demands for a divorce with the stipulation that she continue to see someone for further counseling. Ann conceded at this point that she would continue to see Chaplain Lee.

However, Ann did not return for approximately two months. Although she had instigated divorce proceedings, she was now having second thoughts about her decision, feeling once again alone and unprotected. She had grown tired of her most recent lover and was in the process of looking around for a replacement. In the process of doing so, she was having sexual intercourse with a number of males from many walks of life. The previous week, she had gone to bed with a bus boy in one of the local restaurants on the spur of the moment. She had been seeing an engineer from a neighboring state for several weeks, and it was with him that she seemed to place most of her hopes at the present time.

For the next six months, Ann would show up occasionally for an appoinment with Chaplain Lee. On each occasion she discussed her continuing sexual escapades with several different people, each ending in the same way, disgust with men and her way of life. Her most recent involvement included sexual relations with a sixty-five-year-old uneducated itinerant handyman. She was currently living with another man but denied any sexual involvement, living with him only for convenience. She continued to use drugs and showed no inclination to really change although she was unhappy with things as they were. When things improved, she would stay away for several weeks only to return when she became upset and depressed to see Chaplain Lee again. On several occasions, she described bizarre incidents which included, among other things, the feeling that her father was interested in having sexual intercourse with her. At other times, such feelings involved other relatives. She was also convinced at one time that she had homosexual inclinations and expressed a desire to become involved with some female. On one occasion, she asked Chaplain Lee if he found her discussion of her sex life exciting to him and asked on another occasion if he would hold her and appeared to go out of her way to entice Chaplain Lee in a sexual fashion. Although going to some lengths to do so, she continued her attack on males, describing her disgust and distrust of all men indicating, on various occasions, that her lips or eyes would swell up when sexual involvement seemed imminent. In spite of such feelings, however, if the male did not make any sexual advances, Ann would instigate sexual overtures herself. Although she found such a pattern repeated again and again in her life with the same results, she continued to place herself in situations where similar situations were sure to develop. Her stated reasons for doing so were the low opinion she had of herself, feeling that sex was all she had to offer a man and her only hope for sustaining a relationship.

In the seventh session, Ann stated that she was considering going back to Richard and had contacted him the previous week. Richard, feeling that a husband should stick by his wife in sickness and in health, had responded by saying that he would be willing to do so. After further thought, however, Ann decided against such a choice.

In the final session with Chaplain Lee, Ann indicated that she could no longer tolerate the sessions since Chaplain Lee was a male and hinted that she might see a female psychologist. Although apparently void of any feelings of wrongdoing or remorse in any of the sessions, Ann was becoming more and more concerned with her thoughts and dreams, indicating that she was having difficulty in determining what was real in her life.

Discussion

While Ann appears to be more disturbed than Richard, both seem to have emotional problems serious enough to warrant psychiatric referral. Richard, apparently a passive individual, tolerated behavior which should not have been tolerated. His unwillingness to place restraints on Ann would suggest that they are two emotionally unhealthy people who are probably making each other even sicker by continuing to live together.

With individuals like Ann, who ignored social conventions and seemed unable to learn from past experience, it is unlikely that counseling alone with Chaplain Lee will be of help. She appears to be a person who is incapable of establishing and maintaining a responsible and caring sort of relationship. She uses extremely poor judgment and apparently seeks excitement with little concern for the consequences. She does not appear to have adequate emotional control as evidenced by her impulsive behavior which includes unsuccessful sexual relationships and two unwanted pregnancies. Her long history of sexual acting out, along with her lack of motivation to change, is discouraging. Needing restraints, she continues to resist any attempt to provide such.

Such persons must often be confined to a more structured environment until emotional control can be reestablished. While Ann appears to be growing more confused, her suggestion that she see a female psychologist is evidence that Ann realizes that she needs professional help.

Anyone who attempts to help other individuals must recognize his limitations and not hesitate to refer when these limits are reached. Chaplain Lee's willingness to encourage the referral enabled Ann to re-establish a relationship with a mental health professional trained to deal with the more extensively disturbed individual.

Libby and Tim

Libby and Tim, both twenty-eight, came in to see Chaplain Lee in an attempt to reach some decisions about their three year old marriage. Libby indicated that she did not know what she wanted, but felt inclined toward getting a divorce. Tim, on the other hand, with a great display of feeling, stated that he was altogether opposed to the divorce and insisted that things could be worked out. He also insisted that they still loved one another, which his wife failed to verify but which he ignored. When the matter of divorce had been first introduced by Libby, Tim had responded with disbelief, anger, and ridicule. When this failed to change his wife's position, he began to cry and became depressed, indicating that he did not know what he would do if his wife left him. When his wife insisted in bringing the matter up, he eventually began to threaten suicide and had, on several occasions, implied to his wife that he might harm their two-year-old daughter. Becoming more and more depressed in appearance, he began to miss work.

In discussing her reason for wanting a divorce, Libby focused on a lack of communication which had become increasingly more of a problem in recent weeks. While dating, both indicated that they felt close to one another in many ways. Describing the sexual part of their marriage as good in the early stages of their marriage, both indicated that it was now almost nonexistent. Noticing that Tim's interest in her had begun to decline several months after their marriage, Libby had felt crushed as a woman. Trying to revive Tim's interest by being more aggressive sexually, she indicated that her overtures only seemed to turn him off more than before. However, with the talk of divorce, Tim had become more interested. Due to the breakdown of communication in other ways, Libby had responded to his sexual advances with indifference, indicating that she could no longer bear to have him touch her. Both Tim and Libby denied any involvement with anyone outside their marriage.

Discussing the breakdown of communication further, Libby said that Tim had withdrawn more and more into himself and that any feeling expressed on his part she had to extract as if pulling teeth. Their backgrounds and interests, which had always been different, now appeared to be even further apart with Tim more interested in solitude in some rural area, with Libby preferring the city where she could become involved in numerous activities with different people.

During the third week in which Libby and Tim were seeing Chaplain Lee, Libby came alone, indicating that Tim had refused to come back since marriage counseling had not improved their relationship. During the session alone with Chaplain Lee, Libby was even more negative about her feelings toward Tim, stating that only the fear of having Tim's suicide on her conscience kept her around. Later, in the same week, she called Chaplain Lee in tears explaining that Tim had a pistol and had placed the gun to his head when she had asked him to leave. After she promised to let him stay, he relinquished the pistol. Convinced for the moment that Libby would not leave him, he appeared to calm down. However, such behavior, according to Libby, only made her more certain that she could no longer live with him.

The next week Tim showed up for his appointment with Chaplain Lee quite calm in manner and indicated that he did not know where his wife was. After leaving the baby with her mother two days earlier, she had disappeared. Later in the week, Libby's parents called to inform him that Libby was in another state where she had met an Air Force officer whom she had been seeing in secret for the past three months. Several months later Tim received a letter from Libby announcing her intentions of seeking a divorce, giving custody of the child to Tim.

Much to Chaplain Lee's surprise, Tim took Libby's leaving and her plans for a divorce much calmer than he had anticipated. Verbalizing his willingness to take her back even then, if she would only return, he stated that at least he knew where things stood and some of the reasons behind her recent behavior toward him. Almost immediately, Tim began to make new plans for his life and several weeks later informed Chaplain Lee that he had decided to move to another city with his child to get away from the painful memories. He made no further references to suicide.

Discussion

Obviously much of Tim's behavior was an attempt to hold onto Libby in an immature and manipulative fashion. Giving in to such blackmail usually accomplishes nothing more than to aggravate an already intolerable situation and is certainly a poor base on which to build a marriage. Nothing rouses more anxiety than the threat of suicide. Individuals like Tim, who have a history of getting their way through threats, are quick to capitalize on the anxiety and fear aroused by threats of suicide. Libby's leaving without notice and her willingness to abandon her baby suggest that she is also not a responsible person. Unless both get professional help, one can only wonder what will happen to the child as well as to Libby and Tim in the future.

Lynn and Paul

Paul initially came alone to see Chaplain Lee because of depression and dissatisfaction with his work. During the session, he appeared to be severely depressed and worried, with little self worth. Though thirty-five years of age, he still was undecided as to what he wanted to do in regard to his vocation. He was currently working as an assistant manager in a local store by day while taking courses in law at night with some vague notion of eventually practicing law. He described a long history of depression going back to his early high school days when his mother died after a lengthy illness with cancer. Always shy and reserved, he found it difficult as a student to relate to others and to meet people and attributed some of his depression and anxiety to his work which required that he remain in frequent contact with the buying public. Considered for promotion to manager on two occasions, he had turned it down feeling that the additional pressure on him would be intolerable.

Married for twelve years, he had one son, age eight. He stated, with considerable guilt, that his moods were affecting, not only his work but his relationship with his wife and child as well. His son had already been seen in a child guidance clinic where his parents were told that family tensions were the major contributing factors to his difficulties in the home and at school.

In the second session, Paul began to discuss more in detail, his relationship with his wife, Lynn, thirty-three years of age, indicating that she was becoming fed up with his lack of ambition and unwillingness to snap out of his depressive state. He described his wife as a nagging person who viewed him as a failure with little respect for him as a husband and a father. Not only did she confront him with his impotence in his work and in social relationships, but with his loss of sexual interest and ability as well. Although he denied such, he also indicated that she was extremely jealous and had often accused him of having affairs with other women and refused to let him go anywhere unless she went along also. His lack of interest in her sexually, she interpreted as evidence that he was having sexual relationships with other females. His attempts to convince her that his anxiety and depression were contributing factors to his declining sexual interest, along with the physical fatigue of long hours in the store, failed to satisfy his wife.

At this juncture, Chaplain Lee requested that both husband and wife come in together for the next session. For the most part, Lynn verified the events and feelings expressed by Paul in the two previous sessions. After some moments of silence and with both Lynn and Paul insisting that the other bring up the subject, Lynn, with considerable reluctance, stated that she had been involved with another man two years earlier and had asked Paul for a divorce. When Paul refused to give her a divorce, Lynn took an overdose of sleeping pills. Paul found her when he came home for lunch and rushed her to the hospital where she remained overnight. Upon her return home, they agreed to see a marriage counselor when Paul insisted life would be unbearable for him if Lynn left him. After visits covering a period of several months, both indicated that the marriage improved somewhat with things going fairly smoothly until Paul's most recent episodes of depression. In spite of the hurt and disappointment over his wife's infidelity, Paul insisted that he had forgiven her and that the affair was completely forgotten on his part. On the other hand, he could not understand why Lynn remained so suspicious of him when it seemed to him that he should be the suspicious one in view of his wife's unfaithfulness.

Lynn not only described her husband as experiencing emotional problems but accused him of being a hypochondriac as well, continuously complaining of headaches, chest pains, stomach problems, backaches, insomnia, and constant fatigue. He refused to go out socially or even to associate with the neighbors. Their only social activity was an occasional movie and fairly regular attendance at church on Sunday. His irritability with both her and their son and his moping around the house she found more difficult to tolerate with each passing day.

Though critical of Paul, Lynn was also critical of herself, feeling that she had let her husband down by being unfaithful and with her impatience and lack of understanding during his depressive periods. Neither did she believe that he had forgotten her affair, although he refused to discuss it or permit her to mention it in his presence.

In subsequent sessions, Paul continued to discuss his unhappiness with his work. He still refused, however, to consider other job opportunities though several had been offered to him. Although Lynn indicated that money and financial security were of great importance to her, she insisted that she would be content with anything Paul chose to do if it would only make him happy. Her husband's passivity and refusal to act, however, only tended to infuriate her even further.

At Chaplain Lee's insistence, Paul agreed to see a psychologist for the purpose of taking vocational tests with the hope that they could be of some assistance in regard to his choice of work. According to the test results, Paul appeared to be more suited for vocations which did not entail any significant degree of involvement with people. His scores indicated that he definitely was not suited for sales work. In spite of this, Paul still refused to change jobs, although he continued to talk of doing so in each session.

As the sessions continued, it became apparent that Paul

had considerable difficulty in making decisions and relied
heavily on others for this purpose. He was also strongly in-
fluenced by other people's opinions of him and refused to consider a more menial type of work, even though he felt he was
better suited for such, due to his fear that his sisters and
father would be disappointed in him.

After eight sessions, Chaplain Lee, now discouraged with
Paul's passivity and seeing little evidence of change, recommended that Lynn and Paul join a therapy group composed of
married couples meeting in the city on a weekly basis. Although they agreed to do so, he later learned that they had
missed the first two meetings and attended other sessions
sporadically, eventually dropping out altogether.

Approximately seven months later, Chaplain Lee heard
again from Lynn and Paul. At this time, Lynn called quite
concerned about her husband, indicating to Chaplain Lee that
he was more depressed than ever and talking of suicide. She
requested that Chaplain Lee see him as soon as possible. An
appointment was arranged for that evening at which time
Paul showed up accompanied by his wife. Though she had not
planned to accompany him, Lynn indicated that Paul had refused to come without her and even then did so with great
reluctance, feeling that counseling offered little hope for improvement in his condition. Paul did indeed appear to be quite
depressed and unable to mobilize any energy to do anything
about his situation. Exuding a spirit of hopelessness and helplessness, he only requested that he be referred to someone who
practiced hypnotism. He expressed the feeling that hypnosis
was his last hope and felt that it might provide him with the
ability to relate to people in a better fashion. He saw his inability to do so as the crux of all his problems.

The question of his despondency and the possibility of
suicide were discussed at some length with Paul saying that
he saw no reason for living if life had no more to offer than
it had for him in the recent months. According to both Paul
and Lynn, he had continued to be unable to relate to his wife
in any meaningful fashion and found his son more and more a
source of irritation. His screaming and unfair treatment of his
family only served to make him feel more guilty and worthless
as a human being. He had now reached the point where he
depended on his wife more than ever to make decisions concerning the family and had missed a number of days of work.
When he did go in to the store, he often came home early or
refused to return after lunch, complaining that he was ill to

the manager. Consequently, his income had fallen substantially due to a drop in commissions, resulting in more unpaid bills. This only added to his worries.

At this point, concerned that Paul was on the verge of a nervous breakdown, Chaplain Lee gave in to his request that he be referred for hypnosis. Acquainted with a psychiatrist in a nearby town who used hypnosis in his practice, Chaplain Lee made the necessary arrangements. Although Paul and Lynn made no further appointments with Chaplain Lee, he was informed by the psychiatrist that Paul was not considered to be a likely candidate for hypnosis and was encouraged to join a therapy group where he might receive help in acquiring the skills necessary to facilitate some degree of social growth on his part. Although he had agreed to do so, Chaplain Lee was able to learn several weeks later that Paul had made no effort to become involved in a group and his condition continued to be pretty much the same as when seen earlier.

Discussion

Although Paul's responses would not be labeled as bizarre or "crazy," there are some disturbing factors in the destructive and unhealthy way he related to his family, his work, society, and to himself. These attitudes and moods seem to be so pervasive that psychiatric referral should definitely be recommended for Paul and probably for Lynn and the child as well. The Band-Aid type of help provided by Chaplain Lee apparently enabled Paul to show temporary signs of improvement, but a more massive and intensive program of therapy seems indicated if he is to improve significantly or the family to survive as a unit without further damage to the parents or child. Paul's efforts to seek help through hypnosis suggest that he is still looking for a way of bringing about change in his life without accepting the responsibility for such or making any real effort to do so.

From the events described above, there are several reasons why psychiatric intervention is indicated. Paul, at age thirty-five, still undecided about his career, still trying to please his sisters and father, seems to be an immature individual who is still struggling with unresolved childhood and developmental problems. His extreme passivity, dependence, and inability to make decisions are further evidence that at age thirty-five, he wants others to accept responsibility for his life. His long history of depression, feelings of worthlessness, thoughts of suicide, impotence, somatic complaints, anxiety, loss of interest, job performance, and so on are all causes for concern. His inability to relate to people in general and to his wife and son are further reasons to believe that a more intensive and long-term therapy program is needed. Even though there are difficulties in the marriage, the situation appears to be much more serious than just a marital problem. Strong evidence suggests that both individuals have personality problems which cause them difficulty in all interpersonal relationships, including marriage.

While not appearing to be as disturbed, Lynn seems to need help in regard to her feelings about her husband. Her affair suggests that things were not as she wished with her husband. Neither Paul nor Lynn seem to have dealt with this traumatic event in their lives in an adequate manner with Paul still having many strong feelings about Lynn's involvement with another man. It is particularly disturbing that Paul continues to insist that all is forgotten when it is obvious that he has not been able to forgive or forget. Lynn's excessive jealousy and her previous attempt at suicide also suggest that she needs help. As with most children living in a chaotic and unstable environment, the child will also, probably, need counseling.

If not immediately, Paul may, in the future, need to be hospitalized in order that more direct intervention may be possible in attempting to change the pattern of failure he has fallen into. The need for a rather substantial restructuring of personality seems to be so great that it would be difficult to accomplish in one hour per week out-patient therapy.

Karen and Jack

Karen and Jack had been married for approximately six months when they first came to see Chaplain Lee for marriage counseling. They had moved to the community shortly after their marriage where Jack was stationed at a nearby Air Force base as a student pilot. They had elected to see Chaplain Lee rather than a base chaplain or psychiatrist due to Jack's concern that an awareness of his need for counseling by his superiors might interfere with his career.

Karen was an extremely attractive twenty-two-year-old female who had some previous experience as a model and appeared to be somewhat older than she was. Although well-dressed and intelligent, she was quiet during the session and spoke so softly that Chaplain Lee had to ask her to speak louder on several occasions. Although smiling continuously, she had tears in her eyes during the first session as she indicated that she was upset and depressed about Jack's upcoming over-seas assignment which would leave her alone. In discussing this further, she indicated that she had no close friends or family nearby to whom she could turn and had no faith in herself to make it on her own.

Although four years older than Karen, Jack appeared to be younger and noticeably less attractive physically than Karen. In addition to being smaller in stature and physically frail in appearance, which he detested, he also had problems with his complexion which added to his woes. In spite of this, he appeared to be the stronger partner and both agreed that Karen was completely dependent on him and that all decisions, even minor ones, were made by Jack.

In the initial, as well as in subsequent sessions, Karen focused on her fear of losing Jack and her intense jealousy which had reached such proportions that she became depressed and withdrew for hours if she saw Jack even looking at a magazine featuring girls. Further discussion revealed that these intense feelings of jealousy and insecurity had persisted long before her marriage to Jack. In recent months, however, they had become even more intense to the point that the picture of an attractive girl would upset her even if Jack was not present to view the picture. Although outstanding in face and figure, Karen perceived herself as woefully inadequate by comparison. In recent weeks, she had begun to openly accuse Jack of running around with other girls and going out of his way to go places without her for this purpose. However, when Jack attempted to get her to accompany him on these occasions, she usually refused to go and, if she did, felt miserable while in attendance. She refused to associate with other wives on the base for the most part, choosing to remain alone in her apartment, even when they made friendly overtures toward her. When Jack came home for lunch or dinner, she immediately began to accuse him of ignoring her and having affairs with other females. Although Jack attempted to explain that such was impossible since he spent all of his off-duty time with her, she continued to find herself unable to shed her doubts and suspicions. On numerous occasions, she would lock herself in the bathroom or bedroom and sit for hours on the floor, paying no attention to her husband's pleas to open the door. On several occasions, she had become so threatened by other females that she had written letters to stores and businesses asking that they ban the sale of all "girlie" magazines as well as forbid the wearing of mini skirts and shorts in places of business. She also reported that when walking with Jack she would become upset if they passed a pretty girl whether he looked at her or not. On these occasions she said that she had an almost uncontrollable urge to hit Jack. Jack, unable to understand his wife's feelings of jealousy, indicated on several occasions that he was unable to comprehend how anyone so beautiful as Karen could possibly entertain the idea that he would ever do anything to jeopardize the relationship with her.

Due to her striking physical appearance, Karen received considerable attention and numerous invitations from other males on the base which she did not know how to handle at all. Her usual reaction was panic and withdrawal. Being a jealous person himself, Jack had cautioned his wife to be wary of any man who expressed any interest in her, sexual or otherwise.

In spite of Jack's attempts to reassure Karen that he would never leave her for another woman, Karen persisted in her accusations to the point that Jack had resorted to physical violence on several occasions, striking Karen with his fists. Although this served to reinforce Karen's opinion that Jack did not love her, the thought of losing him terrified her and made her even more possessive and unrealistic in her demands and attacks. She saw the overseas assignment as the final step in the dissolution of their marriage.

As the sessions continued, Karen appeared to become more unstable with each visit. Her discomfort in social situations became even more evident. Even a trip to the supermarket she found almost unbearable. Although apparently making some attempt to understand his wife's behavior, Jack was becoming more and more frustrated. Their sexual relationship, which was never enjoyed by Karen, was now nonexistent. When Chaplain Lee suggested psychiatric referral, Karen interpreted this as further evidence of rejection, indicating that she had seen a psychiatrist for a brief time shortly before her marriage, but had not returned when he suggested that they limit her visits to one per week rather than the two per week to which she had become accustomed.

For the most part, in the session with Chaplain Lee, Karen blamed her troubles on her husband, insisting that he did not care for her. She had considered running away from him or drowning herself in the bathtub. Although she insisted that she had made no attempts at suicide up to this point, she stated that she did not know what she might do when her husband left for overseas. On several occasions, she appeared to be convinced by Chaplain Lee that her reasoning was faulty, but eventually returned each time to the conclusion that her suspicions concerning her husband were correct. In moments of stress and doubt, she indicated that her thoughts and behavior were those of someone else with her voice and feelings being manipulated by some external force. The more her husband attempted to compliment her and to make her feel worthwhile, the less she trusted him.

In describing her family situation as a child, Karen's earliest and strongest remembrances were those of a rather chaotic and unpredictable marriage in which her parents fought frequently, with the threat of divorce always present. In addition to the unstable environment in her immediate family, the situation became even more upsetting when Karen's aunt, recently divorced, decided to move in with Karen's family. Karen, ten years of age at the time, was bombarded by both her mother and aunt with warnings that all men were alike and could never be trusted. She described her parents as paying little attention to her, though she was an excellent student and model child, choosing instead to shower her younger brother with love and attention. Even though she tried to please her parents, she was never permitted to make any decisions affecting her life. When displeased with Karen, which happened with unfailing frequency, they would resort to cruel and sadistic modes of punishment. Some of these were described by Karen as being forced to stand in a tub of hot water, eat garbage, wear diapers to school, appear in front of other family members nude, or remain silent with other members of the family for days at a time.

In the several weeks that Chaplain Lee saw Karen and Jack, Karen's suspiciousness, insecurity, and depression continued to worsen with the result being that she alienated herself more and more, viewing others with increasing hostility and distrust. Her lack of self-esteem, obvious from the begining, became even more apparent as the days passed. In the latter sessions with Chaplain Lee, she would sit quietly with a smile on her face, as if in a stupor, speaking only when spoken to and even then with little show of emotion or feeling. Having displayed a great need for affection and attention in the earlier meetings, she had now reached the point where she made no effort, either in the sessions or at home, to get her needs met in any way.

No longer able to ignore Karen's withdrawal and deteriorating condition, Chaplain Lee insisted that Jack arrange for Karen to see one of the base psychiatrists. Although Karen had earlier refused to consider such a request, she had reached the point that she showed little interest in anything and offered no resistance to being seen by a psychiatrist. The following week, Karen was transferred to another Air Force base where psychiatric facilities were available for hospitalization.

Discussion

Jealousy in male and female relationships is universal. It is so prevalent that some social scientists have likened it to the concept of "territoriality" among other animals. In Karen's case, however, the degree of jealousy is far out of proportion to the circumstances, with suspicion and distrust so rampant that she is unable to function in her daily living. Her insecurity, almost total withdrawal from people, and her unreasonable attacks on her husband tell us something of the seriousness of her situation. Her dependence on Jack is so extreme that she finds herself paralyzed with fear that he will leave her. This degree of dependency strongly suggests that any sense of self-integration is almost totally lacking.

There seems to be little hope that this can be achieved

without extensive restructuring of Karen's basic personality patterns. Due to the seriousness of her illness, immediate referral for psychiatric care is recommended for Karen with hospitalization likely.

Summary

Unfortunately, by the time many couples seek marriage counseling, it is too late to save the marriage. With the increase of divorce in addition to the many unhappy couples who stay together for various reasons, the need for marriage and premarriage counseling is obvious. Except when one, or both, of the partners is seriously ill emotionally, clergymen seem to work more effectively than many mental health professionals with marriage and pre-marriage counseling. For some clergymen, the matter of divorce remains a thorny issue, with each clergyman having to decide for himself if he can deal with the issue in clear conscience. Whether we approve or not, divorce is now a fact of life for millions in our society. If some clergymen still feel uncomfortable with the subject, then referral should be made to one of the many community agencies available for such counseling. In larger cities, there are clinics that do nothing but counseling with couples or individuals after the decision to divorce has been made.

Although there are others who would not agree theologically, we believe that separation and divorce should be encouraged in certain cases, if for no other reason than that of self-preservation for the people involved. For reasons not always obvious, sick individuals are often attracted to other unhealthy or emotionally unstable individuals. When such occurs, both may need to be seen together or individually for counseling. Even when only one of the partners involved is emotionally disturbed, it may be necessary for both to be seen at some point together in order that the healthier spouse may learn more effective ways of coping and living with an unstable spouse.

Where children are involved, family therapy is often

recommended when either or both of the parents are experiencing difficulty. Some agencies insist on seeing the entire family when any one member comes in for help, whether adult or child. In cases where severe psychopathology is suspected on the part of either partner, psychiatric referral should be made.

Clergymen should consider referral if: (1) the couple continues to relate to each other in a destructive fashion; (2) either partner resorts to the excessive use of drugs or alcohol to escape the pressures of marriage; (3) either inflicts unduly harsh punishment, either physically or mentally, on the other or on the children; or (4) either displays other symptoms of being emotionally disturbed.

Chapter 10
Etcetera

We are well aware that mental illness covers such a broad spectrum of human behavior and manifests itself in so many ways that it would be impossible to cover all types of psychological disturbances. In the preceding chapters we have attempted to touch on some of the more common types of problems encountered by mental health workers, clergymen, and others in the helping professions. In this chapter we will present cases in which physical complaints or symptoms play a major role. In some cases they contribute to or cause the psychological problems discussed. In other cases the physical difficulties and symptoms are the result of psychological problems.

Val

Val, a twenty-nine-year-old bookkeeper, asked to see Chaplain Lee due to recurring stomach problems which had not been relieved by many visits to his family physician. Informing Chaplain Lee that he had a spastic colon, he wondered if his stomach pain might be the result of his guilt feelings about his extra marital affair which had been going on for about six months. Describing his wife as a nagging female who screamed and yelled either at her husband or two children most of the day, he had found himself turning more and more to interests outside the home to get his needs met. The few times he found himself standing up to his wife, he always lost the argument. Sexually things had become so bad that he seldom attempted intercourse anymore and when he did often found himself impotent. When such occurred, it only seemed to make his wife more prone to level insults and nag. So angry at times that he felt he would explode, Val revealed that he never permitted himself to show anger, not only at home but in other situations as well. Whenever he felt angry, his reaction would be numbness with stomach pains usually occurring. Not only was he upset about the affair and relationship at home, he had recently been told that he was being considered for office manager with a good chance that he would be offered the position. While he wanted the job and felt that he could handle the added responsibility, he indicated that he also had many doubts. In later sessions Val described himself as a person with strong feelings of inferiority, especially intellectually and physically. He revealed that he had grown up in a home with a domineering mother and passive father who ignored his wife's outbursts as well as his children's attempts to get close to him. Disagreement with his mother was never tolerated and when he did work up the courage to oppose her, he lost so often that he quit trying. When she would become angry and begin to yell, he would lock himself in his bedroom and cry.

With Chaplain Lee's assistance, Val was able to learn that many of his physical problems were a product of his inability to express his anger and hostility. This turning inward toward himself led not only to stomach problems but frequent spells of depression as well. On other occasions he had experienced a skin rash for which the doctors could find no physical cause and had suggested it was probably due to emotional stress. At Chaplain Lee's suggestion Val was referred for group therapy where he could begin working on the need to ventilate feelings. Several months later after noticable improvement Val and his wife returned to see Chaplain Lee for marriage counseling.

Discussion

A large host of physical complaints may stem from psychological problems and concerns. These include stomach ulcers, spastic colon, skin rash, headaches, low back pain, and some types of asthma. While there is a psychological component involved in all physical disease to a degree, some individuals are more prone to suffer from psychosomatic disorders than others. In Val's case there seems to have been a strong correlation between his inability to express his emotions, especially anger, and his physical symptoms. Anger which is not ventilated properly can result in many of the symptoms listed above. For example, depression has been defined in some cases as "anger turned inward." If one gets angry enough at one's self then suicide can occur as a result of anger improperly handled. While most people do not go to this extreme, many do suffer from depression, ulcers, and skin disorders which may be traced to unexpressed anger. It is for this and other reasons that individuals need to know that it is just as important to learn "how to fight" as it is to learn "how to love." Everyone gets angry at times. Individuals who say they never get angry are either liars or in serious trouble emotionally. Christ, although portrayed as loving and compassionate, openly and directly let people know when he was upset, once becoming so angry that he overturned tables and used a whip to drive wrongdoers from the church. Individuals who manage to short circuit or bypass their emotional feelings are often the same people who show up on a regular basis in doctors' offices with physical complaints for which no organic cause can be found. They have locked their feelings inside their bodies and their bodies are crying.

Val seems to have been one of these. He apparently suffered from a lack of a good role model in childhood in that his father was described as a passive individual who never stood up to his wife or otherwise expressed his feelings. No matter how successful such people are in suppressing their anger there are limits as to how much of such behavior can be tolerated before anger comes out in some form or other. In addition to physical symptoms discussed above unexpressed anger sometimes results in extreme violence. This accounts, in some cases, for the person who suddenly goes berserk, killing several people without any apparent reason. Such individuals are often described by neighbors and friends as having been meek, quiet, and exceptionally nice people who would never harm anyone. While such violence is rare, there are many individuals who, rather than express their anger in a direct and healthier fashion, resort to more subtle ways of expressing hostility. Sometimes consciously, often unconsciously, individuals may become involved in affairs not only for sexual reasons but to get back at their spouses. Children, unable to stand up to their parents, often do poorly in school as a means of getting back. It is possible that Val's inability to have sexual relations with his wife and his subsequent affair fall in this category though he would probably deny such if asked.

Chaplain Lee was wise to get both Val and his wife involved in marriage counseling as well as group therapy. The group could possibly expose them to healthier people than they experienced in their relationship with each other and in their families as children. Nonmedical people should again be cautioned, however, unless they assume that headaches, ulcers, or other physical complaints can be helped by counseling alone. While counseling may help in many cases, physical complaints should first be evaluated by a person trained for such, a physician. While psychiatric referral is not always necessary in cases similar to Val's medical opinion should be obtained.

Art

Art, a forty-two-year-old carpenter, was referred to Chaplain Lee by his family physician after he had been arrested for the third time for drunk driving. Having a three year history of alcohol abuse he had been diagnosed as alcoholic and had attended AA meetings for a short time but with little commitment. Though he drank a lot, he was a good worker and provider for his wife and three children.

In the several sessions Art had with Chaplain Lee, he revealed that he suffered from severe headaches and had spells in which he had seen friends on his front lawn when they were in reality not there. His father and two sisters had died with cancer and Art was convinced that his spells and headaches were proof that he was also dying with cancer. On other occasions he was convinced that people were hiding in his closet with the intention of killing him or that someone was in the back seat of the car waiting for an opportunity to do him harm. At other times he would become irritable with his wife and children for no apparent reason. While he had experienced these and other similar fears and feelings while drinking he had also experienced them when sober. Concerned about the irrational content of Art's fears and the fact that he experienced them often when not drinking, Chaplain Lee suggested that Art see a psychiatrist. After two sessions the psychiatrist recommended that Art have a neurological examination. Art returned several weeks later to see Chaplain Lee and informed him that he had been diagnosed as having temporal lobe epilepsy. With medication begun, there was a noticeable improvement in Art's condition.

Discussion

Chaplain Lee's alertness in referring Art for psychiatric and medical evaluation is another example of the need for clergymen and other nonmedically trained individuals to ask for help whenever there is some doubt or suspicion that emotional problems may stem from organic causes. In this case, what is presented as a drinking problem also involves an underlying medical problem which will in all probability require ongoing medical supervision. As with other cases, it is important that Art discuss with his doctor the possible dangers of combining alcohol and other drugs, in this case medication prescribed for epilepsy. Since Art will still need counseling to adjust to the fact that he has epilepsy, as well as a drinking problem, this is another situation in which Chaplain Lee can be a valuable member of the treatment team.

Mr. Evans

At the end of their rope, the wife and daughter of Mr. Evans, a seventy-four-year-old retired cab driver, came to see Chaplain Lee with the complaint that they could no longer handle him or cope with his outbursts of temper. Things had come to a head the previous night when Mr. Evans, always noted for his gentle spirit and kindness to others, had hit his daughter for no apparent reason. On another occasion he had threatened his wife with a shotgun. Appearing to be completely normal at times, on other occasions he would make no sense at all. He was frequently found wandering around the home at night in a confused state. At other times he would be convinced that friends and acquaintances were deliberately trying to lock him away in the attic or that the police were coming to carry him away. Much to the embarassment of his wife he had appeared twice in the last month in the living room attired only in his underwear in the presence of company. On another occasion he had urinated in the backyard in full view of the neighbors. Convinced that her father was emotionally ill his daughter had arranged to see Chaplain Lee.

Having been a member of Chaplain Lee's church for some years, Mr. Evans agreed to talk with Chaplain Lee. During the session he wandered around the office and had difficulty keeping his thoughts together. At times he would not recognize Chaplain Lee and insisted that the police were coming to lock him up.

Feeling that any attempts to work with Mr. Evans would be fruitless, Chaplain Lee continued to see his daughter for several weeks. During this period he encouraged her to make an appointment for her father with a physician. Tests and examination showed that Mr. Evans suffered from arteriosclerosis. It was suggested that he be placed in a nursing home. Unable to agree to this suggestion, his daughter, along with financial help from other family members, arranged to have a young man stay with her father during the day. With the medication provided by the doctor, Mr. Evans became less prone to outbursts and slept well during the night.

Discussion

Not all old people react to the aging process in the same fashion. Many remain physically active and mentally alert as long as they live. However, in Mr. Evans's case the physical changes resulted in emotional changes severe enough to disrupt not only the patient's life but that of the family as well. As with many older people, the aging process results in a decreased blood supply to the brain with symptoms or behavior displayed similar to those of Mr. Evans. They may be disoriented or confused, make up stories, talk incoherently, be uncoordinated, or unable to remember. Quite often there is a religious flavor in the thinking of such patients in which they feel that God has given them some particular insight which they must share with others.

Clergymen often find themselves in a position to work with the patient's family in regard to the guilt they may feel if nursing home care is required. In situations in which the elderly family member's condition is progressively worsening they may need a more extensive care plan or a more protective environment than the family can provide. In some cases, families will hold on to the aging person even when he is no longer manageable. Such may prove to be not only detrimental to the patient, but in some cases, quite damaging to the remaining family members.

While few relish the idea of removing a loved one from a cherished environment, there are situations in which this seems to be the best for all involved. Again it is recommended that older people remain active, involved, and as independent as circumstances will allow for their own good as well as that of the family.

Clay

Clay, a forty-two-year-old executive, came in to discuss problems in his marriage. He quickly informed Chaplain Lee that he had only come because his wife insisted. She had wanted to come in together but Clay had refused to let her accompany him. Clay opened the session by saying that he was so anxious and tense as a result of pressures in his work that he could not relax at home with his wife and two boys. He indicated that he had been this way as long as he could remember. He had been taking tranquilizers for years but received little relief. While only a junior college graduate he had managed to reach the executive level through dedication to the company and a compelling determination to succeed. Stating that the competition for the job next in line would be unbelievable, he had thrown himself into his work with even greater fervor. To his dismay, however, he seemed to be going nowhere, even losing ground in his struggle to advance. At this point Clay volunteered the information that he suffered from a type of seizure in which he became paralyzed and blacked out, often falling to the floor. Never losing consciousness, he was at all times aware of what was going on around him. Having experienced these attacks for years, he had seen a number of physicians and been told that they were a form of anxiety attack. They usually occurred in periods of stress and tension, often with his wife, and never at work. His wife, apparently a gifted person, had taken a job selling real estate when her sons reached junior high school. Quite successful, she seemed to bother Clay, who perceived of her as being in competition with him. In an attempt to relieve his tensions Clay had taken up handball and tennis. Rather than serving this purpose however, Clay stated that his desire to be the best only made him react in sports pretty much the same as he did in his work.

At the end of the hour, Clay expressed a desire to be seen again the following day. When Chaplain Lee informed him that he already had a full schedule, Clay replied that his problem was of the greatest urgency and could not wait. When Chaplain Lee failed to respond to his demand that he be seen the next day, Clay collapsed in his chair with his head falling against the wall and his eyes closed. From all outward appearances, he seemed to be unconscious. However, when Chaplain Lee asked him if he could hear, he responded yes. A doctor called in from a nearby office stated that Clay's blood pressure and pulse rate were normal. With the doctor's encouragement Clay opened his eyes and stood up. Insisting that everything was all right now, Clay continued to complain of cold legs and feet and numbness in his right arm. When asked to describe his feelings, Clay responded that he had been paralyzed. However, he refused to accompany the doctor to his office for further examination. Apologizing for his attack, he again asked about the time of his next appointment and agreed to return in one week.

Returning one week later, he appeared hostile and belligerent, indicating that he had been unusually tense after the last session for two days. He reported a return of the tension several hours prior to his session with Chaplain Lee and stated that his stomach was tied up in knots. As the session progressed his anger and uneasiness seemed to increase. When Chaplain Lee suggested at one point that he might be better off if he looked for a less demanding job, he accused Chaplain Lee of encouraging him to run away from the problem rather than facing up to it.

At one point in the session he stood up to leave, angrily saying to Chaplain Lee that they obviously were not able to communicate and that the conversation should be terminated. Attempting to confront him with his anger, Chaplain Lee convinced him to return to his chair. At first denying that he was angry, Clay insisted that people who have control over themselves do not show emotion. Viewing any display of anger as a sign of weakness Clay stated that he never got angry in public. "Whenever I have allowed myself to do so I have always come out on the losing end." Many times in his work he admitted that he wanted to tell people to go to hell but indicated that you did not become a successful executive this way. Chaplain Lee's suggestion, for the second time, that he pursue work which did not require him to conceal his real feelings to such a degree was again met with anger. Though he was able to say that his current situation was destroying him, as well as his marriage, Clay said that he had no intention of quitting. When Chaplain Lee suggested that nothing was worth the agony he put himself through Clay looked and acted as if he were about to have another of his attacks. Instead, rising from his chair he informed Chaplain Lee that he would not return since he left the sessions feeling worse than when he came.

Discussion

Because of physical manifestations Clay should be referred to a psychiatrist. Individuals suffering from any sort of convulsion or seizure should be seen by a physician. While Clay's behavior appears to be manipulative, somewhat like a temper tantrum suffered after his request was denied, seizures can indicate that some serious neurological problem exists. Once evaluated medically, the individuals may be referred back to a clergyman for further counseling. However, in Clay's case there does not seem to be much motivation to change. He does appear to be an immature and insecure individual who has to prove something to others as well as to himself. Despite the suffering they seem to endure, many patients of this sort receive some sort of secondary gain from their suffering and are often reluctant to change. Clay's refusal to return and his threats to walk out of the sessions suggest that therapeutic success will be limited at this time in his life.

Monty

Mrs. West, the mother of Monty, a nine-year-old boy, came to see Chaplain Lee the day after she had lost her temper

and slapped her son in the face. Sobbing deeply, stating that
she knew it was wrong of her to have done so, Mrs. West informed Chaplain Lee that Monty was about to drive her crazy
with his constant chatter, ceaseless activity, and boundless
energy. His conflicts with other children in the neighborhood,
along with complaints from neighbors about the damage he
did to their property, had become so frequent that she hated
to answer the phone, always fearing the worst. He failed two
years in school though he was bright; his teachers complained
that his attention span was extremely short and that he dis-
rupted other students. As a result he was sent home from
school on a number of occasions. With his two younger sisters,
he would become irritable when not permitted to have his way
and had hurt them seriously on several occasions. When his
parents attempted to discipline him, he would fight back and
if restrained scream and curse. Rather than have such a scene,
they would tend to ignore his behavior until it became intolerable. Even while watching television, he was restless and easily
distracted. Never seeming to think of the consequences of his
behavior, he usually acted quickly and impulsively, often in the
most unexpected fashion. By this time in tears again, Mrs.
West wanted to know where she had failed as a mother in
rearing a child so unlike her two daughters who were quite
normal. Though difficult to do, she had begun to consider the
possibility that Monty was emotionally disturbed.

Having worked with the parents of children with similar
problems in the past, Chaplain Lee suggested that Monty see a
child psychiatrist. This done, Mrs. West was informed that
Monty was a hyperactive child. With medication, he became
less active and aggressive. With Chaplain Lee's help Mrs. West
was able to see that, while she was not a bad mother, Monty
did need a firm hand and discipline. Deciding to see Chaplain
Lee as a family, they were helped to understand and tolerate
Monty's behavior with more realistic expectations.

Discussion

It is difficult for some parents who expect their child
to become an Albert Schweitzer and Mickey Mantle rolled
into one to accept the truth that the child is instead mentally retarded or emotionally disturbed. In some cases, parents overlook obvious clues that something is wrong rather
than admit to themselves or others that all is not well with
their child. Most children at times place a strain on their

parents with their seemingly untiring, aggressive, hyperactive behavior, common to most healthy well-adjusted
youngsters. Monty's behavior, however, goes beyond that
of an exuberant and energetic child. Fortunately, relief may
be obtained through medication in many cases. While the
medicine may be needed for many years, taking it is generally safe under proper medical supervision. However, not
all doctors agree with this statement.

It is not unusual for parents to react as Mrs. West did
and to assume that they have done something wrong resulting in some abnormality in their child. Clergymen can be extremely helpful to parents in whom such guilt feelings arise.
They can also help parents to accept and learn to live with
a disease when there is no cure. If parents are unaccepting
and guilty, such feelings can be transmitted to the child who
also learns to feel ashamed and guilty. As in previous cases
Chaplain Lee took appropriate action in referring to a physician when physical problems were involved.

Summary

We can only re-emphasize again the need for medical
evaluation wherever physical symptoms are such that the
patient's health or life may be in danger. Even when the patient's life is in no immediate danger, various symptoms,
which may appear to be the result of emotional problems,
can be a signal that something is wrong physically. For example, the hyperactive child may be overly abusive in his
relationships with other children, engaging in such frantic
activity to the point that even his parents find him hard to
tolerate. In some cases their frantic pattern of behavior involves sexual activities far beyond what is normally expected of children in a younger age group. The epileptic
child without convulsions may display symptoms of extreme
irritability, throw temper tantrums, or occasionally engage
in violent forms of behavior. Or he may appear to be in a
fog or daze, staring off blankly into space for only a moment, after which he resumes his activities as if nothing

had happened. As discussed in other chapters, the person suffering from hypoglycemia may be depressed or irrational with bizarre behavior. Individuals suffering from thyroid deficiency may be depressed and lethargic. Some years ago, many individuals in certain parts of the country suffered from pellagra, a disease with various mental as well as physical symptoms. Caused by a deficiency of niacin, their mental conditions improved once proper diet was begun. There has been a surge in recent years in which vitamin deficiency has been cited as a cause of certain mental illnesses with some therapists resorting to megavitamin therapy. There is still much controversy as to whether schizophrenia results from some chemical imbalance or from environmental conditions. Some still believe that homosexuality is the result of physiological aberration rather than a learned, sexual lifestyle. While we realize that some of these viewpoints are controversial, they do serve the purpose of reminding us that where one is confronted with the etiology of physical or emotional problems there is no sure line of demarcation. In many cases a combination of psychotherapy and medical care provides a partial, if not total, alleviation of the distressing symptoms or behavior. If it is determined that the problem has no organic base, counseling can often provide relief. In either event, cases similar to those discussed in this chapter demonstrate the need for cooperation between clergymen, physicians, and psychiatrists.

Chapter 11
When Not
to Refer

Psychologists and psychiatrists do not have all the answers to the world's problems. Neither do they possess some magic power or super pill capable of curing all mental illness. True, there are some who have become so awed with their own importance that they dare to stand before the world and pontificate, sometimes so persuasively that they convince a sizeable audience that they do indeed possess answers not yet discovered by the less gifted. On the other end of the continuum, psychologists and psychiatrists have come in for their share of ridicule serving as the butt of never-ending jokes. Some punster has, for example, defined psychology as the study of the id by the odd. It is not uncommon for critics to inject the "physician heal thyself" bit, citing the high suicide rate among psychiatrists as evidence that they cannot handle their own problems much less help others with theirs.

Ignoring these extremes, most of us would agree that psychology and psychiatry have made significant contributions to our understanding of human behavior and to the treatment of mental illness. Theology itself has not escaped the impact of psychological theory and practice as seen in the following statement by Paul Tillich.

Theology has received tremendous gifts from these movements [existential philosophy and psychoanalysis], gifts not dreamed of fifty years ago or even thirty years ago. We have these gifts. Existentialists and analysts themselves do not need to know that they have given to theology these great things. But the theologians should know it.[1]

Koehler, a minister writing some years ago in the *Journal of Pastoral Psychology*, says:

Parish ministers should recognize their indebtedness to the behavioral sciences and psychotherapy for the dynamic contributions these fields of study are making to the control of human behavior. . . . Church executives have carefully weighed the recommendations of scientists in the field of human relations, psychology, and sociology. In the light of said recommendations some church bodies have restructured denominational procedures, rewritten religious education curricula, pioneered new approaches to the needs of individuals and societies.[2]

While it is good that clergymen are aware of the contributions made by the behavioral sciences and avail themselves of the insights gleaned from the psychological study of human behavior, they should not neglect their own special gifts or forget that many other clergymen and theologians have made significant contributions to our understanding of human behavior. While the death of a theologian most often goes unnoticed in the field of psychology, the death in recent years of three of the most respected theologians in the world, Paul Tillich, Martin Buber, and Reinhold Niebuhr, is cause to stop and reflect on the impact which such theological giants have had on psychology and counseling. While none of these would probably refer to himself as a psychologist, they have all demonstrated more expertise in the field of human relations than many psychologists or psychiatrists. In view of the contributions already made by these three and the vast potential possessed by other clergymen in the area of human relationships and behavior, it is discouraging to read that many psychologists and psychiatrists ignore or belittle the works of theologians and pastoral counselors. In a generation in which those things that cannot be weighed, measured, or put in a test tube are cast onto the slag pile of superstition or fiction, we must remember that some of the most necessary and redeeming commodities for human health and survival cannot be subjected to the scientific method. We speak of faith, hope, love, trust, kindness, goodness, responsibility, and sensitivity. All of these are of great concern to most individuals. And it is with these issues that religion is or should be vitally involved.

Those psychiatrists who are themselves not religiously oriented should recognize that religion is a vital force with widespread repercussions in the lives of millions. As D. E. Trueblood once said: "Belief in God ... may be false, and it may be true, but it cannot possibly be trivial."[3] Gordon Allport in his book on *The Individual and His Religion* says concerning religion:

> Scarcely any modern textbook writer in psychology devotes as much as two shamefaced pages to the subject even though religion, like sex, is an almost universal interest to the human race. The psychologist has no right to retire from the field. Fully two-thirds of the adults in our country regard themselves as religious people, at least nine-tenths, by their own report believe in God.[4]

As disturbing as the avoidance of religious concerns by some psychiatrists and psychologists may be, even more disturbing is the "retirement" of many clergymen and theologians "from the field." These clergymen, apparently attempting to remain in vogue in a growing skeptical and scientifically oriented universe, seem anxious to rid themselves of much that is not only the heart and cornerstone of theology, but of immense value in the treatment of human emotional ills as well.

A study conducted by Schneider and Dornbusch in

which they surveyed the religious literature for the last seventy-five years led them to conclude:

> A dominant trend in the literature through the decades is secularization ... the deity in the literature is in process of transformation, his existence in some objective sense is no longer insisted upon, and he often approximates a consciously useful fiction. Finally there is a strong bias against the "unscientific" and for equating religion and science.[5]

As one reviews the events of recent decades in which religion and science have had a common interest, one fact emerges above all else—almost without exception it has been religion which has been forced to rethink or modify its position in moments of conflict. Science has come a long way indeed from the age in which Copernicus and Galileo engaged in debate with the spokesmen for religion, not infrequently coming off second best and recanting under threat of excommunication or physical punishment. With the frontiers of the unknown receding before the advances of modern science, however, theology has reformulated and redefined many of its concepts in an effort to retain its credibility. It is almost as if on rare occasions some scientist steps from his laboratory to issue an ultimatum to some theological gathering as to what it must surrender or subscribe to if theology is to be accepted by modern science. Even though such offerings are rare, strangely enough, theology, just a short time ago in the position of issuing ultimatums, now finds itself in the position of "accepting crumbs from the master's table." Not only has religion been relegated to the bargaining table where it is now willing to barter away much that once was important, it also finds itself in a situation analogous to the suitor who awakens to find his overtures to romance repulsed by a partner no longer desiring his affection. Science could hardly care less. Theology is no longer the Queen of the Sciences, and no one is forced to recant.

Not all clergymen are jettisoning their more traditional

theological beliefs while opting for a more socially acceptable and scientific theology. There are voices raised in dis-
sent. One such a voice is that of Dr. Robert M. Brown, professor of religion at Stanford University. His works were
discussed some years ago in newspapers throughout the
country by the late religious writer, Louis Cassels.

> Teaching in a great secular university, Dr. Brown is
> well aware of the "appalling irrelevance of Chris-
> tianity to the vast majority of modern men" and he
> has tried hard in his books, articles, and lectures to
> present the gospel in terms which educated people
> will find comprehensible. But interpreting the good
> news is one thing; abandoning it is another. "It is
> not the task of Christians to whittle away their heri-
> tage until it is palatable to all.... Faith has never
> been easy.... Scandal is the term used nearly 2,000
> years ago to describe the reaction of Jewish and
> Greek intellectuals to Christian claims that God
> dwelled among men in the person of an humble Gali-
> lean teacher. But the apostle would not tone down his
> shocking story to make it more respectful in the ears
> of his audience.... The coming generation had better
> make sure that it does not succumb to the temptation
> Ronald Knox once described as the willingness to
> settle for whatever Jones will swallow.[6]

We are by no means advocating a return to many of the
questionable religious practices or beliefs of the past, nor
do we favor the suppression of any theory, scientific or
otherwise, which might conflict with any theological belief.
We are painfully aware of the potential for psychological
damage which religion possesses in the hands of the misin-
formed who use religion to stifle human growth and to promote shame and guilt in staggering proportions. Anyone
who has worked in a mental health clinic has seen the results of well-intentioned but misguided religious workers
passing on personal convictions as fact or dogma to young
children.

Well aware that religion has at times been guilty of
such inappropriate practices, we are still of the opinion that

no other group or profession has more to offer than clergymen in the prevention and treatment of emotional illness.
We are even more convinced of the church's potential in this
area as we become more aware of the particular problems
being seen by psychotherapists in recent years. When describing the problems they are treating today more and
more psychiatrists and other analysts of the human condition seem prone to use such terms as loneliness, emptiness,
depersonalization, alienation, meaninglessness, hopelessness, rootlessness, valuelessness, anomie, detachment, isolation, goallessness, and lack of meaning and purpose in life.
Long considered the baliwick of theologians and moral philosophers, such matters have in recent years become of increasing interest to behavioral scientists as they attempt
to combat the seeming mass neuroses of our age.

Such a drastic switch in the types of problems seen is
obvious in even a cursory examination of psychotherapeutic
or counseling literature. As a result of this trend, many psychologists have made adjustments in their thinking and interests. It is interesting to note, for example, that one of the
most provocative books on sin to come off the press, *Whatever Became of Sin*, was written, not by a theologian, but by
Dr. Karl Menninger, one of the most eminent psychiatrists
in the world. Hobart Mowrer, a psychologist, has written
extensively on such topics as guilt and repentance. Some
years ago Carl Jung said:

> Among all my patients in the second half of life—
> that is to say, over thirty-five—there has not been
> one whose problem in the last report was not that of
> finding a religious outlook on life. It is safe to say
> that everyone of them feels ill because he lost that
> which the living religions of every age have given to
> their followers, and none of them have been really
> healed who did not regain his religious outlook.[7]

There are vast differences in what various writers
mean by religion, but apparently many psychotherapists are
aware of modern man's religious and moral concerns in spite

of the claim that these issues have diminished in importance in our world today. We would like to suggest that it is perhaps not so much that individuals have become less concerned with values or moral principles. Instead it appears they are turning in large numbers to psychotherapists for answers to problems once handled by the church. Viktor Frankl says concerning this so-called migration of Western humanity from the priest to the psychiatrist, that such a movement must not be ignored by either the priest or the psychiatrist for this is an emergency which demands that psychiatrists fulfill the function of the medical care of souls.[8]

One of the most striking changes encountered in psychotherapeutic literature is the increasing interest on the part of psychologists in personal values and value systems. One of the most interesting books in recent years is a compilation of writings by recognized authorities in their fields on values. Among the contributors so vitally concerned with the present state of valuelessness, one finds, rather than theologians or philosophers, some of the most respected social scientists in the field, including A. H. Maslow, Erich Fromm, and Kurt Goldstein. Serving as editor, Maslow writes in the introduction:

> This volume springs from the belief, first that the ultimate disease of our time is valuelessness; second that this state is more crucially dangerous than ever before in history; and finally, that something can be done about it by man's over rational efforts. The state of valuelessness has been variously described as anomie, amorality, anhedonia, restlessness, emptiness, hopelessness, the lack of something to believe in and be devoted to. It has come to its present dangerous point because all traditional value systems ever offered to mankind have in effect proved to be failures (our present state proves this to be so).... The cure for the disease is obvious. We need a validated, usable system of human values, values that we can believe in and devote ourselves to because they are true rather

than because we are "exhorted" to "believe and have
faith."[9]

Have all previous value systems proved to be inadequate? It is not, for example, that the values set forth in
both the Old and New Testaments have been "weighed and
found wanting" but rather that they have never been seriously put to the test. While it is good that behavioral scientists have become more interested in values, this increased
interest along with the mass migration to therapists, does
seem to suggest, that for many, the church is no longer ful-
filling its function in regard to such matters of great significance to most individuals.

If it is true that individuals are now turning from clergymen to psychiatrists with problems regarding values and
other matters cited above, then such is most discouraging.
It is discouraging for the simple reason that clergymen with
their theological training are equally, if not more, responsible for and capable of dealing with most of these problems
than are psychiatrists. It would be a great tragedy indeed
if clergymen refuse to accept their responsibility as teachers and leaders in the realm of human values and moral conduct. No other institution or agency is so well equipped as
the church to lead in this area. As Karl Menninger says,
"Not every man or woman is strong and brave and intelligent enough to be a minister, a priest, a rabbi. But these are
our moral leaders and they must lead."[10]

Clergymen possess the tools to work effectively in the
field of mental health. If one is willing to exert the effort,
he can find some parallel in theology for almost any concept
or principle in counseling theory. In any exposure to counseling literature, for example, one is confronted with numerous references to such terms as "acceptance" and "unconditional positive regard." The popularity of the latter
may be traced to Carl Rogers, but it is included in some
form or other in most counseling theories. While there are
differences, it is interesting to compare Roger's "uncondi-

tional positive regard" to the following statement by Paul Tillich's concerning the meaning of "grace."

> And it is indeed important to know that theology had to learn from the psychoanalytic method the meaning of grace. The word grace, which had lost any meaning, has gained a new meaning by the way in which the analyst deals with his patient. He accepts him. He does not say, "you are acceptable," but he accepts him. And that is the way every minister and every Christian should deal with the other person.[11]

While clergymen may gain new insights into the meaning of grace from the analysts, they should also be reminded that grace did abound long before Freud or Rogers came on the scene and that clergymen were emphasizing God's love and acceptance of the sinner while hating the sin long before anyone heard of unconditional positive regard.

Another reference frequently encountered in counseling literature has to do with the relationship between client and therapist. Every age or group has its own language in which certain words or phrases briefly summarize concepts believed to be most significant. As frequently happens, many of these words and phrases are used and abused to the point that they soon lose most, if not all, meaning. In counseling literature one of the phrases most frequently encountered is "meaningful relationship." Unlike most phrases of this sort, which reach peak usage then begin to wane, this one seems to have found a more or less permanent place in the vocabulary of not only psychologists but clergymen, couples, and many other groups and disciplines as well. We would like to suggest that one of the reasons for its continued popularity is that the concept of "relationship" is at the heart of both theology and psychology.

Both human psychology and theology are primarily studies in relationships. Although this is perhaps an oversimplification, human psychology is the study of man's relationship with himself, with his fellowman, and with his total environment. Theology is also a study of man's relationship to himself, to his fellowman and to his total environment which includes his relationship to God. Carl Rogers and others have emphasized again and again the importance of the quality of the relationship between client and therapist if therapy is to be successful. In doing so they have stressed such qualities as warmth, caring, and acceptance. In referring to the prerequisites of a successful therapeutic relationship, some years ago Snyder wrote in the *Journal of Counseling Psychology*:

> What really seems to matter is that the client finds that someone "cares." And most human beings, whether born inherently good or bad, seem to find they need to have someone in life who cares. If they establish such a relationship without benefit of psychotherapy they are the lucky ones. If not, they have to pay their fee and get their caring from a therapist.[12]

As brilliant and to the point as Rogers, Snyder, and others have been, no one has ever been able to improve on the simple statement regarding the importance of relationships made by Jesus almost 2,000 years ago:

> Thou shalt love thy God with all thy heart, and with all thy soul, and with all thy mind. This is the first great commandment. And the second is like unto it. Thou shalt love thy neighbor as thyself. On these two commandments hang all the law and the prophets. (Matthew 22:23-40)

In some form or other, all of the great philosophical, psychological, and theological systems through the centuries have incorporated bits or pieces of the exhortation to "love thy neighbor as thyself." While many psychologists have emphasized in recent years the need for self-respect and have written numerous articles and books correlating love of self and love of others, Søren Kierkegaard the Danish theologian, writing over one hundred years ago, said:

> If anyone will not learn from Christianity to love himself in the right way, then neither can he love his

neighbor.... To love one's self in the right way and
to love one's neighbor are absolutely analogous concepts, are at bottom one and the same.[13]

Living in an age in which the commandment to "love
thy neighbor as thyself" seems to have been superseded
by the more pragmatic and paranoid philosophy of "Do it to
them before they do it to you," we need to heed more than
ever the words of such theologians as Kierkegaard and,
more recently, Martin Buber who has written so tellingly
to our age, on the subject of relationships.

In an era in which church members are more concerned
with affluence than with influence; when man is more interested in laying up treasures on earth than with the more
eternal values of life; when the church is dominated by the
professional fund raiser and public relations expert as opposed to leaders deeply concerned with the moral and spiritual climate of the day; when financial contributions are
a substitute for personal involvement and commitment; and
when building programs are of greater concern than human
rights; is it any wonder that thousands have turned their
backs on the church? Until the church is willing to redis-
cover its real mission to communicate to the world that it
really cares, deeply and sincerely, and to demonstrate a
willingness to speak on the issues of such grave concern to
most individuals, this mass exodus to therapists will most
probably continue unabated with both the church and society the losers. In the final analysis it is the church rather
than therapists which can best provide answers to many of
the problems generating the anxiety and other emotional
disorders so frequently encountered in mental health clinics
today.

Summary

We are in no way suggesting that the pulpit be replaced by the psychiatrist's couch or the Bible by a text-
book in psychology. But we are raising the question as to
whether clergymen are not themselves too prone to do just

this, choosing to refer or turn to psychiatrists whenever psychological or emotional problems arise, ignoring their own gifts and knowledge of human behavior.

We have also attempted to suggest that clergymen need not rid themselves of, nor apologize for, their religious values and convictions in order to preach, teach, or counsel effectively. In truth it might well be that in an attempt to become more scientific clergymen have surrendered some of their most potent weapons for combating feelings of emptiness, alienation, estrangement, amorality, and lack of meaning and purpose in life. While it is only common sense to refer or call for assistance when needed, clergymen should realize that psychiatrists do not have a monopoly on care and treatment for the mentally ill. Some of the best therapy is provided by individuals who have never had a course in psychology.

In the final analysis, no other group is so well endowed historically as are clergymen to bring hope and comfort to those afflicted with emotional problems. As Menninger says:

> No psychiatrists or psychotherapists, even those with many patients, have the quantitative opportunity to cure souls and mend minds which the preacher enjoys. And the preacher also has a superb opportunity to do what few psychiatrists can, to prevent the development of chronic anxiety, depression, and other mental ills.[14]

While we are aware that not all clergymen desire to, or even believe that they should, devote even a small portion of their time to the emotional concerns of their congregations, not to do so is most unfortunate, for man is thus treated as something less than a total person. In the final pages of his book on sin, Menninger writing, not as a theologian, prophet, or sociologist, but as a "doctor ... speaking the medical tongue with a psychiatric accent," says:

For doctors, health is the ultimate good, the ideal state of being. And mental health—some of us believe—includes all the healths: physical, social, cultural and moral (spiritual).[15]

If mental health does indeed include these all encompassing areas of man's existence, and we believe it does, for clergymen to ignore their responsibilities in these areas is tantamount to admitting that the church has nothing to offer in some of the most serious moments and conflicts in man's lifetime.

Notes

Chapter 1—Introduction

1. Nina Ridenour, *Mental Health in The United States* (Cambridge, Mass.: Harvard University Press, 1961), p. 135.
2. Ibid.

Chapter 4—Suicide

1. Robert C. Drye, M.D., Robert L. Goulding, M.D., and Mary E. Goulding, M.S.W., "No-Suicide Decisions: Patient Monitoring of Suicidal Risks," *American Journal of Psychiatry* 130, no. 2 (February 1973): 171–74. Copyright 1973, the American Psychiatric Association. Reprinted by permission.

Chapter 11—When Not to Refer

1. Paul Tillich, "Psychoanalysis, Existentialism, and Theology," *Pastoral Psychology* 9, no. 87 (1958): 9–17.
2. John G. Koehler, response to article by Carl Rogers and B. F. Skinner, "Control of Human Behavior," *Pastoral Psychology* 13, no. 128 (1962): 32–35.
3. David E. Trueblood, *Philosophy of Religion* (New York: Harper Brothers, 1957), p. 6.
4. Gordon W. Allport, *The Individual and His Religion*

(New York: Macmillan, 1950), pp. v-x. Copyright 1950 by Macmillan Publishing Co., Inc.

5. Louis Schneider and Sanford M. Dornbusch, "Inspirational Religious Literature: From Latent to Manifest Functions of Religion," *American Journal of Sociology* 62 (1957): 476–81. Reprinted by permission of the University of Chicago Press.

6. Louis Cassels, "Protestant Voices Concerns at Trend," *Atlanta Journal*, 12 August 1965, p. 30.

7. Carl Jung, *Modern Man in Search of a Soul* (New York: Harcourt, Brace, 1933), p. 264.

8. Victor E. Frankl, "The Will to Meaning," *Pastoral Care* 12 (1958): 82–88.

9. Abraham H. Maslow, *New Knowledge in Human Values* (New York: Harper Brothers, 1959), p. vii.

10. Reprinted by permission of Hawthorne Books, Inc. from *Whatever Became of Sin?* by Karl Menninger, M.D., pp. 220–21. Copyright © 1973 by Karl Menninger, M.D. All rights reserved.

11. Tillich, "Psychoanalysis, Existentialism, and Theology," p. 16.

12. W. U. Snyder, "Comment," *Journal of Counseling Psychology*, 3, no. 2 (1956): 91–92.

13. Robert Bretall (ed.), *A Kierkegaard Anthology*, p. 289. Copyright 1946 by Princeton University Press. Reprinted by permission of Princeton University Press.

14. Menninger, *Whatever Became of Sin?*, p. 201.

15. Ibid., p. 230.

Index

About the authors
All three authors are affiliated with the University of Georgia at Athens. John R. Curtis, M.D. is the director of University Health Services. He has published articles in *The Journal of the American Medical Association* and the *American Journal of Psychiatry.*

Carol B. Currier, Ph.D. is senior clinical psychologist of University Health Services and associate professor of psychology.

Robert L. Mason, Jr., Ed.D. is counseling psychologist of University Health Services and assistant professor of education. He has published articles in *The Journal of Humanistic Psychology* and *Pastoral Psychology.*

DATE DUE

MAY 28 90			